LEGAL INVERSIONS

D1570586

LEGAL INVERSIONS

Lesbians, Gay Men, and the Politics of Law

Edited by Didi Herman / Carl Stychin

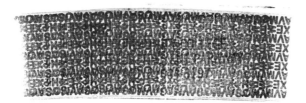

TEMPLE
UNIVERSITY
PRESS
Philadelphia

Temple University Press, Philadelphia 19122
Copyright © 1995 by Temple University
All rights reserved. Published 1995

♾ The paper used in this publication meets the requirements of the American
National Standard for Information Sciences—Permanence of Paper for Printed
Library Materials, ANSI Z39.48-1984

Printed in the United States of America

Text design by Arlene Putterman

Library of Congress Cataloging-in-Publication Data

Legal inversions : lesbians, gay men, and the politics of law / edited
    by Didi Herman, Carl Stychin.
        p.   cm.
    Includes bibliographical references and index.
    ISBN 1-56639-376-0 (cloth) — ISBN 1-56639-377-9 (paper)
    1. Homosexuality — Law and legislation. 2. Lesbians — Legal status, laws, etc.
3. Gay men — Legal status, laws, etc.   I. Herman, Didi. II. Stychin, Carl F. (Carl
Franklin), 1964-
K3242.3.Z9L44   1995
346.01′3—dc20
[342.613]   95-40370

Contents

Acknowledgments

OUR primary acknowledgment is to our contributors. We thank them all for agreeing to contribute and for producing such superb essays. We also wish to acknowledge the Keele University Law Department for its support of our research. Thanks also to Davina Cooper for all her help. A great debt is owed to Doris Braendel of Temple University Press, who has provided this project with unqualified support, even when it was little more than a rather sketchy idea. Thanks also to Sherry Babbitt at Temple for copyediting. Finally, we acknowledge permission to reprint the following previously published works:

Peter M. Cicchino, Bruce R. Deming, and Katherine M. Nicholson. "Sex, Lies, and Civil Rights: A Critical History of the Massachusetts Gay Civil Rights Bill." *Harvard Civil Rights–Civil Liberties Law Review* 26(2)(1991):549–631.

Davina Cooper and Didi Herman. "Getting 'The Family Right': Legislating Heterosexuality in Britain, 1986–1991." *Canadian Journal of Family Law* 10(1991): 41–78.

Introduction

Carl Stychin / *Didi Herman*

Context

This book can be viewed as part of the recent explosion of lesbian and gay studies, which in most if not all academic disciplines has emerged as one of the most vibrant areas of scholarship. Yet until recently the legal discipline has lagged behind in this development. While law reform struggles have always been a part of the grassroots lesbian and gay agenda, academic research and writing on the "politics" of these engagements have been slow to appear. But this has changed gradually, and critical analyses of lesbian and gay legal issues are now found in all but the most traditional legal journals.

Lesbian and gay legal studies takes several forms. Some writers focus on the formal inequities and exclusions in law, and attempt to develop arguments for litigants to make in court. One could note, for example, the exclusion of the category of sexual orientation from a particular piece of human rights legislation, and suggest constitutional or other arguments that could be made to remedy this situation. Or one could develop arguments, based on concepts such as a right to privacy, to assert that laws explicitly prohibiting certain same-sex sexual practices are constitutionally invalid.

Other writers choose to explore the effects, contradictions, and inconsistencies of law. For example, in thinking about a particular law reform campaign, one might ask questions such as: How were lesbians and gay men mobilized by this struggle? What sort of opposition was encountered? Do the arguments made by lesbian and gay rights campaigners have negative implications for the struggles of people with differing identities?

Still other scholars focus on the ways in which subjects are constructed by law and legal actors. A study in this vein, for example, might explore how child custody law represents the lesbian mother. There are also those who have attempted to develop lesbian-centered jurisprudence by constructing new ways of understanding and working with the law that prioritize lesbian experience.

We do not wish to suggest that these various approaches to lesbian and gay legal studies are mutually exclusive. On the contrary, many writers will employ all these perspectives and more. Nevertheless, our own bias is toward the work of those who largely perform the second and third levels of analysis. Thus, this book primarily should be read as a critical, analytic text about the politics of lesbians and gay men engaging with and being engaged by law, rather than a legal manual, a jurisprudential text,[1] or a collection of materials covering every aspect of relevant law.[2]

Indeed, the idea for *Legal Inversions* came about when we found ourselves working in the same institution and discussing how there did not seem to be any published collection of critical essays on this topic. We thought that the possibility of putting together such a publication might help to rectify that problem.

Some years ago, a book bearing this title (assuming a publisher would have accepted it) might well have focused largely (if not exclusively) upon gay male issues, repressive features of the criminal law and law reform struggles for formal legal equality. Those issues remain important, and we seek to pay attention to them. However, we have become increasingly aware that law (like other discourses) is not only prohibitive and repressive, but also shapes the ways in which we know ourselves and in which others come to know us (an insight provided by Foucault[3] and others). Law has both a constitutive and a symbolic role to play in how identities and actions are characterized. The essays in this collection, then, approach law in diverse ways, recognizing its multiplicity of functions in shaping the contours of sexual identities, relations, and practices.

The intellectual tools with which we analyze the law also have changed. While a traditional doctrinal approach to the law still is important for progressive and radical lawyers as well as for lesbian and gay citizens who require legal answers, insights into the construction of sexuality through law as a discourse have been gleaned through a wide range of academic approaches. Deconstruction, poststructuralism, social theory, sociology, and anthropology all make important contributions to our understanding of how law operates. Thus, this collection includes a diverse range of intellectual approaches to the subject.

In broadening their horizons, legal commentators also have been forced to confront the historical exclusions within lesbian and gay legal theory and social practice. For many gay men, the invisibility of lesbians has been a glaring omission that still is being corrected—and often only at the insistence of women. The lack of attention paid to the construction of race and racism also is slowly being challenged. Other issues, such as disparities in wealth and mental or physical ability, remain largely unaddressed by mainstream lesbian and gay theory and practice. While this collection does not rectify all of these imbalances (and may reinforce some of them), it has been prepared with the knowledge that these issues need addressing.

Some mention should also be made of the relationship between legal theory, the law in practice, and the role of legal academics. The contributors to this collection are mainly legal academics rather than practicing members of the profession or of service and activist organizations (although some work in all these realms). This in part is a reflection of the heavy demands on the time of those who do not write articles for a living. It also may suggest that academic legal writing is somewhat removed from the day-to-day world of lesbian and gay law. However, the dichotomy between theory and practice ultimately is an oversimplification of reality. The essays in this collection deal with actual people who have either sought to employ the law to achieve certain ends, been part of law reform movements, or have been subjected to the force of the law. Moreover, the contributors themselves are not divorced from social realities; rather, they are social actors who in various ways are engaged in struggles for social change.

Finally, despite the emergence of a dynamic (and increasingly voluminous) body of lesbian and gay legal theory, the conservatism of the legal establishment should never be underestimated. While we are extremely fortunate to earn a living thinking, writing, and talking about these issues, many engaged in the theory and practice of lesbian and gay law have experienced marginalization and indeed direct discrimination as a result of their work. Thus while much progress has been made, the message of this collection is that many arenas of struggle remain.

Themes

Although the essays in this book are diverse, the concerns of the authors intersect in several ways. While the themes noted below are by no means rigid categories, and while our discussion of an essay under one heading is not meant to suggest that it could not also have been included in another, we hope that readers will find the distinctions drawn here to be useful.

The Subjects of Law

As noted, lesbian and gay legal studies, like other areas of scholarship, has been influenced by postmodern and Foucauldian approaches to the relationship between discourse and socio-political identities.

Several of our authors adopt these perspectives and focus on how the language, categories, and thinking of law produce particular kinds of legal subjects.

Leslie J. Moran, for example, turns his attention to the famous Wolfenden Report, and explores how the legal actors of the period created their "homosexual." He notes that the Wolfenden Committee sought to constitute (and strictly regulate) a coherently defined homosexual. The array of schemes employed to achieve this end, however, also gave rise to unstable and multiple understandings about the nature of homosexuality that threatened to produce incoherence.

In what could be read as a companion piece, Leo Flynn examines the contradictions and partialities in the Irish Supreme Court's construction of male homosexuality. Flynn's concern is to show that the Court, in upholding the constitutionality of laws criminalizing same-sex sexual activity, sought to define the male homosexual by explaining what he was *not*. In creating a series of exclusionary categories, the Court uncovered the "truth" of its subject. Flynn, like Moran, finds that the attempt to constitute the homosexual gives rise to contradictions that potentially destabilize the model being constructed.

Mary Eaton takes a somewhat different tack while similarly employing a postmodern framework. She also looks at how the law discursively constructs the homosexual, but her focus is on how that figure is racially constituted as white. Eaton suggests that the stability of homosexuality not only depends on the maintenance of rigid sexual categories through discourses such as law, but also requires that the homosexual be racially unmodified. This finding in turn means that a more complex theory of the politics of sexuality is demanded, one that interrogates how legal discourse casts the homosexual in racial terms.

The Implications of Strategy

A second theme running through the contributions is a concern with the effects and implications of specific legal strategies.[4] Katherine Arnup, Susan Boyd, and Shelley A. M. Gavigan are all concerned with the political implications of particular strategies. Arnup and Boyd consider the emerging forum of custody battles between lesbian mothers and gay sperm donors, and situate this arena within a larger feminist analysis of the construction of motherhood and the assertion of fathers' rights. Some gay men and lesbians might find unsettling the authors' view that a failure to recognize gay fatherhood "represents an important step in the struggle for women's reproductive autonomy."

Gavigan's essay is primarily concerned with similar battles between biological and nonbiological lesbian mothers. She explores whether arguments made by both litigant mothers in cases such these entrench familial ideology and its attendant oppression of women. Ultimately, Gavigan highlights the particular dilemmas facing the nonbiological mother. In contrast to the more postmodern contributors, Gavigan focuses on understanding the role of ideology and the way in which dominant frameworks of meaning shape the terms of the debate.

Finally, Cynthia Petersen analyzes how current equality discourse fails to capture the complexity of the oppression of lesbians. Turning her attention to the particular issue of race, she argues that current modes of thinking about lesbian oppression are fundamentally essentialist. In other words, lesbian legal theories fail to account for the diversity of lesbian identities and the need for nonuniversalizing strategies.

Law Reform, Struggle, and the State

The final theme explored in this volume is the interaction and engagement of lesbians and gay men with state institutions. Peter M. Cicchino, Bruce R. Deming, and Katherine M. Nicholson offer an analysis of a specific law reform struggle in Massachusetts, exploring the contradictions, mobilizations, and confrontations that occurred. They conclude that while a conservative strategy helped to secure the passage of the Gay Civil Rights Act, this victory came at the price of its reinforcement of dominant conceptions of lesbians and gay men. Their findings also underscore the broader contradictions implicit in the use of a rights discourse to realize social change.

Similarly, Davina Cooper and Didi Herman examine some of the law reform initiatives of the conservative right in Britain. In discussing how the British right legislated heterosexuality, the authors consider several aspects of the process, including the sexuality rhetoric of conservatives and liberals, and why and how the initiatives emerged when they did.

Ruthann Robson explores how lesbians have been constructed and treated within the criminal justice system in the United States. She is particularly concerned with how the dominant equality discourse of lesbian and gay rights campaigners is inapt and ill-suited to the dilemmas faced by lesbians caught up in the criminal process. She argues that in the effort to secure a largely male vision of rights, the situation of lesbian defendants and prisoners remains untheorized and unaddressed.

Finally, William F. Flanagan analyzes the complexity of identity politics in the context of AIDS activism. He finds that the divergent and conflictual interests of activists must be continually (re)negotiated during the process of engaging with the state. At the same time, AIDS activists articulate shared interests that may diverge from other lesbian and gay political struggles. Flanagan thus raises questions about what happens to existing alliances and interests when new identities come to the fore.

The Comparative Legal Context

This collection of essays is unique in that it brings together work from four legal cultures—the United States, Canada, the United Kingdom, and Ireland. This national diversity can facilitate cross-cultural comparisons in analyzing the role of law in the constitution and regulation of sexual identities, as well as in examining how lesbians and gay men engage with law. Although the legal regimes that are the basis for these essays are in some sense fundamentally similar in that they are all Western systems that share a primarily common law tradition, useful comparisons can still be drawn. One obvious absence, however, is material from Third World cultures. This reflects the limits of our own knowledge and contacts, and leaves the book very much a Western collection.

Importantly, three of the four regimes (the United Kingdom being the exception) possess written guarantees of the constitutional rights of individuals, which are enforceable by the judiciary. The role of rights discourse thus assumes a centrality in some (but not all) of the essays in this collection.

For example, in the last decade American constitutional law has been decisively shaped by the decision of the United States Supreme Court in *Bowers v. Hardwick*,[5] which upheld the constitutionality of state laws that criminalize sodomy. For American readers, interesting comparisons can be drawn from Leo Flynn's essay in this collection, which analyzes how the Irish Supreme Court has approached the same issue and has reached the same result. Also of comparative interest is Leslie Moran's analysis of the Wolfenden Report, which is best known for its recommendation of the decriminalization of consenting same-sex sexual activity between males in Britain.

Furthermore, some of the contributions can facilitate comparisons of how social actors engage with law in struggles over lesbian and gay rights in different societies. Whether that engagement is made with the objective of promoting the traditional heterosexual family through law reform initiatives (the subject of Cooper and Herman's essay); manifests itself in attempts to secure formal legal equality for lesbians and gay men (examined by Cicchino, Deming, and Nicholson), or appears in the private legal sphere of the custody battle (documented by Gavigan as well as Arnup and Boyd), an examination of the legal strategies and discursive moves employed in one culture can usefully inform those engaged with the law in another. So too the reader may find enlightening the comparisons in the social movement organizing around HIV and AIDS in the United States and Canada that are highlighted by Flanagan.

Thus, one aim of this collection is to broaden the frame of reference of those involved in an area of study that to some extent has been dominated by the American legal experience. The inclusion of essays with European and Canadian perspectives will hopefully facilitate this process, and make an important contribution to cross-cultural lesbian and gay legal studies generally.

Concluding Remarks

We conclude with a short note on ourselves and our contributors. Our choice of authors was not scientific—we wrote to people we knew and whose work we admired. While we hoped to have a diverse collection—intellectually eclectic, attentive to the intersections of different relations of power, somewhat international (Britain, Canada, Ireland, and the United States)—we leave it to others to determine how well we have realized those aims. Finally, we also aimed to provide some space for young scholars whose work may not yet have achieved a wide, international exposure. We likewise included two previously published pieces (revised and much edited for length) that, in our opinion deserve a broader audience, which we hope their publication here will facilitate.

NOTES

1. See, e.g., Ruthann Robson, *Lesbian (Out)Law: Survival under the Rule of Law* (Ithaca, NY: Firebrand, 1992).

2. See, e.g., William B. Rubenstein, *Lesbians, Gay Men, and the Law* (New York: New Press, 1993).

3. Michel Foucault, *The History of Sexuality, vol. 1, An Introduction*, trans. R. Hurley (London: Penguin, 1976).

4. One of the debates not addressed directly in this collection is that of essentialism versus constructionism, and the strategic implications of deploying immutability arguments in lesbian and gay rights struggles. These matters have been well explored elsewhere. For an excellent discussion, see Janet E. Halley, "Sexual Orientation and the Politics of Biology: A Critique of the Argument from Immutability," *Stanford Law Review* 46(1994): 503–68.

5. 478 U.S. 186 (1986).

PART I

THE SUBJECTS
OF LAW

ONE

One of the functions of the Wolfenden Committee, established by the British government in 1954, was to review the law and practice relating to homosexual offenses. While its recommendations eventually led to the partial decriminalization of same-sex sexual acts between men, Leslie J. Moran's essay focuses on how the "homosexual" and his "offences" were defined by the committee. He finds that while the terms had no legal history, the committee "discovered" the meaning of homosexuality as sexual identity, as sexual acts, and ultimately as a knowledge of the (male) body produced by authorized speakers. Thus, a new category of legal wrong was invented in order that it might be decriminalized. Moran argues that in so doing the committee revealed the incoherence of its own knowledge about homosexuality. As a result, that knowledge became vulnerable as a site of contestation.

The Homosexualization of English Law

Leslie J. Moran

ON THE first of November 1953 the editor of the *London Sunday Times* directed the attention of readers to "A Social Problem." The specific topic was male homosexuality. The problem was said to be evidenced in a dramatic growth in the number of prosecutions and convictions of men for buggery, gross indecency, and the offence importuning of male persons. The editorial noted that trial agendas were said to be "packed full of cases of indecent assault and gross indecency between men." The judiciary had spoken of the shock and indignation of having to deal with "gang[s] of homosexuality." In response to this, on August 24, 1954, the British government inaugurated a review of the criminal law and the penal system to be conducted by a committee, later known as the Wolfenden Committee after its chair, Sir John Wolfenden. Its assignment was to consider the law and practice relating to homosexual offenses and the treatment of persons convicted of such offenses by the courts, and the law and practice relating to of-

This research has been undertaken with the financial assistance of the Nuffield Foundation and the British Academy. Special thanks are due to Alain Pottage, who commented on an earlier draft of this essay, and to Anne Barron, Lucia Zedner, Peter Rush, and Alison Young, for their conversations and support.

3

fenses against the criminal law in connection with prostitution and solicitation for immoral purposes.[1] An immediate and enduring problem
that dominated the review was the meaning of the phrase "homosexual offences." On the one hand, the committee found that the term was
neither defined by the government ministers who had set the agenda
for the committee nor already known within the law; it neither referred to a particular named offense nor to a discrete category of criminal offenses known to English or Scottish law.[2] Nor was the task of the
committee assisted by the contemporary enactment of a wider general
legal category of "sexual offences." While the Sexual Offences Act of
1956 (4&5 Eliz.2 c.69) purported to bring together all of the existing
offenses in England and Wales relating to the sexual, it did not organize those offences by way of a division between heterosexual and homosexual offenses.

On the other hand the phrase "homosexual offences" was deployed as an organizing category by the committee and by many of the
organizations[3] and individuals who contributed to the review. This
drew attention to the fact that the term already had a certain legibility
and currency, at least within popular discourse, and certain specialist
official discourses, if not formally within the law. However, the repeated citation of the phrase did not appear to resolve the difficulties
over its meaning. In an early draft of its final report the committee
commented that

> at every stage we have been driven to face the question of terminology.
> From the literature of the subject, from the memoranda submitted to us,
> from our conversations with witnesses, and from our own discussions, it
> has become clear that an accepted terminology is an essential precondi-
> tion to any useful discussion of this tangled and complicated matter.[4]

As such "homosexual offences" appeared to be not so much a phrase
that had no meaning but more a phrase that had many different and
problematic meanings. The repeated use of "homosexual offences"
seems to have sustained and compounded the committee's problems
regarding the meaning of the phrase.

In the final instance, the problem of the meaning of "homosexual offences" plays an important role as the enigma in need of resolu-
tion at the heart of the Wolfenden review. It is thus important to recognize that the phrase forms part of the mechanics that promoted a
great proliferation of speech about homosexuality in general and about
"homosexual offences" in particular that dominated not only so much
of the proceedings before the committee but also its own deliberations
and its final report. The phrase also has a significance beyond the

Wolfenden investigations. "Homosexual offences" appeared not only in the committee's reform proposals but, as a result of the enactment of some of those reforms in the 1967 Sexual Offences Act (15&16 Eliz.2 c.60), now also has formal significance in the law. More specifically, its use in the 1967 act is the first formal appearance of the word "homosexual" in English law.[5] As such it installs a very specific idea of the body by way of its intergenital relations in the law. It is a sexed and gendered body. This "homosexual" does not refer to genital relations between women but only to those between men. In this context the Wolfenden review has particular importance, as it provides a snapshot of the process whereby this already sexed and gendered "homosexual" comes to be imagined as the "homosexual" of law. This essay is concerned with plotting the emergence of that "homosexual." The analysis will first consider how the enigma of "homosexual offence" was formulated by the committee and will then follow the committee's deliberations whereby the riddle was resolved.

The Enigma of "Homosexual Offences"

One important formulation of the enigma is to be found in the committee's consideration of the conjunction of the words "homosexual" and "offence," which, they noted, was particularly problematic: "It is important to make a clear distinction between homosexual offences and homosexuality. . . . Homosexuality is a sexual propensity for persons of one's own sex. Homosexuality, then is a state or condition, and as such does not, and cannot come within the purview of the criminal law."[6] While the word "offences" referred to acts designated as criminal and thereby within the general agenda of the review, the addition of "homosexual" rendered that problematic. "Homosexual" seeks to define the wrongful acts by way of "homosexuality," a term that refers to a "state or condition." Homosexuality was not and never had been illegal. As such, they concluded, it was not an object of concern of either the law in general or the criminal law in particular. But the conjunction of "homosexual" and "offences" brought together in one phrase a term that appeared to be primarily a reference to matters outside the law and thereby outside the legal interests of the committee, with another term that referred to an object firmly within the purview of their investigations. The enigma was that in the combination of terms, "homosexual offences" threatened to name an object that was unintelligible within the law and thereby outwith the committee's agenda.

The committee followed two strategies in their attempts to understand and resolve the relationship between "homosexual" and "offence." The first pursued the meaning of "homosexual offences" by analyzing its association with "homosexual acts" and "homosexuality." The second strategy was to name "homosexual offences" by producing a list of those offenses.

The Homosexuality of "Homosexual Offences"

The attempt to discover the meaning of "homosexual offences" through a consideration of the relation between "homosexual offences," "homosexual acts," and homosexuality led the committee to address the causes and nature of homosexuality. This brought them up against the limit of their agenda: How could the committee consider homosexuality when the law had no interest in that state or condition?

They found the solution to this problem in the terms of reference that dictated the parameters of the review, which directed the committee to consider not only the law and practice relating to homosexual offenses but also the treatment of persons convicted of such offenses. It was in the context of the treatment of offenders that they found that the questions of the nature and origins of homosexuality already had a currency within the legal system. Therefore it was legitimate for the committee to engage with that general domain of knowledge through which such questions might be asked and answered, and with the numerous submissions that addressed the question of the nature and causes of homosexuality.[7]

The management of this material and its application to the task at hand were, for much of the review, delegated to two psychiatrists sitting on the committee, Drs. Desmond Curran and Joseph Whitby. On behalf of the committee they formulated an analysis of the homosexuality of acts and offenses by way of an exegesis that flowed from two propositions. The first was that not all homosexuals indulge in homosexual acts. The second was that not all those who engage in homosexual acts are homosexuals. Their analysis produced interesting results.

The analysis of the first proposition began with the category of overt homosexual behavior. While Dr. Curran accepted that the level of participation in homosexual acts by homosexuals might vary, he concluded that in the final instance total abstinence from such acts would be extremely rare.[8] He reached this conclusion on the basis that few would abstain from the most common homosexual act: homosexually motivated masturbation.[9] Thus the review rejected the first proposition as it applied to overt homosexual behavior. It was to proceed on the basis that all homosexuals indulged in overt homosexual acts.

However, this did not exhaust the consideration of the first proposition. The matter was complicated by the introduction of a new dimension—the concept of latent homosexuality. This threatened to problematize the conclusion that all homosexuals indulged in homosexual behavior in two respects. First, homosexuality now could be something absent or invisible, a mere potential for presence and visibility. Likewise, the homosexual act was rendered problematic, as an act might now be an act of homosexuality even though it did not appear to be an overtly sexual act. Thus homosexual acts might take many forms. For example, the experts suggested that latent homosexuality might be expressed in poor relations with a wife, in a completely unsuccessful heterosexual love affair, in neuroses of various kinds, or in psychopathic manifestations.[10] In the first instance the invisibility of both homosexuality and homosexual acts associated with latent homosexuality threatened to make it more difficult to support the conclusion that all homosexuals engaged in homosexual acts. However, latent homosexuality did not so much disturb Dr. Curran's conclusion that all homosexuals indulged in homosexual acts but rather reinforced and elevated the importance of that conclusion by creating the possibility of discovering homosexuality in acts that had heretofore been thought to be outside the boundaries of the sexual. Thus the homosexuality of individuals who had fallen outside that category of identity might be produced.

The introduction of the distinction between overt and latent homosexual acts draws attention to some important features of homosexuality. Here homosexuality is shown to be not just a self-evident quality of certain acts or individuals but an effect of interpretation. While it may be a practice of self-definition, it is also shown to be a practice of reading and naming an individual's actions that is undertaken by others. Through these practices of naming, others may give the name "homosexual" to a person's behavior even though that person has neither defined himself or his acts as homosexual, nor had any awareness of the possibility of his or their homosexuality. Finally, through the concept of a latent homosexuality, homosexuality is liberated from any discrete notion of sexual (genital) acts.

The addition of latent homosexuality and its effects to the discussion generated some concern. W. C. Roberts, the secretary of the committee, expressed his concern over the notion of latent homosexuality in a handwritten marginal note to his redraft of the report's general chapter on homosexuality in the following terms: "The difficulty about a homosexual is that according to some psychos [sic] we're all homosexuals on this definition." The problem appeared to be that the idea of latent homosexuality in general and of the sexuality of nonsexual acts in particular threatened to transform homosexuality and homosexual acts from an ontological essence peculiar to a distinctive, exceptional, and aberrational class of persons, whose identity was made manifest in a strictly limited range of gestures or acts, into an ontological category that was universal and the norm. In turn this threatened not only to increase the importance of Dr. Curran's original conclusion that all homosexuals engage in homosexual acts but also to render it less important, as it appeared to explain less about the distinctive and peculiar nature of homosexuality and homosexual acts.

While in the final report the Wolfenden Committee accepted the idea of latent homosexuality, the members also demonstrated a determination to limit the great homosexualizing potential that was found to be associated with the concept. While they concluded that the existence of latent homosexuality was a validly drawn inference, they also commented that it was to be limited in two ways. First, in general latent homosexuality was an inference that could only be drawn in specific circumstances by certain individuals—for example, after a formal examination made by a specialist such as a doctor, who had been trained to discover the symptoms of a homosexual component. Second, while certain signs might be read by laypersons as self-evident proof of latent homosexuality, the committee wished to limit the number of such signs. Several examples from which homosexuality might be inferred were given: an individual's outlook or judgment; a persistent and indignant preoccupation with the subject of homosexuality; and participation in certain occupations, particularly those that called for service to others or services that were of great value to society, such as teachers, clergy, nurses, and those interested in youth movements and the care of the aged. By these mechanisms the committee could recuperate and reinstall the idea that homosexuality was an ontological essence peculiar to a distinctive, exceptional, and aberrational class of persons, whose identity was made manifest in a strictly limited range of gestures or acts. In turn this might help to recover the importance of the conclusion that all homosexuals engage in homosexual acts, which suggests that the act is a manifestation of a specific identity.

Having thus suggested that homosexual acts, either overt or latent, were necessarily a manifestation of homosexuality, Drs. Curran and Whitby proceeded to explore the second proposition: that not all those who indulge in homosexual acts are homosexuals. They concluded that on many occasions homosexual offenses (and thereby homosexual acts) were committed by individuals who were not predominantly homosexual. They offered various examples of same-sex acts

that were not the acts of homosexuals, including situational homosexuality, adolescent activities, and the acts of "certain primitive types
who wanted sex and were indifferent as to whether the partner was
male or female."[11] The committee's final report added other examples:

> some of those whose main sexual propensity is for persons of the oppo-
> site sex indulge, for a variety of reasons, in homosexual acts. It is known,
> for example, that some men who are placed in special circumstances that
> prohibit contact with the opposite sex (for instance in prisoner of war
> camps or prisons) indulge in homosexual acts, though they revert to het-
> erosexual behaviour when opportunity affords; and it is clear from our
> evidence that some men who are not predominantly homosexual lend
> themselves to homosexual practices for financial or other gain.[12]

Having discovered that all homosexual acts, both overt and covert,
were the acts of homosexuals, this evidence appeared to suggest that
some homosexual acts might be the manifestation of neither overt nor
latent homosexuality. Drs. Curran and Whitby attempted to capture
this emerging paradox in their conclusion that neither social reputa-
tion nor even legal conviction were sound criteria for what might be
called the percentage of homosexuality in a given case or the Kinsey
rating of that case.[13] Their analysis appeared to suggest that a homosexual act, and thereby a homosexual offense, might be not only the
overt or latent manifestation of homosexuality but also the manifestation of bisexuality or heterosexuality.

Various attempts were made to express this complex state of affairs. One example is to be found in a draft of Chapter 3 of the report:
"Where we refer, in this report to a 'homosexual,' we mean a person
in whom this propensity exists and not a person who indulges in homosexual acts. . . . A person who indulges in homosexual acts is not
necessarily 'a homosexual.'"[14] While the definition of homosexuality
as a "propensity" expresses the idea that the homosexuality of homosexual acts may be both overt and latent, this connection is rendered
problematic in the further observation that a person who performs a
homosexual act is not necessarily a homosexual. In a later draft of the
same chapter we find another formulation: "in this enquiry with the
law relating to homosexual acts, the adjective homosexual as applied
to such acts will be used indifferently whether or not those who engage in them are by nature or disposition of the exclusively homosexual type."[15] Although this definition attempts to preserve the nexus between sexual identity and sexual act, if only in the suggestion that
temporary or transient homosexuality will result in transient or aberrational homosexual acts, at the same time it also suggests that there is
no necessary connection between the sexual identity that is used to

name a category of unlawful act and the sexual identity of the person that performs the act. These attempts to explain the homosexual of "homosexual acts" and thereby the homosexual of "homosexual offences" seem to suggest that it cannot be explained as a reference to the sexual identity of the one who performs the act or offense. Again, as the analysis proceeds toward its object, that object threatens to disappear; the homosexuality of homosexual offenses appears to refer to no sexual identity at all.[16]

Listing "Homosexual Offences"

A second major attempt to explore the meaning of "homosexual offences" occurred in the context of attempts to list such offenses. Several lists are to be found in the papers submitted to the committee.[17] The final report of the Wolfenden Committee had two lists of "homosexual offences," one referring to England, the other to Scotland. In England, "homosexual offences" incorporated the following: buggery, attempted buggery, assault with intent to commit buggery, indecent assault on a male by a male, indecent assault on a female by a female, acts of gross indecency between men, procuring and attempts to procure acts of gross indecency between males, persistent soliciting or importuning of males by males for immoral purposes (where the immoral purposes involve homosexual behavior), and offenses involving indecency contained in by-laws (where the offenses involve acts of indecency between persons of the same sex).[18] The list for Scotland differed from the list for England in that it made no reference to buggery but did include references to sodomy.[19] It also included offenses that were absent from the English list, in particular the Scottish common law offense of lewd and libidinous practices and behavior between males, which has no equivalent in England.

These two lists differ in various ways from other lists of "homosexual offences" found in memoranda submitted to the committee. In general the lists in the final report of the Wolfenden Committee are more expansive. For example, they include an offense that is notably absent from most others presented to the committee: genital acts between women.[20] This is in sharp contrast to the lists of offenses produced by the central government; both the Home Office and the Scottish Home Department had commented that homosexual acts between women were not criminal offenses. Second, the Wolfenden lists are more expansive in that they include a potentially extensive range of offenses (by-laws) created by town, city, and regional governments. Third, they show a sensitivity to jurisdictional differences between Scotland and England that are notably absent from the memoranda submitted by the Home Office and the Scottish Home Department. In particular they take note of the distinction between buggery (a term of English law) and sodomy (a term of Scottish law) and of the existence of offenses in Scotland that have no equivalent in England.

The committee provided no overt explanation of the common denominator that joined these offenses together under the title of "homosexual offences." However, the papers of the committee's deliberations offer some evidence of the factors that informed its production. The issue was addressed by Drs. Curran and Whitby, who noted that the phrase "homosexual offence" already had currency as a rubric for a list of offenses: "Taylor, a prison medical officer . . . stated that in his experience [homosexual offenses] can be divided into four main groups namely (1) indecent assaults on boys under the age of 16, (2) importunity [sic], (3) buggery, and (4) gross indecency."[21] Drs. Curran and Whitby concluded that this classification had certain virtues. First, it was simple. Second, if the majority of cases appearing in the criminal statistics could be brought under this scheme, it would also have the virtue of intelligibility.

While the catalogue of wrongs found under the heading "homosexual offences" in the Wolfenden final report might be explained by reference to the criteria used by the prison medical officer, it differs in various ways. For example, it appears to have a greater intelligibility, incorporating a wider range of offenses. In particular the list includes all indecent assaults by men against men and by women against women as well as a wider range of lesser offenses. However, this still tells us little about the factors that brought the offenses together under this common rubric.

An attempt to formulate a statement of the common denominator is to be found in a letter by Dr. Curran attached to a draft of the chapter on general considerations relating to homosexual offences. He suggested that

> at least the majority of offences would I think fall into the general statement "a meeting between two or more male persons during which the genital organs of one party are deliberately brought into contact with or pressure against any part of the body of another or wilfully exhibited or inspected with intent (admitted or reasonably presumed) to obtain sexual excitement."[22]

This definition of "homosexual offences" has interesting characteristics. Of particular note is the absence of any reference to the sexual identity of the participants and to women. Furthermore, while this definition might explain the presence of some of the offenses on the list, it is problematic with regard to most of them. At best it would appear to be directly relevant to only two of the offenses named: gross indecency and importuning. The definition of gross indecency is to be found in Section 11 of the Criminal Law Amendment Act of 1885 (48&49 Vict. c.69):

> Any male person who, in public or private, commits, or is a party to the commission of, or procures or attempts to procure the commission by any male person of, any act of gross indecency with another male person, shall be guilty of a misdemeanour, and being convicted thereof shall be liable at the discretion of the court to be imprisoned for any term not exceeding two years, with or without hard labour.

As it is an offense exclusive to men, such behavior would appear to fall within Dr. Curran's definition of "homosexual offence." Further, the word "indecency," while undefined in the 1885 act, is a term in law that might include genital contact or display.[23] However, it is important to note that Section 11 does not itself define the illegal act as a homosexual offense but as an act that is an outrage on decency.[24] Nor is this section to be found in a statute whose main focus is sexual relations between men, for as is described in its preamble, the purpose of the act is "to make further provision for the Protection of Women and Girls, the suppression of brothels, and other purposes." The 1885 legislation is thus primarily concerned with cross-sex relations in general and cross-sex prostitution in particular. The naming of gross indecency as a "homosexual offence" would appear to be at best a post-hoc classification.

The incorporation of the offense of importuning in the committee's list is more problematic still. Importuning is defined in Section 32 of the Sexual Offences Act of 1956: "It is an offence for a man persistently to solicit or importune in a public place for immoral purposes." The section itself does not specify the sex of the object of the accused's soliciting or importuning. The reduction of the offense to behavior between men is unique to English law and an effect of English police practice and judicial interpretation, which the history of the statutory provision suggests is far from either the necessary or inevitable meaning of the terms of the prohibition.

The incorporation of other offenses into a list of "homosexual offences" presents even greater difficulties. Both buggery and sodomy are problematic. Contrary to expectations generated by the rubric of "homosexual offence," neither buggery nor sodomy is exclusive to male-to-male intercourse. In England and Wales buggery is made an offense by virtue of Section 12(1) of the Sexual Offences Act of 1956: "It is a felony for a person to commit buggery with another person or with an animal." By virtue of the paragraph heading, buggery is an unnatural offence. Section 44 of the act further defines buggery in giving a meaning to the phrase "sexual intercourse": "Where, on the trial of any offence under this Act, it is necessary to prove sexual intercourse (whether natural or unnatural), it shall not be necessary to prove the completion of the intercourse by the emission of seed, but the intercourse shall be deemed complete upon proof of penetration only." As such buggery is a wrongful act that may be performed by one man with another, by a man with a woman, and by a human with an animal. In Scottish law the definition of the criminal act of sodomy differs from this in that it does not include acts of unnatural intercourse between a man and a woman. These acts are not an offense in Scotland. The common incorporation of bestiality in the definition of these two offenses also draws attention to the fact that neither offense is sex/gender (or species) specific.[25] Similarly, the laws that define acts of indecent assault on a man or a woman do not limit these wrongful acts to situations where the wrongdoer is the same sex as the object of the assault. Section 14(1) of the Sexual Offences Act of 1956 merely declares that "it is an offence . . . for a person to make an indecent assault on a woman."[26] Section 15(1) states that "it is an offence for a person to make an indecent assault on a man." Furthermore, while the Wolfenden Committee did not give details of the by-laws that might fall under the rubric of "homosexual offences," they did note that these laws, made by town, city, and regional governments for the "good rule and government" of their areas, provide penalties for indecent behavior that are neither sex, sexuality, nor gender specific.[27]

These factors draw attention to the fact that in order for Dr. Curran's definition of "homosexual offences" to work as an explanation of the factors that connect the items listed, much has to be ignored and forgotten. In particular it is necessary to forget that the most common overt homosexual act, solitary masturbation with homosexual fantasies, has never been criminalized.[28] It is necessary to forget that most of the offenses on the list are equally applicable to heterosexual relations and might equally be described as "heterosexual offences." It is necessary to pass over the jurisdictional idiosyncrasies of England and Wales on the one hand and Scotland on the other, thereby erasing the cultural and historical differences in their practices of criminalization. It is necessary to ignore the fact that Dr. Curran's definition cannot explain the absence of any reference to sexuality in a definition that purports to name a category of offenses by way of a particular sexuality. It is necessary to disregard the general absence of women from the definition of both homosexuality and "homosexual offence." Nor can his definition explain the one reference to wrongful acts between women in the final Wolfenden list of "homosexual offences." It is necessary to

forget that when viewed in terms of sexuality in general or more specifically in term of the binary of hetero- and homosexuality, as a reference to genital acts performed with the opposite sex versus those performed with the same sex, the criminal calendar appears to be absurd
and incoherent.

The production of a list of "homosexual offences" is an attempt to
install a new configuration within the law. This citation of "homosexual" appears to be a reference to a complex process of selection and re-
organization that works to create a new coherence and incoherence in
the law by filling in gaps between wrongs that otherwise have little or
no connection and separating out offenses that had previously been
proximate to each other. It partially reorganizes elements of the law by
means of selection and addition, producing dramatic rearrangements,
making drastic new connections, and censoring knowledge of previous
practices, histories, and cultural differences. It is by this process that
"homosexual offences" is made to appear as a category that makes
sense in law. It is also by this process that the traces of other, earlier
ways of making sense of prohibitions are now to become part of a new
nonsense or a new unintelligibility. To be a success, the phrase "homosexual offences" depends upon and seeks to install a certain amnesia in the law and demands a certain forgetfulness by those who cite
the term.[29]

Forgetfulness is also a theme to be found in the earlier analysis of
homosexuality, homosexual acts, and "homosexual offences" conducted by way of the proposition that not all those who indulge in homosexual acts are homosexuals. As the analysis demonstrates, in using
the phrase "homosexual offences" it is necessary to forget that the "homosexual" in that term is not necessarily a reference to the sexual identity of the actor made manifest in the wrongful act. At best it might be
said to be a mere reference to the fact that both parties who perform
an act that attracts a penalty are of the same (male) sex. Furthermore,
the analysis of the proposition that not all homosexuals indulge in homosexual acts draws attention to the importance of recognizing that
the citation of "homosexual" is not so much the use of a term that describes the essential nature of an act or the truth of the identity of the
actor, but rather a reference to a practice of naming that attributes a
particular truth that purports to refer to the essence of the object(s) so
named. More specifically, the Wolfenden analysis draws attention to
the fact that the citation of "homosexual" is a reference to "a whole
machinery for speechyfying, analyzing and investigating."[30] It is a reference to a set of practices and a particular knowledge of the (male)
body and its desires that is produced and enforced not so much by the
one who is placed in the position of the object of consideration,[31] but,

as the Wolfenden Committee noted, by authorized and duly qualified speakers such as psychiatrists and prison doctors. The Wolfenden analysis suggests that as the machinery works toward the discovery of the essential truth of the thing that is the object of knowledge (homosexuality), it is faced with the prospect of discovering that rather than being a reference to a specific identity, homosexual(ity) refers to no specific thing. This is not to suggest that the "homosexuality" of "homosexual offences" has no meaning but it does draw attention to the way nothing can give rise to something, as "homosexuality" becomes a fantasy space or a kind of screen onto which are projected desires, memories, and anxieties.[32]

Finally, the analysis shows that the "homosexual" of "homosexual offences" is a reference to a machinery of naming that has a great capacity not only to incite, extract, distribute, and institutionalize the discourse of (homo)sexuality, but also to put sex into a discourse that has unruly tendencies, produces unexpected meaning, and is in need of control. The final report of the committee draws attention to two mechanisms through which that control might be produced: the distribution of those who are and are not authorized to speak the name "homosexual," and the designation of a specific lexicon or code that may be spoken and read as the signs and symptoms of that identity. The Wolfenden review suggests that the "homosexual" of "homosexual offences" is nothing more than a reference to the machinery through which the very legibility of homosexuality and "homosexual offences" is produced.

The use of "homosexual" in the phrase "homosexual offence" focuses on the fact that by the time of the Wolfenden review a machinery for speechifying, analyzing and investigating homosexual(ity) in law was already a possibility. The references to treatment, to the prison medical service in general, and to the prison medical officer's use of the category "homosexual offence" in particular demonstrate that these naming practices implanted within the legal system had already produced a possibility of the legibility of "homosexual" and "homosexual offences" within the substantive law.[33] The use of "homosexual offences" as a central category in the Wolfenden reform proposals seeks to formally deploy these practices and knowledges developed elsewhere for a different purpose: the invention of a new category of wrong in law. The remainder of this essay will consider the machinery of naming and the knowledges that it produced and deployed.

"Homosexual" as a Technology of Production

One mechanism of the process of naming homosexuality is of particular importance: the examination. It is a complex apparatus that brings together technologies for observing, questioning, listening, formulating and recording. The British Medical Association's (BMA) memorandum to the Wolfenden Committee[34] shows the importance of the examination as a naming practice through which medical knowledge of the (male) body and its desires was deployed and produced. It also provides a valuable snapshot of the uses of the technologies of examination within the processes of the law at the time of the Wolfenden review. The report notes that in general the examination might operate in two contexts: first, in the context of the offense itself; and second, in what the BMA described as a medicopsychiatric context. In the former, an examination might be undertaken to facilitate the process of detection and/or to assist the court in deciding whether there was sufficient evidence to justify conviction. In the latter case the examination might occur at various points in the legal process—before trial, after conviction but before sentencing, or after sentencing—and might be commissioned by the prosecution, the defense, the court itself, or the penal authorities. The BMA suggested that this second type of examination might have various uses. Before the trial it could be used to assess the quality of the case. Postconviction it might be used to determine the causes or reasons underlying the conduct or to inform the court's disposal of the offender. This attempted categorization of examinations ilustrates three important points. First, the two functions need not necessarily be carried out in separate examinations; there is evidence of overlap between, for example, the fact-finding function and the pretrial medicopsychiatric function. Second, an individual might be subject to many examinations; he might be examined upon arrest, before trial, before sentence, after sentence, in the course of entrance and placement in prison or in other institutions of punishment/treatment, and even during the period of punishment/treatment, especially before release on parole. Finally, examination may take place after release as a condition of that release.[35] Thus by the time of the Wolfenden review, the technologies through which the (male) body and its desires might be put into discourse were well implanted within the processes of the law.

While the BMA document details the many uses of examination, it tells little about the techniques deployed within the examination itself. A document submitted to the Wolfenden Committee by the Admiralty provides an example of some of the practices associated with the fact-finding examination.[36] Having stressed the importance of the examination, the Admiralty orders explained its purpose. The general objective was to produce a written record that contains a clear and definite opinion. The written record should always incorporate certain information. It must record the detail of the act[37] and establish whether it occurred on one occasion or on several occasions. It must record all signs and symptoms, whether direct or indirect; all findings, both positive and negative; and all participation, both active and passive. It must contain a record of any physical signs and symptoms of venereal disease and include the venereal history of the man. The Admiralty orders also state that the report shall contain the appropriate conclusions and gives explicit instruction as to what that evidence shall be: the only certain medical evidence of the commission of the offense of buggery "is the presence of semen in the anal canal."

The orders require that the practices of interrogation and documentation are in general to be carried out by specific personnel, medical officers, or, in certain situations, particular specialists—psychiatrists and venereologists. Each in turn must have complex training: the completion of a medical course, with supervised clinical experience, contact with the psychological disciplines, the creation of particular attitudes, and the installation of particular personality characteristics. All have their place in the production of the art of observing, questioning, and listening.[38]

The orders then detail three examination procedures: one for the passive "partner," a second for the active "agent," and a third for the self-confessed homosexual. In general each individual is to be subject to two examinations, both the passive and the active. Where two persons are suspected of a "guilty relationship," they are to be kept apart during the examination and given no opportunity to communicate.

The orders declare that the passive examination should be conducted in the following manner:

(1) Note the general appearances. Look for feminine gestures, nature of the clothing and the use of cosmetics, etc.

(2) Visual external examination of the anus for:
Appearance of bruising or inflammation.
Whether redundancy or thickening of the skin is present.
Evidence of irritation, inflammation or presence of thread worms.
Recent tears, lacerations, fissures and piles, old scars due to previous ulceration, or any physical sign that might be present and might cause dilation or relaxation of the anal sphincter.

(3) Examine the anus for size and elasticity (it is useful to measure the size of the opening by some standard measure such as the number of fingers) and note any discomfort or otherwise during the examination. A speculum may be used.

(4) A swab must be taken from inside the anus with the aid of a proctoscope or speculum for demonstration of spermatozoa, and another from surrounding parts for identification of lubricant and spermatozoa.

(5) The anus should be examined most carefully for the presence of V.D. The presence of any discharge from either the anus or urethra should be noted and slides and swabs taken for the identification of gonococci. . . . When possible all cases in whom V.D. is suspected should be sent to the venereologist for examination at the earliest opportunity.

(6) If it is alleged that the practice has been carried out recently, the underpants and shirt should be examined for the presence of stains which may still be damp. Any suspected stained articles should be wrapped in cellophane or brown paper and sealed for transmission to a laboratory. If it is possible to collect a specimen of liquid semen from an article of clothing, it is desirable to send this in a suitable container. In some cases the blood group of the donor can be detected.

(7) Other suspicious objects such as tins of lubricants, should be sent to a laboratory for examination for the presence of spermatozoa or pubic hair.[36]

In the case of the active (agent), the examining officer is instructed that the examination is to have a particular focus: the penis. The purpose of the examination is to establish whether the penis has in fact been subjected to friction and is contaminated with feces, lubricant, and spermatozoa, which are strong evidence of an offense having occurred. Here the examiner is instructed to pay particular attention to clothing, in this case the front of the underpants, trousers, and shirt, for fresh stains and again for a mixture of semen and feces.

The third interrogation procedure is specific to the examination of the self-confessed homosexual. Here the orders direct that the examination should be conducted by particular specialists: a venereologist and a psychiatrist. The examination must be carried out on the general lines already indicated as far as appropriate but must be modified to exclude those procedures applicable only to a recent act. The objective here is not the documentation of a single act but the documentation of a life history and an identity. Again the examiner is directed to document negative as well as positive findings with supporting reasons for any conclusions reached at any stage. The examiner is specifically required to state in his report whether he believes that the man is telling the truth or lying, or whether he cannot give an opinion on this point.

Finally, the orders contain certain cautions. For example, the examiner is warned that the "classical" appearance of the anal sphincter described in many books is most uncommon and that the conical anus occurs only in the confirmed homosexual practitioner. The orders go on to advise that the anus, which is the object of so much attention, is problematic in other respects, since the "dilation of the anus by itself is not a specific sign of the homosexual and . . . can be due to other causes, e.g., old standing piles, or it may follow operations on the rectum, or it may be due to some disease of the nervous system, etc." Further difficulties are noted in the context of the examination of the self-confessed homosexual. The examiner is warned that "medical evidence may be completely negative even in a well established case; and as the rating who voluntarily confesses may not be a confirmed addict, abnormal physical signs are unlikely to be met."

While the examination procedures appear to be of general significance, applicable to the fact-finding process for a wide range of "offences of immorality,"[39] they seem to have a very particular focus. This is demonstrated by the emphasis given to the distinction between active and passive, which in turn repeatedly concentrates the interrogation procedures upon the anus and the penis, respectively. The technology thus appears to be oriented to the production of evidence of one particular offense—buggery (the only one on the list that directly involves the penetration of the anus by the penis)—rather than upon the full range of offenses. In general the orders also purport to be concerned with setting out an examination procedure dedicated to the detection of an unlawful act. However, it is apparent that this is not the only goal. For example, the direction to examine appearances in general and the presence (or absence) of feminine gestures, the nature of clothing, and the use of cosmetics in particular suggests that the examination is designed to discover evidence not merely of the act itself but also of the signs or symptoms of an identity that is produced through the act and installed behind the act to be named as its cause and essence. Nor is identity only to be read from signs remote from the wrongful act. Act and identity are presented in close proximity by an assumption that the "unnatural offence" (buggery) and more specifically particular uses of the anus are manifestations of homosexuality.[40] Here the fact-finding and the medicopsychiatric functions are not necessarily separate aspects of separate examination procedures but one and the same. These orders suggest that, if the fact-finding examination is concerned only with establishing the fact of the offense, then the sexual desire and thereby the sexual identity of the accused have become facts of the offense to be established.[41] Thereby they suggest that the nature and cause of homosexuality are not matters confined to postconviction deliberations.

The technology's concern with identity is also confirmed by the presence of a psychiatrist as an officer in the fact-finding examination of the self-confessed homosexual. Here the interrogation is concerned primarily with the production of a sexual biography rather than the detail of a particular act. The examination procedure applicable to the self-confessed homosexual is of interest in other ways. In particular,

Admiralty orders emphasize that the authenticity of identity is an effect not so much of self-identification but of the machinery of examination, subject to the scrutiny and the endorsement of specialists. Thus while the technology of examination incites the self-confessed homosexual to speak of his homosexuality in the first instance, it then questions the authenticity of that speech. Where the homosexual names himself, that naming appears to become more rather than less problematic. Thus the orders warn the examiner of the dangers of self-definition, with the homosexuality of the self-confessed homosexual threatening to disappear in the process of examination. Contrary to expectations, the presence of the self-confessed homosexual does not so much undermine the need for the technology of examination as reinforce the importance of that technology. Here self-confession is only an ambiguous sign of homosexuality. The examiner is warned that the self-confessed homosexual may become more difficult to detect, as he may carry none of the signs of homosexuality.

Thus the self-confessed homosexual poses a threat, in part because he is not an authorized speaker, and in part because he may present his homosexuality in ways that do not comply with the canonical code by which homosexuality is represented and that therefore may disturb and disrupt that code. The Admiralty orders show that in the final instance homosexuality is to be produced or authorized by a designated speaker and through a particular code of representation dedicated to the discovery of "the truth" of homosexuality. As a particular specialist, a psychiatrist is required to determine the truth or falsity of the self-confession, and, by means of the examination, document the self-confession according to the requirements of the canonical discourse.

Again, the Admiralty papers only provide evidence of a fragment of the technology of examination. Other papers presented to the Wolfenden Committee illustrate other aspects of that technology. In particular they offer evidence of the knowledges of homosexuality according to which the outpourings incited by the examination machinery might be organized, presented, and absorbed. For example, in a memorandum submitted to the Wolfenden Committee by the Institute of Psychiatry the knowledge of homosexuality is tabulated as a scheme of classification.[42] This classificatory grid operates with five main categories and a number of subcategories. It incorporates references to various treatments: analytical therapies, psychiatric teamwork, sexual sedative medicine, social work supportive measures, and penal. The grid evaluates their suitability with a crude scale (+ = useful; ++ = very useful; +++ = essential). Like all of the classificatory schemes presented to the Wolfenden review, this grid has both an individualizing and a totalizing dynamic.[43] It seeks to name homosexuality in general by way of its causes, origins, and manifestations, and to name the nature and causes of the homosexuality of the particular individual. The grid demonstrates the interface between the classificatory schemes and treatment regimes, which shows that these knowledges of homosexuality are closely linked to projects of control and eradication. When deployed through the process of interrogation, the naming process attempts not only to incite and extract but also to distribute and institutionalize the (male) body and its desires by attributing to it a particular nature and connecting it to a particular project of treatment that might further encode it in certain practices or work toward its eradication.

Conclusion

The term "homosexual" in the phrase "homosexual offences" is in the Wolfenden review a reference to technologies of examination, schemes of classification, and projects of management and eradication. The phrase "homosexual offences" points to the existing implantation of these devices through which homosexuality might be spoken about and induced to speak for itself within various practices of the law. The use of this term indicates the installation of these technologies within regimes of containment, treatment, and punishment. While particular attention has been paid to the technologies of homosexuality in the prison medical service, this was not the only site of the production of homosexuality at the time of the Wolfenden review. Another particularly important location, which I consider elsewhere, was police practice.[44] This draws attention to the dispersion of sites of production, which in turn illustrates how the review worked as a nexus connecting these disparate sites and facilitating their further extension into substantive law. The Wolfenden proposals and the later inclusion of the phrase "homosexual offences" in the Sexual Offences Act of 1967 sought to install these technologies and knowledges in a different context, within the practices through which substantive law is imagined and more specifically through which the (male) body and its desires are both criminalized and decriminalized.

There is much evidence to suggest that the Wolfenden Committee hoped to install a technology of homosexuality within English law that would both limit the meaning of homosexuality and further promote its eradication. Two strategies of eradication are proposed by the Wolfenden reforms. The first is juridical eradication. By arguing that certain homosexual offenses should be decriminalized when they occur in private, the committee hoped that homosexual acts might disappear into a space beyond the law. The second project of eradication is also connected to the proposal to decriminalize certain offenses, which the committee hoped would encourage homosexuals to seek treatment for their condition. In turn that treatment would lead to heterosexuality, abstinence, or the performance of homosexual acts in private. Finally, the Wolfenden review proposed that a major project should be launched to discover more about homosexuality, which again might be dedicated to eradication.

However, there is ample evidence in the Wolfenden papers that a project to install these technologies of production was doomed to failure. Thus it is important to note that the above descriptions of the technologies of examination outline the optimum conditions for success. These descriptions ought to be placed in the context of their actual operation. Day-to-day practice might not mirror these formal requirements. Evidence before the Wolfenden Committee suggests that the use of the examination was a partially realized and idiosyncratic practice rather than a systematic one. For example, a survey of homosexual offenders remanded to Brixton prison in 1946 showed that the magistrates had called for a report in only 39 of 66 cases.[45] The Cambridge survey,[46] conducted immediately prior to the Wolfenden review, found that the courts called for medical reports in only 20 percent of cases. Evidence indicated that the use of medical examinations by the courts depended upon the offense charged. Thus the Cambridge survey suggested that the use of medical examinations was higher (31.7%) where the accused was charged with indecent assault. Dr. Snell, the Director of the Prison Commission Medical Services, also noted that the courts asked for reports much more frequently in cases of indecent assault, but he added that the same pattern emerged with regard to persons charged with importuning.[47] The courts therefore had a discretionary power rather than a duty to order medical examinations. Finally, medical officers did not undertake such examinations uniformly.[48]

Other instances of the failure of these technologies abound. For example, in its references to available treatments the classificatory grid demonstrates that the success of the treatments was problematic. Furthermore, the memoranda submitted to the committee show that while many classificatory schemes might have certain features in common, they also differed in many respects. It should not be forgotten that the difficulties facing the Wolfenden committee in part arose out of the need to make sense of the multiplicity of classificatory schemes that had produced a proliferation of categories of homosexual. This proliferation of categories points to the effects of the tension between the totalizing tendency and the individualizing tendency, which promotes the proliferation of new categories and subcategories, which in turn threatens to undermine the technology and invalidate the knowledges it seeks to produce and disseminate. As Dr. Landers, the prison medical officer for Wormwood Scrubbs, noted, the "over classification of the different types of homosexual adds nothing to our knowledge and, if anything, leads to confusion."[49] Thus in some respects the multiplicity of classificatory schemes, fragmentation of ontologies, and multiplication of etiologies designed to clarify the nature and origins of homosexuality made it more difficult to talk about its nature and origins, which indicates that these knowledges are not monologic.[50] These technologies are capable of producing knowledges that are not only partial but also problematic, multiple, and unstable. The knowledges may emerge as sites of contestation rather than as exhaustible and stable expositions of the truth. The post-Wolfenden era attests to this fact. Rather than being a successful project to limit speech in law on homosexuality by confining it to authorized speakers, by imposing a code of representation, and by relegating it to the silence of a private space or total eradication, the Wolfenden review was the inauguration of a new era that formally installed an incitement to put homosexuality into the discourse of English law and of other legal systems within the United Kingdom.

NOTES

1. Sir John Wolfenden, *Report of the Departmental Committee on Homosexual Offences and Prostitution, Cmnd 247* (London: H.M.S.O., 1957), p. 7, para. 1. Several histories of the period have been published recently. Some focus on the Wolfenden review and the subsequent reforms, such as Anthony Grey, *Quest for Justice: Towards Homosexual Emancipation* (London: Sinclair-Stevenson, 1992); and Stephen Jeffrey-Poulter, *Peers, Queers, and Commons* (London: Routledge, 1991). Others deal with the review as part of a wider study of sexual politics in the U.K. in the 1950s and 1960s, such as Tim Newburn, *Permission and Regulation: Law and Morals in Post-War Britain* (London: Routledge, 1992).

2. English law refers to the law applicable to England and Wales. The review did not include a consideration of the law in other parts of the U.K., in particular, Northern Ireland, the Isle of Man, or the Channel Islands.

3. The first memoranda received by the committee from the Home Office—*Memorandum Submitted by the Home Office, 2. Homosexual Offences* PRO HO 345/7 CHP/2—and from the Scottish Home Department—*Memorandum Submitted by the Scottish Home Department, Homosexual Offences*, PRO HO 345/7 CHP/4 —deployed the phrase "homosexual offences" as an organizing category. The Scottish Home Department document declared that "The following offences known to English law may be regarded as 'homosexual offences' . . ." (CHP/2, p. 1). The use of "may" and the quotation marks that frame "homosexual offences" draw attention to the problematic and tentative use of the term, but at

the same time the text demonstrates the legibility of that phrase and its use as a citation to produce a list of offenses.

4. PRO HO 345/11 CHP/DR/3.

5. These reforms have subsequently been applied to other parts of the U.K.: to Scotland in 1980, Northern Ireland in 1982, the Channel Islands in 1990, and the Isle of Man in 1992.

6. Wolfenden, *Report*, p. 11, para. 18.

7. Papers submitted to the Wolfenden review that addressed the question of the nature and causes of homosexuality include: *Memorandum from Paddington Green Children's Hospital Psychological Department on Homosexuality and the Law*, PRO HO 345/7 CHP/37; *Evidence Submitted by Dr. Winifred Rushworth, Honorary Medical Director of Davidson Clinic Edinburgh*, PRO HO 345/7 CHP/36; *Royal College of Physicians, Evidence Presented to the Departmental Committee*, PRO HO 345/7 CHP/30; *Interim Report of a Sub-Committee of the Public Morality Council Appointed to Study the Problem of Homosexuality*, PRO HO345/19; *Memorandum of the Institute of Psycho-Analysis*, PRO HO 345/8 CHP/42; *Memorandum Submitted by the Institute of Psychiatry*, PRO HO 345/8 CHP/57; *Memorandum Submitted by Dr. Eustace Chesser, Harley Street*, PRO HO 345/8 CHP/67; *Comment on Fifty Cases of Homosexual Personalities Submitted by Dr. R. Sessions Hodge*, PRO HO 345/8 CHP/84; *Note by the Prison Commissioners for England and Wales*, PRO HO 345/9 CHP/86; *A Memorandum of Evidence Prepared by a Special Committee of the Council of the British Medical Association for Submission to the Departmental Committee, November 1955*, PRO HO 345/9 CHP/95; *Memorandum from Drs. Curran and Whitby*, PRO HO 345/9 CHP/107; *Memorandum Presented to the Departmental Committee on Homosexuality and Prostitution by a Joint Committee Representing the Institute for the Study and Treatment of Delinquency and the Portman Clinic (I.S.T.D.) London*, PRO HO 345/9 CHP/90.

8. See Dr. D. Curran and Dr. D. Parr, "Homosexuality: An Analysis of 100 Male Cases Seen in Private Practice," *British Medical Journal* 1(1957): 797–801. In the final instance the committee were much more optimistic about the possibility of abstinence. They observed that "many persons, though they are aware of the existence within themselves of the propensity, and though they may be conscious of sexual arousal in the presence of homosexual stimuli, successfully control their urges towards overtly homosexual acts with others." As such the homosexual condition never manifests itself in overtly sexual behavior. This, the committee concluded, was due to various factors, including "ethical standards, or fear of social or penal consequences, . . . a happy family life, a satisfying vocation, or a well-balanced social life." They went on to conclude that "our evidence suggests however that complete continence in the homosexual is relatively uncommon—as, indeed it is in the heterosexual—and that even where the individual was by disposition continent, self-control might break down temporarily under the influence of factors like alcohol, emotional distress or mental or physical disorder or disease." (Wolfenden, *Report*, p. 12, para. 23).

9. While the main thrust of the argument was that homosexual acts were the manifestations of homosexuality, the committee also noted that this might not always be the case. Since homosexual persons have heterosexual in-

tercourse with or without homosexual fantasies, homosexual persons may perform heterosexual acts. Ibid., p. 11, para. 19.

10. *Memorandum from Drs. Curran and Whitby*, PRO HO 345/9 CHP/107, p. 12. As an example they refer to "the well known case of Lord Castlereigh," who developed a paranoid melancholia in which he believed he would be caught and imprisoned for homosexual offenses, which led to his suicide.

11. Ibid.

12. Wolfenden, *Report*, p. 11, para. 19.

13. *Memorandum from Drs. Curran and Whitby*, PRO HO 345/9 CHP/107, p. 6. Some members of the committee met Professor Alfred C. Kinsey in 1955. His work proposed a heterosexual-homosexual rating scale. The memorandum of Dr. Kinsey's meeting with members of the Wolfenden Committee can be found at PRO HO 345/9 CHP/93.

14. PRO HO 345/17.

15. PRO HO 345/18 CHP/DR/11 (replacing CHR/DR/3).

16. See Slavoj Zizek, *Looking Awry: An Introduction of Jacques Lacan Through Popular Culture* (London: MIT Press, 1991), pp. 3–12.

17. See *Memorandum Submitted by the Home Office, 2. Homosexual Offences*, PRO HO 345/7 CHP/2; *Memorandum Submitted by the Scottish Home Department, Homosexual Offences*, PRO HO 345/7 CHP/4; and *A Memorandum of Evidence Prepared by a Special Committee of the Council of the British Medical Association for Submission to the Departmental Committee, November 1955*, PRO HO 345/9 CHP/95.

18. At the time the Wolfenden review was initiated, in English law the offense of buggery was defined under the heading "Unnatural Offences" in Section 61 of the Offences Against the Person Act of 1861 (24&25 Vict. c.100), in the following terms: "Whosoever shall be convicted of the abominable crime of buggery committed either with Mankind or with an Animal shall be liable, at the discretion of the Court to be kept in Penal Servitude for life or for any term not less than ten years." The offense was reenacted in 1956 in the Sexual Offences Act, where it appears under the heading "Unnatural offences" in Section 12(1): "It is a felony for a person to commit buggery with another person or with an animal." The Sexual Offences Act of 1956 appears to bring the act of buggery within the definition of sexual intercourse (whether natural or unnatural) in Section 44 as complete on penetration. This repeals a similar provision in Section 63 of the Offences Against the Person Act of 1861.

19. David Hume, in *Commentaries on the Law of Scotland*, vol. 1 (Edinburgh: Law Society of Scotland, 1986, pp. 469–470), defines sodomy as "unnatural lusts." He goes on to discuss the crime only in the context of proceedings against John Swan and John Litster. He treats bestiality as a separate matter. G. H. Gordon, in *The Criminal Law of Scotland* (Edinburgh: W. Green and Son Ltd., 1978), p. 894 ff.5, defines sodomy in Scotland as "unnatural carnal connection between male persons," and continues that "it is submitted that it is not sodomy, nor indeed a crime at all as such to have anal intercourse with a consenting adult woman.

20. Both the Home Office and the Scottish Home Department had noted that "homosexual acts between women are not criminal offences."

21. PRO HO 345/9 CHP/107.

22. While this definition does not appear in the final report of the committee, it does appear in a proposed amendment to an early draft of "Part 2—Homosexual Offences, Chapter 1 General Considerations," submitted by Dr. Curran. See PRO HO 345/11 CHP/DR/3.

23. On gross indecency see *R. v. Hornby and Peaple* [1946] 2 All E.R. 487; and *R. v. Hunt* [1950] 2 All E.R. 291. On indecency see *R. v. Court* [1987] 1 All E.R. 120; and Leslie J. Moran, "What Is Indecency?" *Liverpool Law Review* 11(1)(1991):99–109.

24. For an excellent discussion of the incidents that gave rise to the legislation, see Judith R. Walkowitz, *City of Dreadful Delight: Narratives of Sexual Danger in Late-Victorian London* (London: Virago Press, 1992). For other histories of Section 11, see F. B. Smith, "Labouchere's Amendment to the Criminal Law Amendment Bill," *Historical Studies* 17(67)(1976): 165–175; and Jeffrey Weeks, *Sex, Politics, and Society* (London: Longmans, 1981), chap. 6.

25. Janet E. Halley has also noted, in the context of the United States, that buggery is sexualized in a very particular way by the courts so as to render heterosexual buggery invisible. See Halley, "Misreading Sodomy: A Critique of the Classification of 'Homosexuals' in Federal Equal Protection Law," in Julia Epstein and Kristina Straub, eds., *Body Guards* (New York and London: Routledge, 1991), p. 351–377; Halley, "*Bowers v. Hardwick* in the Renaissance," in Jonathan Goldberg, ed., *Queering the Renaissance* (Durham, NC: Duke University Press, 1994), p. 15–40; and Halley, "The Construction of Heterosexuality," in Michael Warner, ed., *Fear of a Queer Planet* (Minneapolis: University of Minnesota Press, 1993), p. 82–104.

26. Thus the offense applicable to acts of indecency between women does not prescribe the gender of the wrongdoer.

27. Wolfenden, *Report*, p. 45, para. 125.

28. In part this is very surprising, especially since in the nineteenth century "self-pollution" had been named as the cause of homosexuality as well as other sexual perversions. See, e.g., Richard von Krafft–Ebbing, *Psychopathia Sexualia* (New York: Pioneer Publications, 1948). Nor can it be explained by the public/private distinction. None of the offenses incorporated in the list work with that distinction as a limit to the criminalizing potential of the law. The idea of privacy as a limit to the criminal law applicable to genital relations between men entered the law of England only in 1967 with the Sexual Offences Act.

29. On amnesia and the law, see also Leslie J. Moran, "Buggery and the Tradition of Law," *New Formations* 19(Spring 1993): 109–125.

30. Michel Foucault, *The History of Sexuality*, vol 1, *An Introduction*, trans. Robert Hurley (London: Penguin, 1990), p. 109.

31. As Foucault notes, this does not lead to the conclusion that the object of consideration must remain mute or unconscious, but rather that he must speak according to a particular code: "a certain reasonable, limited canonical and truthful discourse" (ibid., p. 29). See also Halley, "The Construction of Heterosexuality," p. 82.

32. Zizek, *Looking Awry*, pp. 3–12.

33. See Michel Foucault, *Discipline and Punish: The Birth of the Prison*, trans. Alan Sheridan (London: Peregrine Books, 1979), p. 17.

34. PRO HO 345/9 CHP/95.

35. Albert Ellis, "Interrogation of Sex Offenders," *Journal of Criminal Law* 45(1954): 41.

36. PRO HO 345/7 CHP/21.

37. It is important to note that the Admirality fleet orders do not talk about "homosexual offences" or "homosexual acts." The offenses and acts are instead variously referred to as "unnatural acts," "unnatural vice," "unnatural offences," and "offences of immorality." The orders were submitted as an appendix to the *Memorandum from the Admiralty*. In that memorandum the offenses are referred to as "homosexual offences," which shows that some papers were presented in response to requests from the committee. In making such requests the phrase "homosexual offences" was invariably used. Responses worked to that agenda even though this was a departure from their existing classificatory practice. PRO HO 345/9 CHP/95.

38. These issues are discussed in greater detail in Leslie J. Moran, *The Homosexuality of Law* (London: Routledge, forthcoming). See also Ellis, "Interrogation of Sex Offenders."

39. "The offences of sexual immorality between males that Naval Officers may be called upon to investigate are: (1) Buggery; (2) Assault with intent to commit buggery; (3) Indecent assault; (4) Act of gross indecency with a male person; (5) Procuring the commission of an act of gross indecency with another male person; (6) Attempts to commit offences (1), (4) and (5) above; (7) Inciting to commit either (1), (3), (4) or (5); (8) Uncleanness, or other scandalous action in derogation of God's honour and corruption of good manners." PRO HO 345/9 CHP/95.

40. See Leo Bersani, "Is the Rectum a Grave?" *October* 43(Winter 1987): 197.

41. Ellis, "Interrogation of Sexual Offenders," p. 41. Foucault also makes the point: " 'crime' the object with which penal practice is concerned has profoundly altered: the quality, the nature, in a sense the substance of which the punishable element is made, rather than its formal definition. It is these shadows [such as perversions] lurking behind the case itself that are judged and punished" (*Discipline and Punish*, p. 17).

42. PRO HO 345/8 CHP/57. Other examples are in the Wolfenden papers: PRO HO 345/9 CHP/86, Appendix I and IV (both relate to different classificatory schemes deployed by medical officers in the Prison Medical Service); PRO HO 345/9 CHP/95 (BMA memorandum, Appendix A); PRO HO 345/9 CHP/84 (Dr. Sessions Hodge, of the Neuro-Psychiatric Department, Musgrove Park Hospital, Taunton, offered an analysis of 50 cases that he had seen in his criminological practice). These are explored more fully in Moran, *The Homosexuality of Law*.

43. See Michel Foucault, "The Subject and Power," in Herbert L. Dreyfus and Paul Rabinow, eds., *Michel Foucault: Beyond Structuralism and Hermaneutics* (Brighton, UK: Harvester Press, 1982), pp. 208–26; and Foucault, *Discipline and Punish*, pp. 135–95.

44. The police have a particularly significant place in the review process and in the production of homosexuality in the law. The call for a review of the law and practice relating to homosexual offenses and the treatment of persons convicted of such offenses by the courts was a response to what was perceived to be a dramatic increase in the incidence of homosexual offenses generated by the police. This analysis is developed further in Moran, *The Homosexuality of Law*.

45. F. H. Taylor, "Homosexual Offences and Their Relation to Psychotherapy," *British Medical Journal* 2(1947): 525.

46. L. Radzinowicz, *Sexual Offences* (London: Macmillan, 1957).

47. PRO HO 345/9 CHP/95.

48. PRO HO 345/9 CHP/86, Appendix I.

49. PRO HO 345/9 CHP/95, Appendix III.

50. Foucault, *Discipline and Punish*, pp. 26–29.

T W O

Leo Flynn analyzes the reasoning of the Irish Supreme
Court in Norris v. Attorney General, which, in 1984,
held (by majority) that legislation criminalizing same-sex
sexual activity between men was constitutional. Flynn
interrogates the status of homosexuality constructed by the
Court, a status premised upon the inherently criminal
nature of homosexual conduct. Both majority and minority
judges read homosexual desire as individual disorder, and
Flynn demonstrates how the framework deployed by the
Court is incommensurable and contradictory. For American
readers, comparisons can be drawn to the U.S. Supreme
Court's treatment of same-sex sexual acts in Bowers v.
Hardwick. Of particular interest may be the fact that
neither lesbian sexual activity nor consenting sexual acts
between unmarried heterosexuals was criminalized in
Ireland. As Flynn shows, this difference allowed the Irish
Court to justify the criminalization of male homosexual sex
by differentiating it from lesbian sex and heterosexual sex
outside of marriage.

The Irish Supreme Court and the Constitution of Male Homosexuality

Leo Flynn

Introduction

In many Western societies, same-sex erotic activity is problematized
in moral, legal, and medical discourse at several sites, such as education, health, employment, and sexual activity itself. In that final locus
it is described as "homosexuality," a word of recent provenance linked
to a concept that is equally recent.[1] During earlier times there were
"homosexual acts" that did not establish "homosexuality" but were positioned and divided under various other defining heads, such as
sodomy, acts against nature, intimate friendships, or the legitimate engagement in particular sensual acts. Such acts were incidents within an
economy of pleasures, not distinguished from other manifestations of
desire. If they were differentiated from nonhomosexual acts, it was
through social censure attracted because of their position in other discourses. These acts did not in themselves speak the truth of persons
who participated in them; that identification functioned as an interplay
of other discourses. The discovery of "homosexuality" has not totally

displaced those earlier categories that assert themselves in vestigal form, submerged layers capable of disrupting the dominant discourse that has succeeded them. The contemporary impact of the rhetoric and vision of otherwise anachronistic discourses is significant, and a multiplicity of overlapping systems of classification, each of varying strength, may interact in the narratives of law. The judicial constructions of homosexuality are one area in which one can see these mechanisms at work.

The Irish Supreme Court, in *Norris v. Attorney General*,[2] has wrestled with the homosexual man, carefully laying out the nature of his desire. The Court held by majority that legislation criminalizing same-sex sexual activity between men was constitutional. The plaintiff, Norris, had claimed rights to privacy and to bodily integrity, and asserted that the relevant legislation failed to uphold equality before the law. This essay does not focus on the doctrinal arguments employed in the majority and minority judgments. Instead, it is an attempt to understand the homosexual constructed by the Court. The nature of homosexuality was a crucial element in the complex of "facts" that informed the legal reasoning accompanying the final holding.

Norris v. Attorney General

David Norris was a thirty-eight-year-old lecturer in English at Dublin University, when his action was heard in High Court. He was aware of his sexual orientation at an early age and of public and state attitudes toward that orientation, including the sanction of the criminal law. This environment caused him anxiety and distress, leading to nervous illness that required medical care and counseling. After his recovery he publicly declared himself a homosexual and helped to found the Irish Gay Rights Movement.[3] He was never prosecuted for having engaged in homosexual activities but decided to undertake a constitutional action. His challenge was directed at Sections 61 and 62 of the Offences Against the Person of Act of 1861 (24&24 Vict. c.100) and Section 11 of the Criminal Law Amendment Act of 1885 (48&49 Vict. c.69), which criminalized same-sex sexual acts between men.

Norris's principal claim was that the criminalization of consensual, private sexual activity between men infringed a right to privacy that was protected constitutionally, although that right was not to be found on the face of the Constitution's text. Irish judges had previously held that the text of the Constitution merely states, in general and inexact form, rights that inhere in the person by virtue of a higher natural law or the nature of the Irish State. Therefore, there are individual rights that, although not explicitly set out in the Constitution, enjoy protection because they are to be found interstitially in such phrases as "the personal rights of the citizen." This position was upheld in the landmark case of *Ryan v. Attorney General*,[4] where Mr. Justice Kenny accepted that a plaintiff had a constitutionally protected right to bodily integrity that was not specifically mentioned in the Constitution. He said, "I think that the personal rights which may be invoked to invalidate legislation are not confined to those specified in Article 40 but include all those rights which result from the Christian and democratic nature of the State . . . [T]he right to free movement within the State and the right to marry are examples of this."[5] Norris, aside from arguing on privacy grounds, also alleged that the legislation breached expressly guaranteed rights to equality before the law, given that, while all sexual activity between men was criminal, sexual activity between women was subject to no criminal sanction. His case was unsuccessful in the Irish courts. Initially, in the High Court, Mr. Justice McWilliam rejected his claim. On appeal, the Supreme Court split three to two, the majority holding that Norris had no such right to privacy, while the two dissenting judges, Mr. Justice Henchy and Mr. Justice McCarthy, held for Norris in separate judgments.[6]

The majority of the Supreme Court agreed with the judgment delivered by Chief Justice O'Higgins, who first reviewed the moral status and the possible consequences of male homosexuality:

(1) Homosexuality has always been condemned in Christian teaching as being morally wrong. It has equally been regarded by society for many centuries as an offence against nature and a very serious crime.
(2) Exclusive homosexuality, whether the condition be congenital or acquired, can result in great distress and unhappiness for the individual and can lead to depression, despair and suicide.
(3) The homosexually oriented can be importuned into a homosexual lifestyle which can become habitual.
(4) Male homosexual conduct has resulted, in other countries, in the spread of all forms of venereal disease and this has now become a significant public-health problem in England.
(5) Homosexual conduct can be inimical to marriage and is *per se* harmful to it as an institution.[7]

He then went on to hold that "on the ground of the Christian nature of our State and on the grounds that the deliberate practise of homosexuality is morally wrong, that it is damaging to the health both of individuals and the public, and, finally, that it is potentially damaging to the institution of marriage, I can find no inconsistency with the Constitution in the laws which make such conduct criminal."[8]

The remaining two judges dissented strongly on the ground that Norris had a right to privacy that could be invoked outside marriage. Mr. Justice Henchy described the right to privacy as

> a complex of rights, varying in nature, purpose and range, each necessarily a facet of the citizen's core of individuality within the constitutional order. . . . There are many other aspects of the right of privacy, some yet to be given judicial recognition. It is unnecessary for the purpose of this case to explore them. It is sufficient to say that they would all appear to fall within a secluded area of activity or non-activity which may be claimed as necessary for the expression of an individual personality, for purposes not always necessarily moral or commendable, but meriting recognition in circumstances which do not endanger considerations such as State security, public order or morality, or other essential components of the common good.[9]

He located the source of constitutional protection of the right by "having regard to the purposive Christian ethos of the Constitution."[10] Mr. Justice Henchy went on to review expert evidence presented on behalf of Norris, and then held that the impugned legislation was unconstitutional because it intruded "on an area of personal intimacy and seclusion which requires to be treated as inviolate for the expression of those primal urges, functions and aspirations which are integral to the human condition of certain kinds of homosexuals."[11]

The other dissenting judge in the case, Mr. Justice McCarthy, made explicit the potential stresses between Christian and democratic purposive readings of the Constitution. Whereas the Chief Justice merely referred to the Christian nature of the State in giving the reasons for his holding, Mr. Justice McCarthy said that

> in so far as the judgment of Kenny J. in *McGee's Case*, in referring to the Christian and democratic nature of the State, is a relevant identification of source, I would respectfully dissent from such a proposition if it were to mean that, apart from the democratic nature of the State, the source of personal rights, unenumerated in the Constitution, is to be related to Christian theology, the subject of many diverse views and practises, rather than Christianity itself, the example of Christ and the great doctrine of charity which He preached.[12]

Reading *Norris*

The preliminary task of the Supreme Court was to place the male homosexual within legal discourse, to determine his rights-bearing potential, and to scrutinize specific claims made in light of this knowledge. At various points in the judgments in both the High and Supreme Courts the homosexual male is set alongside the lesbian, the married couple, the adulterer, and the fornicator. Using these figures as reference points, the Court can outline the homosexual to its own satisfaction. In addition, the Court notes that different levels of truth reside within the homosexual subject. He may be exclusively homosexual, he may be congenitally homosexual. On the other hand, it is recognized that his homosexuality may simply be superficial, a veneer that is acquired but does not accurately represent the person it purports to illustrate. The Court also identifies the contours of homosexuality by reference to the nature of sexual acts themselves. It can trace the meaning of these acts, position homosexual acts and desire on a grid underpinned by these truths, and so allow law to comprehend the sexual domain that it has uncovered.

The Homosexual and the Lesbian

In examining Norris's arguments, Chief Justice O'Higgins first looks at the contention that a right to equality is breached because the prohibition is confined to same-sex sexual activity between males. A woman cannot commit buggery, nor can she be guilty of gross indecency. The Chief Justice dismisses the idea that this is discriminatory because actions that constitute buggery can only be committed by males. If females are defined as being incapable of committing the offense, then Norris is robbed of this ground of complaint. Careful isolation of a necessarily sex-specific meaning of buggery by the Chief Justice allows him to dispose of the issue. This definitional disability ignores the fluidity of the concept of buggery.[13] The futility of the Chief Justice's attempt to fix the word's meaning in an ahistorical fashion is underscored by reference to the crime of rape. Traditionally only men may commit rape because the common law crime centered on penetration of the vagina by the penis. In Section 4 of the Criminal Law (Rape Amendment) Act 32 of 1990, which defines statutory rape, the Irish legislature accepted the point first made by feminist writers, that rape should include penetration by objects other than a penis. The plasticity of the elements of both buggery and rape belie his justification of a sex-specific offense as natural consequences of biology and the nature of the act.

However, in examining the offense of gross indecency, a crime reserved to men by the 1885 Act, Chief Justice O'Higgins did find differential treatment but not impermissible discrimination between the sexes. The requirement of equality before the law under the Irish Constitution is based on an Aristotlean concept of equality.[14] Equality does

not amount to uniformity; not only may laws legitimately differentiate, in some situations they are *required* to do so by justice, and a distinction between persons is prima facie legitimate if it corresponds with
a real difference of capacity or social function.[15] Chief Justice O'Higgins was of the opinion that "the legislature would be perfectly entitled
to have regard to the difference between the sexes and to treat sexual
conduct or gross indecency between males as requiring prohibition because of the social problem which it creates, while at the same time
looking at sexual conduct between females as not only different but as
posing no such social problem."[16] Although unsupported, no explicit
authority is needed to reinforce his stance. Common sense affirms its
validity. The Report of the Wolfenden Committee on Homosexual Offences and Prostitution indicated that homosexual and lesbian desire
were qualitatively distinct; they could find no assault by one woman
on another that exhibits the libidinous features that characterize sexual acts between males.[17] That observation was reiterated by the
United Kingdom's Criminal Law Revision Committee's Working Paper
in 1980 and in the U.K. government submission to the European Court
of Human Rights in the *Dudgeon* case, where it was clear that "[t]he difference in treatment between the two forms of homosexuality reflects
. . . a genuine difference both in the nature and the scale of the social
and moral problems presented by male and female homosexuality."[18]
Placing the male homosexual beside the lesbian reveals that his desire
manifests itself in aggressive and promiscuous behavior, and that male
homosexual acts directly disrupt societal order. The silence and passivity of lesbian sexuality as conceived in this schema contrast with the
essential qualities of male homosexual acts and desires.[19] The construction of male homosexuality at this point in the judgment associ-
ates male same-sex desire with excess, while lesbian desires are un-
registered and, possibly, unregistrable to the sensitivities of the
judiciary. Notwithstanding that male homosexuality is a monstrous
sexuality for the Irish Supreme Court, it can be grasped, while lesbian
desires and relationships escape comprehension because these are conceived as a lack of those qualities that constitute any sexuality, no matter how abhorrent.

The Homosexual and the Married Couple
The judgment of the Chief Justice is quite clear that "for the small
percentage of males who are congenitally and irreversibly homosexual, marriage is not open or possible. They must seek such partnerships
as they can find amongst those whose orientation disposes them to homosexual overtures."[20] According to the Court, such men are in fact
incapable of contracting a valid marriage, as they suffer from an emo-

tional disability or incapacity. This incapacity may derive from an inherent quality or characteristic of the person's nature that is not vol-
untary or self-induced. In some circumstances, as the Supreme Court
recognized in a later case, "the existence in one party to a marriage of
an inherent and unalterable homosexual nature may form a proper legal ground for annulling the marriage."[21]

The marital relationship is a privileged locus for sexual activity
and the manifestations of desire in law. In fact, it is deemed to be
uniquely proper, and no other site of expression is legitimate.[22] A notable judicial manifestation of this propriety is evidenced by the circumstances in which the right to privacy is recognized as benefiting
from constitutional protection. Although not expressly set out within
the Constitution's text, the right to privacy does come under the umbrella of those rights protected by the Irish legal system. However, that
right was not recognized in an unqualified form. In *McGee v. Attorney
General*,[23] Mrs. McGee brought an action challenging the constitutionality of legislation prohibiting the importation and sale of contracep-
tives. She claimed that it infringed her rights to privacy, specifically, a
protected right to marital privacy. The Supreme Court held by a mar-
gin of four to one that the legislation was unconstitutional. For the majority, Mr. Justice Budd said, "Whilst the 'personal rights' are not described specifically, it is scarcely to be doubted in our society that the
right to privacy is universally recognised and accepted with possibly the
rarest of exceptions, and that the matter of marital relationships must
rank as one of the most important of matters in the realm of privacy."[24]
One of the other majority judgments made clear that the right to marital privacy flowed directly from the right to marry located by *Ryan v.
Attorney General* in the Christian and democratic nature of the State.[25]

However, male same-sex relationships are not simply one of
many nonmarital expressions of sexuality occupying a site in the
penumbra of propriety for the legal system, a position that is determined by their collective antithesis, the marital union. Such relations
are the forbidden "other" of that unique union. The Chief Justice notes
that such conduct can be inimical to marriage and is per se harmful to
it as an institution.[26] Through that opposition one can elaborate the nature of homosexuality. Chief Justice O'Higgins quoted the Wolfenden
Report's comments on the temptation that homosexual activity offers
men who might otherwise marry, noting that "there are also cases in
which a man in whom the homosexual component is relatively weak,
nevertheless, derives such satisfaction from homosexual outlets that he
does not enter upon a marriage which might have been successfully
and happily consummated."[27] The male homosexual is presented here
as driven by the need to satisfy sensual desires in a non(re)productive

way. His sterility is manifested both individually and societally. The family based on marriage, the fundamental unit of society, is undermined by homosexual activity, diverting some men from entering into marriage, while some of those who do marry may cause marital breakdowns. It is interesting that just as the Court was clear that lesbian desire was not dangerous to society, it was sure that such desire was not dangerous to marriage. The possibility of the lesbian leaving her marriage because of the temptation offered by the congenitally lesbian is not canvased.

A juxtaposition of the homosexual and the married couple, however, has a double function. In addition to exposing the adverse side effects of homosexual relations on the foundation of collective stability, the homosexual relationship is itself constructed as an unstable and temporary liaison, satisfying the libidinous desires of the homosexual male but without creating a permanent association in addition to the manifestation of desire. The dangerous, short-term, and pleasure-centered nature of homosexual desire is emphasized in the formula presented by the Chief Justice, where the pleasure available even for a man whose homosexual inclinations are weak outweighs that which is offered legitimately within marriage. No attempt is made by the Chief Justice to locate this latent homosexuality within the contending fields of acquired and congenital homosexuality, which animate much of the judgment. However, his concern about the attractive qualities of same-sex relations opens the possibility that all men might carry within themselves the potential for homosexuality. Notwithstanding that the marital state is a natural one, the potential for pleasure inherent in homosexuality is seen as seductive and potentially more attractive. In this ordering of the legitimacy of pleasures, male homosexual acts are associated implicitly with an excess of desire, a representation that signifies their disruptive potential on the parallel levels of individual and group.

The Homosexual and the Fornicator

The judges also invoke the fornicator and the adulterer, both of whom engage in sexual conduct outside marriage. As such their actions are not privileged in the eyes of the law and could be viewed in the same light as the man who has sex with another. That tactic is adopted by the minority, who would have held that Norris had a constitutional right to privacy that was infringed by the existence of the impugned statutes. One of the minority judges, Mr. Justice Henchy, gives an account of the life style that is forced onto the homosexual man, "a role of furtive living, which has involved traumatic feelings of guilt, shame, ridicule and harassment and countless risks to his career

. . . and his social life generally."[28] These consequences do not follow on the actions of "the fornicator, the adulterer, the sexually deviant married couple," and others whose behavior may be thought to be no less inimical to the upholding of individual moral conduct, necessary standards of public order, the needs of a healthy family life, or social justice.[29] However, the majority make it clear in summary fashion that the attempt to place the male homosexual on the same plane as these others is misguided. The Chief Justice simply states that, given the fact that sexual conduct outside marriage between men and women gives rise not only to different social problems but indeed to no social problem similar to that which results from homosexual activity, "there is no discrimination in the fact that the laws of the State do not apply to heterosexual conduct outside marriage between consenting adults."[30] For the majority it is clear that homosexual acts and desires are of a completely different order than their heterosexual equivalents. In fact, the possibility of describing the acts as equivalent is precluded as they are positioned in different spheres which removes any ability to map one onto the other. Ultimately, Mr. Justice Henchy implicitly concedes this point when, leaving the privacy claim to one side, he responds to Norris's claim that the failure to criminalize acts comparable to (criminal) male homosexual activity amounts to an unconstitutional discrimination: "The sexual acts left unaffected are for physiological, social and other reasons capable of being differentiated as to their nature, their context, the range of their possible consequences and the desirability of seeking to enforce their proscription as crimes."[31] The movement from arguments of privacy to arguments of equality undertaken by the minority judges ultimately destabilizes the attempt to couple the homosexual and the fornicator.

By placing the homosexual along that which is obviously different—the lesbian, the married couple, and the fornicator—the Court reveals his characteristics, circumscribes his boundaries, unveils his features. This process of delineation establishes that his desires are violent and disruptive of society as a whole and of individual relations. This discovery also grounds the Court's claim that his acts are different from those in which heterosexuals engage. However, this strategy of opposition and contrast is not enough. The Court goes on to invoke a second strategy, of analogy and metaphor, to capture the interior identity of the homosexual as well as the signs that he leaves through his acts.

The Nature of Homosexuality

The different conceptions of homosexuality used by the Chief Justice are fourfold, namely, a perversion of nature, a species of sinful and immoral conduct, an instance of criminal behavior, and, an individual disorder.[32] Those elements of understanding are also present in the judgments of the minority, but their favorable conclusion on Norris's claims become possible through the additional conception of homosexuality as an identity. At no stage in any of the Court's judgments does another possible concept—of homosexuality as a normal variation on human sexuality—arise. The remainder of this essay examines the judicial exegesis of the internal nature of, and relations between, homosexual acts and desires, and scrutinizes the authorities employed by the members of the Supreme Court.

The Chief Justice opens his judgment by a description of homosexual behavior as "sexual acts and conduct of a kind usually regarded and described as abnormal or unnatural."[33] He later expands on this observation, noting that such conduct is "a perversion of the biological function of the sex organs."[34] In the High Court, Mr. Justice McWilliam had given a more explicit treatment of the nature of sex, a reading derived from "common sense" observations of nature:

> It seems to me that it is not unreasonable for the assumption to be made, whether correctly or incorrectly, that the primary purpose of the sexual organs in all animals, including man, is the reproduction and perpetuation of the respective species. If that is so, it seems to follow that there are some grounds for reasonable people to believe that sexuality should be confined to lawful marriage, that sexuality outside marriage should be condemned, and that sexuality between people of the same sex is wrong.[35]

It is not necessary for Mr. Justice McWilliam to import the nature of marriage as the unique locus of legitimate sexual activity in order to derive the unnatural status of same-sex sexual expression. Yet by doing so, he elides two concepts of wrongfulness, those of the unnatural act and the immoral act. These understandings are closely linked as, for the Court, nature demonstrates what is morally correct or otherwise. The moral status of homosexual behavior is highly significant.

Chief Justice O'Higgins establishes the immoral nature of homosexual conduct in the Judeo-Christian tradition.[36] It is not necessary, the Chief Justice points out, to appeal to a single religion or indeed to religion at all, since common sense echoes the tradition that homosexual "conduct is, *of course*, morally wrong, and has been so regarded by mankind through the centuries."[37] That point is conceded even by those judges who dissent from the majority's holding. There is no question of validating any expression of such acts or desires; they emphasize that "the removal of the sanction of the criminal law from an immoral act does not necessarily involve an approval or condonation of that act."[38]

The authority to which Chief Justice O'Higgins appeals is not as unequivocal as he indicates; scriptural and patristic statements used to prove the immoral nature of such behavior are open to a number of readings, not all of which are condemnatory.[39] Societies outside of the Judeo-Christian ethical stream have also tolerated some same-sex erotic activities.[40] His assumption that same-sex sex acts can be viewed through a single frame establishes his claim's historical pedigree and plays an interesting role within his decision. However, it is not a coherent grid to bring to bear on the issue.[41]

The inherently criminal nature of homosexual conduct is also emphasized in the majority judgment, supported by pointing to the consequences of such conduct on the individual and on society. The Chief Justice dwells extensively on the relation between the libidinous homosexual male and disease, making it clear that such a person is potentially dangerous to public welfare.[42] The criminality of homosexual conduct is supported (tautologically) by pointing to the legislative history of the prohibition. The Chief Justice gives a truncated account of the law's treatment of such behavior,[43] though the judge at first instance, Mr. Justice McWilliam, is far more comprehensive, setting out this history in detail.[44] Clearly, buggery has been subject to criminal sanction for a significant period of time. However, to say that all same-sex erotic conduct has been the subject of a criminal prohibition for a similar period is misleading. For example, fellatio does not seem to have been covered in the statute *25 Hen. VIII c. 6*[45] and was also beyond its Irish equivalent. Thus, the statement of the majority on the criminal status of all homosexual conduct is overwide and historically suspect.[46] At a deep level this is another expression of the model of static and uniform responses to sexual acts that they utilize. That constant referential grid reinforces the picture of the homosexual that the judges have established through the series of oppositions posited throughout the judgment. To recognize a possibility of shifting attitudes toward particular sexual acts and forms of desire would allow a reframing of the homosexual and would subvert the foundations of this object on which their holding is based.

To describe homosexuality as criminal conduct, immoral behavior, or an act against the course of nature denotes a concern with individual acts, isolated transactions between men, rather than with relationships or desires. Homosexuality, however, is also conceived of as a form of desire that exists as a coherent and unified entity. In the judgments this strand of analysis runs parallel to the preoccupation with homosexuality as a series of momentary and fractured incidents, and an economy of pleasures. However, majority and minority divide sharply on how this desire is to be formulated. Desire is placed at the core of personhood by a powerful discourse in our society, identified

as that point where the essence of the individual is contained.[47] For
that liberal understanding of the self, it is the ability to develop and
pursue life-projects that is the marker of what is most valuable in individual experience and that grounds proper social ordering. Accordingly, what is desired and sought becomes the best and most-authen-
tic sign of the autonomous subject. The judicial treatment of desire in
Norris is crucial, because the conceptual apparatus used by the Irish judiciary to divine constitutionally protected rights, despite the apparent
silence of the Constitution's text itself, explicitly appeals to the human
personality of those appearing before the Court. The minority use the
theory that such rights derive from the nature of the citizen when mediated through the nature of the State. When Mr. Justice Henchy sets
the homosexual alongside the heterosexual, it becomes clear that "in
a number of subtle but insidiously intrusive and wounding ways he has
been restricted in, or thwarted from, engaging in activities which heterosexuals take for granted as aspects of the necessary expression of
their human personality and as ordinary incidents of their citizen-
ship."[48] The essence of those unenumerated rights, which enjoy constitutional protection, is that they inhere in the individual personality
of the citizen in the capacity of a vital human component of the social,
political, and moral order posited by the Constitution.[49] The right of
privacy is a portmanteau of rights that allows the expression of the citizen's core of individuality and so enjoys constitutional protection.[50]
Because the legislation in question "blights and thwarts in a variety of
ways the life of a person who is by nature incapable of giving expression to his sexuality except by homosexual acts,"[51] it is prima facie in
conflict with the constitutional right to privacy and so cannot stand. It
intrudes "on an area of personal intimacy and seclusion which requires
to be treated as inviolate for the expression of those primal urges, functions and aspirations which are integral to the human condition of certain kinds of homosexuals."[52]

For the minority, homosexuality is central and integral to the personhood of certain men. Paradoxically, this formulation allows a gap
to emerge between the *homosexual,* an individual, and *homosexuality,* an
identity, because that identity is not a universal property of those individuals. Given the partial overlap, only certain kinds of homosexuals
can be said truly to possess a homosexual identity. If homosexual desire is acquired, irrespective of whether through some act of will or by
means of inadvertent contagion, it is probably capable of being dis-
lodged and most certainly not indicative of the *real* desires of the *apparently* homosexual subject. Any license accorded to homosexual behavior by this class of superficially homosexual subjects does not give
them leave to express themselves; their acts will be a form of mimicry
that does not warrant the protection of privacy. The majority defuse

the minority's effort to establish correspondence between the homosexual, his desires, and his manifestation of desire through an alternative schema of the relation between homosexual desire and the individual. That space admitted in the minority's careful consideration of
the situation is exploited by the majority in their treatment of homosexual desire. In the majority judgment, Chief Justice O'Higgins does
concede at one point that "there exists in our society a significant number of male homosexual citizens . . . for whom, sexually, the female offers no attraction . . . For these . . . marriage is clearly not open as an
alternative either to promiscuity or a more permanent sexual relationship with a male person."[53] That position is not used to base a representation of desire as identity, but rather is a tactical admission to
dispose of one of the heads under which Norris challenged the legislation—that it infringed a right to marital privacy. The dominant strategy of the majority and minority is to read homosexual desire as an individual disorder. That in turn enables the majority to exploit the gap
in the homosexual identity that was admitted by the minority; for
some men this disorder is innate and congenital—for others, acquired.
The latter group are not truly homosexual, and given the status of their
desire as a false expression both of themselves and of "true" sexuality,
the majority wish to prevent their contagion.

Identification of the disordered nature and consequences of homosexual desire is neatly established by Chief Justice O'Higgins:

> [O]nly a small number [of homosexual men] are exclusively homosex-
> ual in the sense that their orientation is congenital and irreversible. It is
> this small group (of those with homosexual tendencies) who must look
> to the others for the kind of relationship, stable or promiscuous, which
> they seek and desire. It follows that the efforts and activities of the con-
> genital must tend towards involving the homosexually oriented in more
> and more deviant sexual acts to such an extent that such an involvement
> may become habitual.[54]

Accordingly, exclusive homosexuality, whether the condition be congenital or acquired, can result in great distress and unhappiness for the
individual and can lead to depression, despair, and suicide.[55] It is damaging to the health of individuals, for its known consequences are frustration, loneliness, and even suicide;[56] although some may be unfor-
tunate enough to be afflicted by this condition from birth, it can be
acquired by others. Given the framework within which homosexual
desire is found to lie by the majority, their decision to decisively reject
it is a natural and commendable one.

The minority implicitly challenges the ascription of undeniably
deleterious results to homosexual desires in a homophobic society, raising the issue of whether it is the law's treatment of this condition, rather

than the desire itself, that leads to these results.[57] However, they have made too many concessions to a conception of homosexuality as disorder for that response to be equal to the majority's diagnosis of the problem. Their ambivalence cannot match the certainty possessed by the majority; Mr. Justice McCarthy expresses this attitude by saying at the start of his judgment, "It is a feature of modern society in Ireland that the male homosexual is scorned, denigrated and, to a degree, ostracized by a very significant section of the community; it may be that this is because of apparent effeminacy or because of the criminal guilt which attaches under the relevant sections."[58] The use made by the majority of homosexuality as an illness is not challenged. In fact, that conception is antithetical to the individuating characterization of acts as crimes, perversions, or immoral behavior.[59] The creation of homosexuality as an illness originally functioned to deny the freedom of those men who engaged in such acts to determine their own behavior. Its use by the majority creates tension within their own position and inverts its original meaning as they ignore the partiality of their historical situation.

Conclusion

David Norris was unsuccessful in the Irish High Court and Supreme Court because he was not recognized as fully human. He was a homosexual, a different and alien entity whose truth had to be established before the courts could determine how to deal with him. The strategies employed by the Irish Supreme Court in doing so are open to challenge as incommensurable and contradictory, as partial and inaccurate. To issue this challenge, however, requires a subject who can speak in this forum, who can address the Court. Constructing the homosexual as both minority and majority judges did, as false, self-deluding, or (properly) self-hating, allows no space for that coherent voice to fill. The sound of such a speaker is hinted at by Mr. Justice Henchy's description of Norris's conduct and words since he had come out: "[Norris's] subsequent public espousal of the cause of male homosexuals in this State may be thought to be tinged with a degree of that affected braggadocio which is said by some to distinguish a 'gay' from a mere homosexual."[60] At this one point in the proceedings Norris speaks for himself, and simultaneously his gayness is placed within inverted commas, suspended and displaced. The constitution of the homosexual proceeds apace.

NOTES

1. David Halperin, *One Hundred Years of Homosexuality* (London: Routledge, 1990), pp. 15–40.

2. [1984] I.R. 36 (hereinafter *Norris*).

3. These descriptions of Norris were used in the High Court judgment but were taken from his statement of claim. However, the phrases used were not used by Norris himself but by his counsel (conversation between author and Norris, October 23, 1993).

4. [1965] I.R. 294.

5. Ibid., p. 316.

6. Norris was ultimately successful in an action before the European Court of Human Rights but that decision is not the focus of my analysis here. See *Norris v. Ireland*, October 26, 1988, Series A, no. 142; (1991) 13 E.H.R.R. 146. The decision was not unexpected inasmuch as the European Court of Human Rights had previously ruled that the same legislation that remained in force in Northern Ireland was an infringement of an applicant's human rights. See *Dudgeon v. United Kingdom*, October 22, 1981, Series A, no. 45; (1976–82) 4 E.H.R.R. 149. Norris did raise this point in the Irish courts but the Covention has no force in Irish domestic law; see *In re O Láighléis* [1960] I.R. 93.

7. *Norris*, p. 63.

8. Ibid., p. 63.

9. Ibid., p. 71.

10. Ibid., p. 71.

11. Ibid., p. 79.

12. Ibid., p. 99.

13. See Anne Goldstein, "History, Homosexuality, and Political Values", *Yale Law Journal* 97(1988): 1073, 1083 n. 61: "'Buggery' denotes acts which today seem too dissimilar to be named with a single term; anal intercourse between men, see *Stafford's Case*, 12 Co. Rep. 36, 37, 77 Eng. Rep. 1318 (1607) . . . , or between a man and a woman, see *R. v. Wiseman*, Fortes. 91, 92–93, 92 Eng. Rep. 774, 774 (1716), . . . and any penetration between a human being and an animal, see Coke, *The Third Part of the Institutes of the Laws of England*, 58, 59 (London, 1644)."

14. See *de Burca v. Attorney General* [1976] I.R. 38.

15. See *The State (M.) v. Attorney General* [1979] I.R. 73.

16. *Norris*, p. 59.

17. Sir John Wolfenden, *Report of the Departmental Committee on Homosexual Offences and Prostitution*, Cmnd 247 (London: H.M.S.O., 1957).

18. *Dudgeon*, pp. 140–144.

19. Many writers hold that, for the most part, lesbian acts were ignored by both medieval and modern law. See John Bailey, *Homosexuality and the Western Christian Tradition* (London: Longmans, Green, 1955), p. 161. That reading is disputed by Louis Crompton, "The Myth of Lesbian Impunity," *Journal of Homosexuality* 6(1980): 11, but this survey covering five centuries and more than eight modern states can only point to four trials ending in convictions, including three executions, and the legislation referred to seems to have been infrequently enforced.

20. *Norris*, p. 63.

21. *H. F. (orse H.C.) v. J.C.*, July 11, 1990, Supreme Court, unreported, *per* Finlay C.J., p. 17 of the judgment.

22. The institution of marriage is protected in Article 41.3.1 of the Irish Constitution. See Costello J. in *Murray v. Ireland* [1985] I.R. 532, 535–36.

23. [1974] I.R. 284.

24. Ibid., p. 322. See Leo Flynn, "The Missing Body of Mary McGee," *Journal of Gender Studies* 2(1993):238.

25. It has subsequently been noted that Article 40.3 is the source of the right to marital privacy in *Murray v. Ireland* [1985] I.R. 532.

26. *Norris*, p. 63.

27. Wolfenden, *Report*, para. 55.

28. *Norris*, p. 69.

29. *Ibid.*, p. 60. One might argue that Henchy J. should acknowledge that such adverse consequences may follow for the fornicator and her fellow travelers. However, the account offered by Henchy J. does not seem fundamentally inaccurate, and an equality of social and legal opprobrium would undermine Norris's argument of unjustified invasion of his privacy by the State.

30. Ibid., pp. 70–71.

31. Ibid.

32. Ibid., p. 51 ("sexual acts and conduct of a kind usually regarded and described as abnormal or unnatural"), p. 61 (sinful and criminal), and p. 60 (disorder). The disorder of homosexuality can be congenital, *per* O'Higgins C.J., ibid., p. 60, or acquired through an undefined pattern of transmission.

33. Ibid., p. 51.

34. Ibid., p. 61.

35. Ibid., p. 45.

36. Ibid., p. 61.

37. Ibid., p. 64.

38. Ibid., p. 78, *per* Henchy J.

39. John Boswell, *Christianity, Social Tolerance, and Homosexuality* (Chicago: University of Chicago Press, 1980), pp. 91–168.

40. See K. J. Dover, *Greek Homosexuality* (London: Duckworth, 1978).

41. See Kenneth Moore, *The Formation of a Persecuting Society* (Oxford: Basil Blackwell, 1987), pp. 91–94.

42. *Norris*, p. 62. Given the date of the hearing and the age of the material employed by the Chief Justice to support his position (that is, David West, *Homosexuality Re-Examined* [London: Penguin, 1970]), his failure to link the homosexual community with AIDS and HIV is understandable. McCarthy J., *Norris*, p. 101, challenges this alleged spread of venereal diseases, holding that the State has offered insufficient evidence to show a compelling State interest in this respect.

43. Ibid., p. 61.

44. Ibid., pp. 40–41. See *R. v. Jacob*, Russ. & Ry. 331, 168 Eng. Rep. 830 (1817).

45. *Norris*, p. 69.

46. See Michel Foucault, *The History of Sexuality, vol. 1, An Introduction*, trans. R. Hurley (London: Penguin, 1978).

47. *Norris*, p. 97, *per* McCarthy J.: "It is for the Court to decide in a particular case whether the [unenumerated] right relied on comes within the con-

stitutional guarantee. To do so, it must be shown that it is a right that inheres in the citizen in question by virtue of his human personality."

48. Ibid., p. 71.
49. Ibid., p. 72.
50. Ibid., p. 79.
51. Ibid., p. 58.
52. Ibid., p. 62.
53. Ibid., p. 63.
54. Ibid., pp. 62, 64–65.
55. There are interesting implications of homosexual desire's contagious nature for those who deal with the vulnerable, such as teachers, nurses, doctors, and parents, both natural and adoptive.
56. Ibid., p. 69, *per* Henchy J.: "It is not surprising that the repressive and constricting treatment suffered by the plaintiff affected his psychological health."
57. Ibid., p. 65.
58. See Foucault, *The History of Sexuality*, pp. 116–20.
59. See Goldstein, "History, Homosexuality," p. 1089.
60. *Norris*, p. 70.

THREE

Mary Eaton interrogates the phenomenon of racial absence in equality rights jurisprudence dealing with sexual orientation. She analyzes two American cases where issues of race and sexual orientation surface: Williamson v. A. G. Edwards & Sons Inc. *and* Watkins v. United States Army. *Eaton concludes that the erasure of race in these cases suggests that homosexuality is legally coded as white and, at the same time, that race has been legally coded as heterosexual. More broadly, she suggests that the cases are symptomatic of a mode of reasoning that depends upon the separation of identities. As a consequence, reracializing the homosexual should be seen as necessary to a disruption of the hetero–homo binary itself.*

Homosexual Unmodified: Speculations on Law's Discourse, Race, and the Construction of Sexual Identity

Mary Eaton

Getting There from Here:
An Extended Prolegomenon

As they have done for many years, in 1994 lesbians and gays[1] once again took to the streets of New York City to mark yet another Gay Pride Day. In some respects the 1994 parade was indistinguishable from those of years past. The usual array of leather men, queens, butches, and femmes were in evidence, and once again the same political tensions concerning the purpose of the march and the direction of the movement threatened to install divisiveness in the place of unity without ever actually succeeding in doing so. For two reasons, though, the 1994 queer extravaganza was not at all like those of years past. Because 1969 was the year of the infamous Stonewall riots—riots considered by many to have inaugurated gay liberation as a political movement—1994 marked the twenty-fifth anniversary of the organized quest for political and civil rights. As well, and no doubt because this was the year of the queer silver jubilee, turnout for the parade was unsurpassed. According to the organizers, approximately 1.1 million lesbians, gays, bisexuals, and other sexual "minorities" from 72 countries participated in the march.

If for these two reasons Gay Pride '94 does not make its way into the annals of queer social history, it certainly should for another, perhaps even more important, one: The parade's freedom flag, one mile in length and three tons in weight, which symbolized a level of diversity amongst those gathered under the banner of queer that was nothing short of phenomenal. In an age in which issues of racial and other "differences" have threatened to cut asunder the legitimacy and longevity of many identity-based political movements, the fact that the parade attracted such a broad assortment of participants is remarkable in and of itself. Even if the gay rights movement is no exemplar of bad racial politics, it undeniably has not developed a consciousness particularly well attuned to issues of racial difference/dominance and the challenges they pose. First-person accounts of gay white solipsism seem to be growing each year.[2] The portrait of gays as extraordinarily white is by no means a result of the racial politics of the gay rights movement alone. Ideas about race and culture have played an enduring role in the historical development of antigay sentiments and continue to contribute to the representation of homosexuality as a white phenomenon.[3] The tendency to regard AIDS as a disease peculiar to white society is a particularly tragic example of the way in which heterosexism and homophobia have been racially contoured in contemporary times.[4] In place of this monochromatic image of homosexuality, the 1994 parade revealed a different, more spectral truth about this constituency of queers.

Although the parade thus carried unprecedented potential to call conceptions of homosexuality as culturally confined and racially monolithic into critical question, that promise went unrealized in the claims for reform that emanated from the gathering. Greater sexual freedom for homosexuals through the acquisition of more and better legal rights emerged as the clarion call. Sexual orientation, it was demanded, should be included as a prohibited ground of discrimination in the Universal Declaration of Human Rights along with race, sex, and those other features of personhood already recognized by the international community as illegitimate bases upon which to judge the moral worth and political and civil status of individuals. Since this plea for the recognition of the human rights of homosexuals was pitched internationally, diversity of a geopolitical sort did figure in the claim. Apart from this, though the insistence that sexual orientation be included in the Universal Declaration of Human Rights was wholly indistinguishable from similar attempts to secure civil rights for gays in domestic legislation.

In a sense, things really could not be otherwise. If racial difference registered more on the level of spectacle than on the level of substance, law, rather than those seeking access to its protections, was responsible. Most human and civil rights statutes proscribe discrimination only when directed at individuals or groups of individuals on the basis of their membership in certain specified classes. Membership in these classes is in turn defined by the possession of certain so-called personal characteristics (race, sex, age, ability, and so on) that define the group as such. As a matter of structure, therefore, antidiscrimination law tends to assume a basic commonality of experience amongst those classes to whom its protections extend. If legislation of this sort contained general prescriptives against inequality, it might be possible to craft pleas for reform that acknowledge the nuanced and textured experience of discrimination across various identifications. Given that most do not, however, there are clear statutory obstacles to securing equality protections for homosexuals in a way that does not rest on a notion of a group and hence to a certain degree on group homogeneity. Short of restructuring the existing system in its entirety, expanding the list of enumerated grounds to include the characteristic that sets homosexuals apart and that constitutes them as a distinct class—that is, amending current legislation to include sexual orientation—remains the only viable law reform alternative.

The realities of legal struggle are such that the distinction between the pragmatic and the right is often easy neither to draw nor to defend. Nevertheless, the difficulty that arises when the exigencies of the system are offered as reasons in themselves to shelve questions of difference is that the need to inquire into the nature and extent of difference often is downplayed or dismissed altogether. It is theoretically possible, after all, that the problem of racial exclusivity is mostly nominal and, as such, curable through changes in linguistic practice. In other words, it may be that difference makes no difference in substantive terms, that all homosexuals of whatever hue share a common interest *qua* homosexuals and consequently that the inclusion of sexual orientation would suffice to satisfy the legal needs of all.

Were one to examine litigation patterns as a way of broaching the question of whether the difference of race makes a difference, one would immediately be faced with a racial void so profound as to be virtually tangible. Strikingly, in the mass of judicial opinions concerning the equality rights of homosexuals, almost none refer to the race of the parties involved. I have found but two where the race of the plaintiff surfaced to the level of the text: *Williamson v. A. G. Edwards & Sons Inc.*[5] and *Watkins v. U.S. Army.*[6] The notion that there are no homosexuals of color, that gayness is a white phenomenon, was certainly belied by the 1994 march. It is quite possible, however, that queers of color have good reason to believe that the justice system will not offer them very much in the way of justice and that they choose, quite rationally, to spend their valuable energies and hard-earned dollars on things other than litigation. So, too, it may well be that lesbians and gays of color have not chosen to absent themselves from the juridical field at all, but that, in attempting to combat discrimination through litigation, they, for one reason or another, opted not to make their race an issue.

A very different approach to the question of racial absence is suggested by Foucault's work on the construction of racial identity in the *History of Sexuality*.[7] The book opens with a retelling of the tale of sexual repression, according to which sex came to be stripped of its previously enjoyed status as a generally benign aspect of human nature and was subjected to an ever-more prudish mandate of constraint and control, culminating in its careful confinement under the iniquitous influence of the Victorian bourgeoisie. Foucault never denied that sexuality was proscribed, but he saw in the narrative of the "repressive hypothesis" the elision of the evident fact that a "veritable discursive explosion"[8] about sex had occurred in the nineteenth century. Rather than being the subject of a taboo that demanded sexual silence, sex became the object of prolix and proliferating discourses designed to incite individuals to disclose their sexual truths explicitly and in considerable detail. Sex, in other words, was transformed into discourse. The development and application of procedures for telling the truth about sex, the *scientia sexualis*, generated, amongst other things, the specification of individuals into sexual types, including, of course, homosexual ones.[9]

More was at issue in the revelation that the "repressive hypothesis" was a "fable" than the exposé of an antimony between what society preached and what it practiced. For Foucault, this contradiction suggested that the negative relationship between sex and power assumed by the trope of repression was misconceived. Sex did not exist as a sovereign entity unfortunately distorted and disfigured by the manipulating force of an external power, namely the imperial prude.[10] Rather, "the essential features of . . . sexuality are not the expression of a representation that is more or less distorted by ideology, or of a misunderstanding caused by taboos,"[11] but are instead a "dense transfer point for relations of power."[12] Foucault's reconfiguration of the relationship between sex and power suggests an alternative approach to understanding how and why race seems absent from the jurisprudence of the equality rights of homosexuals. Race may not be present in the case law—regardless of whether it was present in the bodies that pressed those claims—because it has been systematically expelled from the terms within which the courts address homosexual rights. The legal figure of the homosexual, in other words, bears no racial marker because law produces it as such.

It is true, of course, that the *History of Sexuality* was concerned with the ecclesiastical confessional, psychoanalysis, and the sexual sciences generally, not with law.[13] Indeed, it is difficult not to notice the decidedly antistatist and antilegal inflection of Foucault's analysis of the relationship between sex, discourse, and power. He insisted, in fact, that by "power" he did not mean "a group of institutions and mechanisms that ensure the subservience of the citizens," namely, the state and its laws. For him, power was not something that emanated from a fixed point, exterior to the relationships it regulated, nor was it simply repressive.[14] Unlike law, power came from innumerable positions, from below, and always played a productive role. While he allowed that the kind of power he had in mind could be embodied in the state apparatus and the law, these were, to Foucault, only "the terminal forms power takes."[15]

It has been precisely this devaluation of the lasting significance of state power that has inspired legal criticism of Foucault's work, both liberal and leftist. Hunt, for example, argues that by "putting 'little power' onto the agenda, [Foucault] appears to ignore or to understate the importance of the processes that aggregate or condense power in centralized sites," like the law.[16] Walzer complains that Foucault's vision of power offers no account of how it might be contained. Such an account, according to Walzer, would require what Foucault seems intent to resist: some positive evaluation of the liberal state, including the working of its political system, law, and constitution.[17] For Walzer, it is the liberal state itself that allows or refuses those decentralized acts of contestation of which Foucault speaks so favorably.[18]

I wish neither to work out a theory of the relationship between macro- and micropowers nor to resolve the dispute over how much or well law can serve an emancipatory function. It bears remarking, however, that, despite the vast theoretical distance that separates Hunt and Walzer, both seem to share the inclination that law is somehow different from the kind of power that concerned Foucault. While I hesitate to suggest that law can be reduced to discourse or conflated with disciplinarity, it strikes me as somewhat strange to conceive of law as if it did not operate discursively or as if legal discourse were wholly distinct from other sorts of discourses that infuse and constitute the power/knowledge conglomerate.

There is more at stake in this debate over the differences between and the sources of juridical and disciplinary power than theoretical nicety. After all, if law serves merely a reflective function, then there would seem to be little point in investing too much energy in combating its misprisions. Why bother with litigation if the source of the problem behind the absence of race from the jurisprudence of homosexuality resides elsewhere? Even if Walzer is partly right when he insists that law is not simply hegemonic, there are limits to how much litigation can achieve in a contest between different forms of power. Allowing for the *productive* element of law suggests not only a very different way of understanding how it is that race seems so absent from judicial discourse about homosexuality, but also a different way of understanding how law might be deployed to contest the racial contours of that construction. If sexual identity is produced through legal discourse,[19] and if law forms part of the matrix within which the subject is constituted as such, it may be that race is absent from the case law not because the reality of race has been distorted by legal ideology, but because racial erasure from the jurisprudence of homosexuality corresponds to "the functional requirements of a discourse that must produce its truth."[20]

In applying this modified Foucauldian analysis to the problem of the construction of race in relation to sexual orientation through civil rights discourse, my point of departure shall be comparative. Because most of the analysis of legal remedies for complex or intersecting inequalities has been done in the race and gender context, I use this jurisprudence and its critique as a way of approaching the problem of the intersection of race and sexual identity. Through this comparison I hope to show that, unlike the discursive fragmentation of women of color into their constituent race-d and gender-ed parts, queers by contrast have been interned in the juridical category of homosexual, a category apparently so consumed by its status as sexually deviant that there exists no racial remainder.[21] In short, legally speaking, there is no race to homosexuality. This racelessness might be understood as being synonymous with colorlessness. However, given the tendency under conditions of white supremacy to regard whiteness as a norm to which no racial reference need be made, I prefer to read this erasure as signifying that homosexuality has been legally coded as white, or to put matters conversely, that race has been legally coded as heterosexual. Drawing upon the observation made by some queer theorists that the differentiation and expulsion of homosexuality from heterosexuality is necessary to the maintenance of both categories, I suggest that this whitewashing of sexual identity is likewise required to sustain the dichotomized system of straight and queer sexualities. If the aim of legal praxis is not simply to use law's categories but to use them against each other to displace them, then exploiting the mutual reliance of homosexuality and heterosexuality on each other cannot be the only point of critical intervention. If racial erasure is as crucial to the survival of the homo/het divide and the continued containment of homosexuality as an outsider category within it, then reracializing the homosexual body is equally necessary to a strategic disruption.

"Looking for Langston"[22]

In what was perhaps the most well-known (although probably not the first) attempt to bring the multiplicity of identity to bear in civil rights litigation, *DeGraffenreid v. General Motors*,[23] a group of employees challenged their employer's decision to introduce a layoff policy of "last hired, first fired," on the grounds that it discriminated against black women as a unique class in violation of Title VII of the Civil Rights Act of 1964.[24] Their argument, essentially, was that because of General Motors's previous pattern of race- and sex-based hiring, black women composed a substantial proportion of the new recruits in relation to whom the layoff policy would apply and would therefore suffer disproportionately if the rule was permitted to stand. Moreover, if the impact of the policy were not examined in relation to them as a group distinct from all women or all blacks, the statistical profile of GM's work force was such that a discrimination complaint could not be made out at all. Although the legislation under which they launched their claim did not specifically name black women as a protected group, the plaintiffs urged the court to find that the prohibition of race and sex discrimination contained in Title VII could be combined to give them the relief against the policy. In a decision now notorious for having elevated formalism to a high art, Judge Wangelin refused to allow the claim. The complainants, he held, could sue as women or as blacks, but not as black women.[25]

Judge Wangelin's rationale for dismissing the plaintiffs' suit bears scrutiny. The court noted that it had never faced such a request and, indeed, that it was unable to find any indication that other courts had been asked or had agreed to construe the Civil Rights Act in the way the plaintiffs suggested.[26] Thus its first reason for rejecting the request was the sheer novelty of the plea. The second concerned the lack of textual support for the proposed interpretation. Nothing, the court argued, in the legislative history of Title VII suggested that Congress had envisioned, let alone endorsed, the notion that the terms of the statute could be combined. This too indicated that the claim was legally incognizable.[27] Finally, as a matter of practicality, the court reasoned that were it to accede to the plaintiffs' request, this would open the floodgates to an endless array of combinations and permutations of protected classes against whose claims no employer could reasonably defend itself. In a very interesting choice of metaphor, Judge Wangelin described the result of such an interpretative approach as tantamount to opening Pandora's box.[28]

The crude exaltation of form over substance made *DeGraffenreid* an easy target, and criticism of the case is now standard fare in the literature on intersecting identities and civil rights law. By forcing Emma De-Graffenreid and her colleagues to litigate under the single heads of race or sex, the court effectively denied them the protections Title VII was plainly intended to guarantee. Inasmuch as the problem with *DeGraffenreid* was seen to rest in its misapplication of an otherwise sound approach to equal protection law, correction of its error required no more than the most modest kind of change: judicial willingness or legislative permission to combine the grounds enumerated in the Civil Rights Act and similar legislation. But some, quite rightly, identified a deeper logic to the decision that spoke more to the nature of black womanhood than to the technical failings of civil rights jurisprudence.[29] *DeGraffenreid* was said to be emblematic of a more general pattern (legal and political) according to which the interests of women of color were systematically subordinated to those of white women and black men. The effect of this marginalization was that the legal meaning of "woman" or "black" and hence the legal meaning of discrimination on the basis of sex or race really were defined in relation to the experiences and interests of white women and black men, respectively. In this way, not only were the interests of black women marginalized, but black women themselves were effectively erased. In other words, the more far-reaching critique of *De-Graffenreid* emphasized the constructed incongruity of black womanhood as an identity category in its own right.

Although *DeGraffenreid* was concerned specifically with race and gender, the concept of intersecting oppressions that emerged out of its critique has been interpreted and applied much more broadly. Intersectionality has come to stand for the effects that occur whenever two or more identities coalesce, as it were, in the same corporeal space. Consequently, there seems to be a growing tendency, in which I myself have indulged, to assume that the *DeGraffenreid* problem is not unique to race and gender. To the extent that the courts have displayed a similar tendency to interpret the enumerated grounds in human rights legislation as if they were mutually exclusive and to justify their decisions by reference to the same questionable interpretive techniques, there is some foundation for this view. Because no attempt has been made to launch a claim combining sexual orientation with race in a manner analogous to that attempted by Emma Degraffenreid and her colleagues, it is simply not possible to determine in any direct way whether the *DeGraffenreid* problem is of a general order.

There is, of course, an obvious reason why no gay equivalent to *DeGraffenreid* exists: Since sexual orientation has yet to receive widespread legislative recognition, in most jurisdictions it would be statutorily impossible. Presumably, however, if the logic of *DeGraffenreid* applied to all intersectional identifications, the absence of sexual orientation as a prohibited ground of discrimination should not have any bearing on the ability of gay litigants to proceed, perhaps even successfully, on other grounds. In fact, however, the courts have been rigidly uniform in their insistence that the legislative refusal to recognize sexual orientation as an illegitimate basis for judging persons and distributing access to goods and services necessarily means that homosexuals are barred from laying claim to any of the other protections. The prototypical response to this clear jurisprudential pattern has been that statutory amendments are required if homosexuals are ever to get the protection they need and deserve. That this legislative lacunae accounts for the judicial refusal to remedy "true" sexual orientation claims is incontestable—provided that what constitutes such "true" cases can be anticipated or identified. Lost in the jump to such legislative imperatives, however, is an explanation of why the existing categories of prohibited discrimination, including race, so consistently have been interpreted to exclude homosexuals from their ambit, even when the facts do not seem to demand it.

In *Williamson v. A. G. Edwards & Sons Inc.*, for example, an African-American gay man attempted to invoke federal guarantees against race discrimination contained in Title VII and Section 1981[30] when he was discharged from his job. Allegedly, the employer dismissed Williamson because he had engaged in "disruptive and inappropriate"[31] conduct, namely, that he had continually discussed "the details of his homosexual lifestyle" and had worn makeup to work.[32] Williamson never denied that he in fact had done so, but he claimed that since his colleagues who engaged in similar kinds of misbehavior were not released, his dismissal was racially tainted. The court disagreed, saying that Title VII did not "prohibit discrimination against homosexuals," that Section 1981 only prohibited "discrimination on the basis of race,"[33] and that the plaintiff had not alleged facts sufficient to establish that he was fired because he was black. First, Williamson's allegation that some of his co-workers had openly discussed their sex lives with impunity was misplaced, because in making that allegation he compared his behavior to that of other heterosexuals rather than of white homosexuals. The latter group, it was true, had also been disciplined, but the record disclosed that the nature of their misconduct was quite different. Whereas Williamson had dabbled in face paints, these other men had only worn earrings. It followed that the complainant was not "similarly situated" to white employees in a comparable position (i.e., white male homosexuals), and his discharge, therefore, could not be attributed to his race. If anything, the court implied, Williamson's dismissal was a function of his sexual orientation, a type of discrimination not prohibited by the statute under which he claimed relief. He could therefore secure no redress.

Given the court's rather strong intimation that had either Title VII or Section 1981 been differently drafted, it would have been much better positioned to give the plaintiff's complaint more substantive consideration, one reading of *Williamson* is both obvious and simple: Like similar cases, it underscores the need for the statutory enumeration of sexual orientation. In itself, however, the fact that neither Title VII nor Section 1981 made any reference to sexual orientation does not explain why the discharge of Williamson, a black gay man, was a racially uncomplicated matter, nor why the discrimination he faced was not remediable under the prohibition of race discrimination. If we are to believe the court, race was foreclosed as an avenue of complaint for the simple fact that Williamson wore makeup. There is some validity in the court's observation that the sociopolitical significance of wearing makeup and wearing earrings is very different, and more generally that practices of adornment are more than a matter of personal taste. Speaking only impressionistically, it does seem that the figure of the male donning earrings evokes a lesser level of social disapprobation than does the figure of the male who has "done" his face, and in a sense one might be inclined to agree with the opinion on this point. Still, even if we concede that the court's distinction between the forms of aesthetic trespass and their effect has some foundation, that would not resolve the issue of whether Williamson's discharge was racially motivated. Consider, for the moment, the aesthetic dimension of racism. The slogan "black is beautiful" was articulated in response to the hegemonization of the white body as an object of appreciation and admiration and of the black body as a token of ugliness and abjection. Williamson's self-adornment might be understood, then, as an act of proud display reflecting an underlying attitude of bodily worthiness and as an attempt to recuperate the black body as beautiful.[34] That he did so in a manner that we might regard as classically if not stereotypically queer was irrelevant; the fact that Williamson was a queen is relevant only to the extent that race is conceived as a heterosexual construct. By calling attention to and challenging the connection between racism and practices of adornment, Williamson's behavior constituted a transgression against the norms of white aesthetic superiority, and in this way his employer's discipline and the court's acquiescence manifested a racist conflation of whiteness with the beautiful and blackness with the grotesque.

Since Williamson did not cast his claim in such terms, it is perhaps unfair to fault the court for failing to explore the racial aesthetic more fully. Even within the court's limited frame of reference, however, the opinion belies its own substantive finding that Williamson's race and his discharge were unconnected. For the court to apply the "similarly situated" test, the relevant group of employees to which the treatment of Williamson could be compared had to be established. That group, according to the case report, was the class of gay males in the defendant's employ. Why the treatment of his *heterosexual* colleagues was not germane to his complaint was not explained. Further, how the court was able to establish membership in the group it considered relevant for comparison purposes was left largely unstated; the judgment indicates only that these men were subject to less stringent disciplinary measures (reprimand) than the plaintiff (dismissal) for workplace misbehavior that was similarly disruptive. Accordingly, it was this shared departure from the norms of (male) heterosexuality that defined the class "homosexual men" and confirmed Williamson's membership in it. Had the court ended its exegesis on male comportment at that point, even the application of the problematic test of similarity of situation would have compelled the plaintiff's victory. Once an essential *similarity* between makeup and earrings was established, nothing distinguished Williamson from his co-workers except race. The fact that he was treated much more harshly than his colleagues, therefore, should have been sufficient evidence to substantiate his claim that he was discriminated against on the basis of race. As if to forestall the plain implication of its own thinking, the court then introduced a second and conclusive consideration. However much earrings and makeup are the same, they are at the same time different enough to attract and justify different levels of censure. If, however, they both constitute disciplinable departures from the norm—if they both are *qualitatively* queer—we are left to assume that the difference between them must be of a *quantitative* sort. What distinguishes makeup and earrings is, in other words, a question of degree, not of kind. In effect, it was this hyperbolic display of homosexuality that marked Williamson as sufficiently unlike his white colleagues so as to render any fair comparison of treatment impossible. Williamson's race disappears as a concern of any legal consequence because he was much too queer to be black or, to put matters somewhat differently, because the rouge was thick enough to conceal the *noir*.

It is of interest to note that the space between the opening of the *Williamson* court's judgment and its affirmation of the decision of the court below is separated by a sparse three sentences, a space so small that its conclusion that the claim was *really* about sexual orientation had more the quality of an unexamined assertion than a reasoned opinion. The assumption that homosexuality and race are unrelated is echoed in *Watkins v. U.S. Army*. And because *Watkins* was not even launched as a race discrimination complaint, its distancing of race from sexual identity suggests that it is not statutory structure or legislative intent that accounts for the refusal to permit homosexual claims to go forward on other than sexual orientation grounds, but rather judicial understandings of who and what homosexuals are.

From the moment Sergeant Perry Watkins entered the armed services in 1967, the army was well aware that he was homosexually inclined: A preinduction medical form inquired of new recruits whether they had any homosexual tendencies, and Watkins answered this question in the affirmative. Despite its long-standing knowledge that Watkins was queer, the army nevertheless periodically attempted to have him discharged or to otherwise thwart his career. Watkins, however, had served with distinction, earning the respect and praise of his superiors, who seemed prepared to overlook his queer tendencies. His commanding officer judged Watkins "the best clerk I have ever known," asserted that he did a "fantastic job," and insisted that his homosexuality did not affect the company. Because Watkins's presence had neither "a degrading effect upon unit performance, morale or discipline" nor a deleterious impact "upon his own job performance," he was never discharged nor denied important security clearances necessary to his career advancement. However, when the army issued a new regulation in 1981 mandating the discharge of all homosexuals, regardless of the length or quality of their service, Watkins was finally released. He contested his discharge in federal court, arguing that it violated his right to the equal protection of the laws under the Fifth Amendment. By majority vote, the Ninth Circuit found that the amended regulations under which he was dismissed were unconstitutional because they singled out homosexuals on the basis of who they were, a form of status discrimination antithetical to the norms of equal protection. Since Watkins's dismissal was solely premised upon his admission of homosexual orientation, and not on any proven sexual activity, the court found that the army had impermissibly discriminated against him and ordered it to reconsider Watkins's application for reenlistment.

Watkins has been widely lauded as an important legal victory for lesbians and gays, and with good reason. Although others had attempted to compel the army (and militaristic entities like the CIA) to alter its discriminatory practices against homosexuals through litigation, Watkins was the first plaintiff to succeed. Just as significant was the reasoning of the court. In *Bowers v. Hardwick*[35] the U.S. Supreme Court decided that the constitutional right to privacy did not prevent the state from criminalizing homosexual sodomy, even when practiced in the confines of one's own home. On its face, the holding in *Hardwick* concerned only the specific legal issue of the scope of substantive due process and the precise question of the constitutional status of sodomy. Many courts interpreting *Hardwick*, however, read the decision much more expansively. They construed *Hardwick* as a comment on the constitutional rights of homosexuals in general, rights that went beyond privacy to include the equal protection of the laws guaranteed under the Fifth and Fourteenth Amendments. Likewise, the fact that *Hardwick* was specifically concerned with the "crime against nature" was rarely afforded the significance it obviously deserved. No meaningful distinction between sodomy and, for example, simple expressions of homosexual identification such as, "I am a lesbian,"[36] was recognized. In what must be regarded as a neat example of inverted reasoning, many courts seemed to consider that so long as it was a homosexual who performed the act, said the words, or conceived the thought, that fact was sufficient to transform these otherwise commonplace human engagements into *homosexual* activities, expressions, and ideas, and thus to place them beyond the protective parameters of civil rights law. *Watkins* distanced itself from this conservative trend by distinguishing between homosexual *being* and homosexual *doing*, reading *Hardwick* as a comment only on the latter. It endorsed a notion of sexual orientation that would not insulate homosexual practices from discrimination, but would spare homosexuals those inequalities born of antipathy toward homosexual status or orientation.

Perhaps because Watkins did not argue the constitutional prohibition against race discrimination, the standard reading of the decision is that it was a gay rights case and nothing more complicated. Indeed, in the wealth of commentary that the decision generated, Watkins's race is virtually never mentioned. Were it not for the occasional and sparing references to the evidence presented at his original discharge hearing, the fact that Watkins is black would probably never have surfaced. That evidence suggested that the effort to have the good sergeant purged from the ranks was racially charged from the beginning. One soldier, Snook, testified that a black staff sergeant driving a silver or gray car with light-colored license plates had picked him up hitchhiking. Inside the car, the driver was alleged to have made a homosexual advance in the form of squeezing Snook's leg. Snook told his unit commander, Captain Bryan, about the incident and named Watkins as the offender. Bryan accepted Snook's story, and both testified for the prosecution at Watkins's original discharge hearing. On cross-examination, however, it was revealed that neither Snook nor Bryan had much ground for considering that Watkins was the man who had committed the deed. Snook, who should have been well positioned to recognize him, was unable to positively identify Watkins in a lineup of black staff sergeants. For his part, Captain Bryan was forced to admit that the information given by Snook was insufficient to implicate Watkins. He conceded that there were "thousands of black staff sergeants at Fort Lewis, and that probably a couple of hundred of them had cars similar to the one Watkins owned."[37]

It could be argued that the category of sexual orientation is insufficient to comprehend what happened to Watkins. For example, evidence tending to show that lesbians and gays of color seem to suffer disproportionately under the army's regulation could have been led to substantiate a mixed race and sexual orientation claim.[38] Or one could show how the circumstances leading to Watkins's identification as homosexual demonstrate the complex relationship of the visual economies of racism and homophobia. In any event, it is unnecessary to suggest ways of thinking about how the claim might have been presented to demonstrate that race was relevant to Watkins's claim, since the decision itself is absolutely riven with racial references. Watkins's race never rose to prominence because the method by which the court conceptualized his sexual orientation claim presupposed that race and sexual identity were mutually exclusive. The terms within which the *Watkins* majority and minority debated the constitutional status of homosexuality thus were strikingly reminiscent of the reasoning in *Williamson*.

In the majority opinion of Norris J., the parallel between discrimination against homosexuals and discrimination against blacks was so irresistible that he punctuated each of his key findings with a racial analogy. In dealing with the impact of *Hardwick* on the scope of the equal protection guarantee, for instance, the majority reasoned that the Supreme Court could not have intended its words to mean that the government was permitted to outlaw sodomy only when committed by a "disfavored class of persons." His example was racial: "Surely, for example, *Hardwick* cannot be read as a license for the government to outlaw sodomy only when committed by blacks."[39] Having thus rejected the army's contention that *Hardwick* effectively disposed of Watkins's equal protection claim, the court then considered the level of scrutiny to be applied in reviewing the constitutionality of the regulation. One of the criteria it employed was the immutability of the characteristic. Here again the majority invoked "the black experience." Norris J. noted that, by an immutable characteristic, the Supreme Court could not have meant that the characteristic must be completely impervious to change; it would suffice if it was difficult to alter without great personal cost. After all, he reasoned, "[l]ighter

skinned blacks can sometimes 'pass' for white, as can Latinos for Ang-
los, and some people can even change their racial appearance with pigment injections," but this did not make race any less immutable or render the necessity for constitutional protection against racism any less
acute. Indeed, the court underscored the point when it noted that
"[r]acial discrimination . . . would not suddenly become constitutional
if medical science developed an easy, cheap, and painless method of
changing one's skin pigment."[40] This left only the question of whether
the army's reasons for the regulation could pass the test of strict
scrutiny. Race once again proved integral to Norris J.'s thinking. The
army argued that the presence of homosexuals would jeopardize troop
morale and threaten the hierarchical chain of command. That is, heterosexual antipathy toward homosexuals necessitated their exclusion.
The court noted that similar reasoning had sustained the now discred-
ited "separate but equal" doctrine and the discriminatory practices it
rationalized, including miscegenation and of course the historical segregation of black soldiers. Since similarly suspect claims regarding homosexuals could not be judicially credited without lending legal
imprimatur to a mode of reasoning already acknowledged to be constitutionally foul, Norris J. concluded that the difficulty engendered by
prejudice was insufficient reason to uphold the army's zero-tolerance
rule.

　　Reinhardt J.'s dissent recognized that the parallel between discrimination against blacks and homosexuals was key, and, not surpris-
ingly, he spent considerable effort illustrating that no legitimate
analogy could be drawn between the two. In his view, there was a
fundamental etiological difference between the two identities. To be
homosexual necessarily required the intervention of human volition:
One could only become homosexual by choosing to respond to a sexual desire for members of the same sex. For blacks, by contrast, there
was "no connection between the particular conduct and the definition
of the group."[41] They simply are what they are, through no act or fault
of their own. It was the failure to appreciate this basic difference that
permitted the majority to interpret the import of *Hardwick* wrongly.
The Supreme Court in that case had clearly recognized the volitional
quality of sexual orientation; that is why it referred indistinguishably
to homosexuals and to homosexual sodomy. Thus, there was no es-
caping *Hardwick*'s inexorable logic: given that homosexuals are defined
by what they do, and given that what they do is constitutionally punishable, no meaningful distinction could be drawn between substantive due process and equal protection in terms of the constitutional
rights of homosexuals. Hence, when the majority reasoned that sodomy laws directed against blacks and those aimed at homosexuals

would equally run afoul of the equal protection guarantee, it betrayed a misunderstanding of *Hardwick:*

> According to the majority, the race and sexual preference of the defendant are equally irrelevant. The majority says: "Surely, for example, Hardwick cannot be read as a license to outlaw sodomy only when committed by blacks." Surely not. And surely, had Hardwick been black rather than a homosexual, the Court would not, throughout its opinion, have written about "black sodomy" or black sodomists.[42]

For the minority, then, any appeal to the treatment of blacks to advance the constitutional position of homosexuals was fundamentally unsound. Reinhardt J. did not dispute that blacks and homosexuals shared an unhappy history of discrimination, and he appeared slightly moved by the obvious unfairness of extending protection only to the former. More particularly, he recognized that both had been victims of an overly rigid legal regime, slow to realize its mistakes. Noting that it had taken several decades for the Supreme Court to admit and correct its error in *Plessy v. Ferguson*,[43] Reinhardt J. suggested that *Hardwick* may have been misguided and, like *Plessy,* might one day be recognized as a judicial blunder.[44] In his view, however, it was not the function of an inferior court to correct what it regarded as jurisprudential wrongs. It followed that "cases regarding blacks [were] simply irrelevant."[45]

There is nothing especially unusual in the court's use of analogy or, for that matter, in its invocation of race as the appropriate analogical point of reference. After all, a fairly entrenched notion in constitutional jurisprudence is that entitlement to equal protection can be determined by comparing the situation of those seeking inclusion to that of African-Americans, the original suspect class. Black is, in this sense, a civil rights norm, a metonym for a standard of disenfranchisement against which the desert of other "others" is measured. Although this approach is commonplace in equality law, it is not unproblematic. On the one hand, an analogy can be drawn only if one can establish a certain degree of commonality or sameness between the things or persons analogized. To say that race and sexual orientation are analogous is to claim that they are in some sense alike. On the other hand, analogies presuppose a measure of difference or dissimilarity. A double bind between sameness and difference thereby is maintained. Grillo and Wildman[46] point out that the use of racial analogies tends to trivialize the signal role of racism in contemporary social relations, inasmuch as the emphasis on similarity obscures how racism is different from other forms of systemic domination. Difference, however, generates a distinct but equally troubling set of problems. Through its preservation of difference, analogical reasoning inserts a space between the things analogized that may be narrowed according to degrees of logical correspondence, but remains ultimately unbridgeable. The effect of this is plain: The possibility of cross-identification or consubstantial oppression is utterly unintelligible in a mode of reasoning that depends upon a separation between identities or oppressions. "Black homosexual" is therefore an oxymoron in an analogical comparison of blacks and homosexuals.

The difficulties engendered by analogical reasoning hold true in a broad range of contexts. One could generally make the same critique of the comparison of race and sex. However, the specificity of the race and sexuality analogy, and the kinds of assumptions regarding sameness and difference it requires to sustain itself, warrant particular attention. Despite the differences between the majority and minority judgments in *Watkins,* they actually shared substantial common ground in two respects: Both conceptualized race in terms of integumental pigmentation, and neither was prepared to hold that homosexuality bore no relation to conduct. What separated the judgment of Norris J. from that of Reinhardt J. was the extent to which homosexual *orientation* was a meaningful concept. In Norris J.'s view, it was incorrect to reduce homosexuality to the performance of sodomy. He agreed that there was an element of choice involved in the decision whether to engage in acts of sodomitical sex, but it was his contention that homosexuals could not meaningfully control their inclinations. Sexuality, to this extent, was quite a lot like skin. In Judge Reinhardt's schema, by contrast, sexuality was not at all like skin, but not because the former was mutable and the latter was not. In his view, because sodomy was "an act basic to homosexuality,"[47] it was nonsensical, not to mention unfair to homosexuals themselves, to suggest that homosexual orientation really had any meaning. It was this behavioral quality of homosexuality that distinguished homosexuals from blacks and compelled their exclusion from the protected circle of deserving minorities. Notwithstanding their dispute, then, both Norris J. and Reinhardt J. agreed that the analogy between race and homosexuality broke down when it came to sodomy, or homosexual conduct.

There is more than a little irony in the court's insistence that it is the behavioral aspect of homosexuality that marks it as qualitatively distinct from race. On one level, of course, it is exactly when queerness remains at the level of orientation that it is least like race. When not acted upon, desire is knowable only by the desiring subject. Desire is private, secret, and a state that, unlike the unavoidable externality of skin, is wholly internal. When the sexual aim finds expression, by contrast, desire enters the world of others, and becomes a phenomenon to be witnessed and perhaps judged. It is not that activity distinguishes sexual identity from race; on the contrary, it is precisely when desire erupts into conduct that it becomes observable and, like race, a matter of visual appreciation or disdain.

Juridical tradition did not oblige the court to accept, as a broad proposition, that epidermal hue is the *sine qua non* of race and racial inequality. Not only was there precedent that offered an alternative rubric for conceptualizing the meaning of race and racism, it was specifically cited by Reinhardt J. in dissent: the infamous *Plessy* decision. At issue in that case was the constitutionality of a Louisiana statute mandating the segregation of the races in public transportation. Plessy sought to challenge the legislation when, upon refusing to leave the white car of the East Louisiana Railroad, he was forcibly evicted from the train and imprisoned in the parish jail. It was Plessy's contention, in part, that his removal was a violation of the statute itself because, as a person of "mixed descent, in the proportion of seven-eighths Caucasian and one-eighth African blood," the "mixture of colored blood was not discernible in him."[48] In other words, he argued that since he "looked white," he should have been entitled to enjoy all the privileges that attend being white in a race-segregated society. As it happens, the court never determined whether the plaintiff was properly classed as white or colored, but left that matter to be determined according to Louisiana law. Like many other states at the time, Louisiana enacted a legislative formula for differentiating Caucasians from Negroes that was premised upon the amount of "Negro blood" circulating through one's veins, irrespective of whether the mix manifested itself on the visible surface of the body. The *Watkins* court's own precedents suggested that race and racism exist not simply or only in a visual dimension but in a sanguine one as well.

The implications of the court's failure to examine the rationale of *Plessy* more fully go far beyond the role of precedent in a common law system. Blood is much more like desire than is skin color. Both are invisible, both require human intervention of some sort (conduct) to be made known, and perhaps most crucially, both are sexually charged. Miscegenation, let us recall, is an offense against sanguineous purity committed when desire does not observe racial boundaries. My point is not that sexual identity and race could be united by linking desire to blood. The two are obviously not the same and an analogy between blood and desire is faulty. Given the rich connections between them, however, the contradictions engendered in reducing race to skin and homosexuality to desire might have been avoided. The notion that one can become black by doing "black" things, or better still, that one can become "nonblack" by doing "nonblack" things was nonsensical in the court's terms, because skin was immune to the push and pull of behavior. Skin just *is*. If race is grounded in the materiality of the body in this way, is it not then impervious to mere practices of the flesh even or especially of the homosexual sort? The regime of skin is not nearly as intransigent as the court insisted. When black individuals engage in gay conduct, race appears to develop a labile quality it was otherwise said not to possess. Once homosexuality finds expression—when desire is acted upon—it enters the same phenomenal domain as race. At this point, apparently, the difference between race and sexuality becomes so great that the analogy between them can no longer be sustained. Watkins's homosexuality was sufficient to lift him up and out of the circle of his darker-skinned colleagues and into a realm of homosexual desire. Once coded as gay, his race figured only metaphorically, an abstract quality to which his homosexuality might be likened but never related. This is precisely the same fate that met Williamson.

Watkins and *Williamson* concerned claims very different from the one advanced in *DeGraffenreid*. My concern, however, is not with these differences per se, but with what the cases indicate about the identities they adjudicate. In *DeGraffenreid,* the court's rationale for endorsing its cabined approach of "either sex, or race, but not both" stemmed from concerns of a practical nature. This cramped reading of the Civil Rights Act deprived the plaintiffs of any meaningful opportunity to secure redress for the wrong done to them, but it did not result in their legal figuration as unidimensional beings. However fictive the court's insistence that race and gender could be conceptualized as something like the terms in an algebraic operation, being juridically constrained to choose between identifications still implies that either identification standing alone was valid. The legal line is drawn only at the point where the combined identity, black woman, claims for itself a special status and a privileged place under civil rights law.

By comparison[49] with the way in which *DeGraffenreid* fragmented black womanhood into its constituent parts, black homosexuality is erased from the legal field through its subsumation under the undifferentiated and totalizing heading of queer. In *Williamson,* the characterization of the plaintiff's claim as a gay one alone was enabled by the expulsion of race that, according to the court's own rationale, was utterly irrational. There is, admittedly, a certain appeal to the idea that the result in *Williamson* is explicable, if not demanded, by the structure of the legislation under which the plaintiff sought relief. Oddly, however, much the same logic underpinned the decision in *Watkins,* which did not turn on issues of legislative exclusion. Not only did the technique of reasoning by analogy create a conceptual distance between the identities of black and homosexual, but the specific terms within which the analogy between race and sexual orientation was cast ensured that the difference between the two could not be bridged. If black womanhood enjoys a legal life in a fragmented and distorted form, identification as homosexual exhausts the range of identificatory possibilities so that black homosexuality cannot exist in law. In saying this I do not mean that some identities fare worse than others and can or should be ranked hierarchically. The different figuration of black womanhood and black homosexuality does suggest, though, that securing the legal recognition of intersecting identities cannot be approached as if the problem were the same for all. And it is to the question of remedies for the erasure of race from homosexuality that I now turn.

Inside/Out, Outside/In, and Beyond

Halley's review and critique of the regulation of homosexual and heterosexual identities through sodomy law provides one of the most engaging attempts to interrogate the production of sexual identity in law and to suggest how that production might be challenged through litigation.[50] In a close and careful reading of *Hardwick*, Halley demonstrates how sodomy simultaneously serves two somewhat inconsistent functions. On the one hand, it marks identity in that sodomy is metonymically related to homosexuality, much as burglary is related to a burglar.[51] Sodomy, however, also serves as a reference to a particular kind of sexual act, the practitioners of which cross the boundaries of sexual identification. Heterosexuals commit sodomy too, and sometimes they are even punished for it. It is this double meaning of sodomy—its inconsistent function as an index of both acts and identity—that makes it equivocal and, consequently, ripe for exploitation. More specifically, the confused nature of sodomy creates "opportunities for the exercise of homophobic power."[52] That is, it facilitates the shifting status of heterosexuality within the discourse of sodomy—as alternately exempt from the stigma of the sodomite and yet subject to the stigma of criminal prosecution for the commission of sodomitical acts. The conceptual complexity of heterosexuality must be contemplated by pro-gay strategies of subversion if they are to be successful.[53] As part of this more-encompassing agenda for disruption, Halley suggests that destabilizing the identity category "heterosexual" be adopted as a goal that might be met by "an emphasis on acts." It is her proposal, then, that lesbians and gays make a break with identity-based strategies and forge an alliance between heterosexuals and homosexuals along the axis of acts.

Halley's analysis is consistent with a growing trend in queer theory, more prevalent outside legal scholarship, of "interrogating the position of 'outsiderness.' "[54] This focus on the production of the outside has led to the theoretical insight that homosexuality is actually not removed from heterosexuality per se but is instead intimately caught up with it in a relationship that creates and sustains both terms through a process of negation. In somewhat crude terms, the existence of an inside, privileged class and an outside, subordinate class depends on a clear differentiation between those on each side of the divide. It is the demarcation of bodies homosexual that makes possible the delineation and the privileging of bodies heterosexual. As Halperin adroitly remarked, heterosexuality came into being "like Eve from Adam's rib."[55] Because the notion of outsiderness is integral to construction of the heterosexual as normal and the homosexual as other, the necessity of policing the borders between inside and outside, straight and queer, is acute, urgent, and fraught. For Fuss, the heterosexual fear of the homo "concentrates and codifies the very real possibility and ever present threat of a collapse of boundaries, an effacing of limits, and a radical confusion of identities."[56] Exploiting the vulnerability of that boundary thus provides opportunities for resistance to the exercise of homophobic power. Turning the boundary inside out may be a promising mode by which to expose heterosexuality as an assumed but unstable identification, and hence a productive technique by which to bring on the collapse of the straight/queer divide.

Ironically, the position of the outsider *within* the outsider has escaped critical scrutiny in this vision of the construction of sexual identity. Although theoretically figured as open to flux, the categories "homosexual" and "heterosexual" remain unmodified and uncomplicated by issues of racial difference. To that extent the categories acquire a certain constancy or even essentialism.[57] In flagging the tendency within some strains of queer theory to neglect questions of race, by no means do I intend to wag a polemical finger. The difference race makes to our theoretical attempts to understand sexual identity is a very hard question, and what follows is but an initiatory attempt to broach it.

Theoretically, the omission of race from substantive precepts does not in itself prove dispositive of their conceptual force or explanatory value. On the contrary, we might understand the erasure of race from the discourse of homosexuality as in keeping with the preservation of the neat divide between straight inside and queer outside. If the creation and maintenance of homosexuality requires that it be set firmly apart from its normal counterpart heterosexuality, the stability of that bipolarity would be threatened by the admission of other identifications, like race, that openly traverse it. The reduction of homosexuals to their sexuality through the occlusion of race is not only consistent with this, but such identificatory retrenchment is essential to the intelligibility of the distinction itself. The despised class "homosexual" depends upon the superordination of the class heterosexual as well as the preservation of homosexuality itself as normatively colorless/white.

Admittedly, reduction is inherent in any dichotomy: Unless the domain of the relevant is confined to two mutually exclusive and opposed categories, a dichotomy, by definition, does not exist. One might be inclined to conclude that the heterosexual/homosexual dualism is structurally indistinguishable from other kinds of dualisms, such as man/woman or white/black, or that the neat separation of the world into same-sex- and opposite-sex-directed desire is predicated upon the effacing of all differences, not just racial ones. If so, it follows that there is, in fact, nothing exceptional in the elision of race from the discursive contouring of sexual identity and, what is more, that there is little to criticize in the failure of queer theory to attend more substantively to race. Indeed, the fact that, as with race, lesbian and gay litigants have been judicially barred from launching claims under any of the other enumerated grounds of discrimination lends empirical support to this deductive chain. For example, the courts have tended to treat sex as a category reserved for heterosexuals in a fashion quite redolent of the heterosexualization of race in *Williamson* and *Watkins:* Homosexuals, the courts hold, are defined by their sexual orientation, not their sex, and hence sexual orientation is the appropriate heading under which their complaints should be adjudicated.

While the parallels between the legal construction of sex and the judicial eclipsing of race seem fairly irresistible, all that safely can be concluded from this concordance is that the judicial interpretation of categories like sex and race produces the same net effect—the juridical containment of sexual orientation in its own field. To posit a full equality between the expulsion of all differences on such a footing is, however, to privilege the result over the terms through which that result is rationalized. Viewed discursively rather than doctrinally, differences in the way the courts exclude differences from the category of sexual orientation become apparent. To remain with sex as an illustration, human/civil rights opinions tend to enforce a separation of sexual orientation from sex, but a certain ambivalence undercuts the otherwise confident assertions that sex and sexuality are two mutually exclusive phenomena. This discomfort with a radical estrangement between the two categories suggests a recognition, unseen in the racial context, that there is actually some connection between them. Ironically, this is revealed in the very terms through which sex discrimination complaints by lesbians and gays are refused. For example, to say that homosexuals are neither men nor women, but instead comprise a third gender certainly provides a reason, if an antiquated and somewhat silly one, for treating sexual orientation discrimination as legally *sui generis.* What

is significant in the recuperation of this sexological artifact is the reliance upon concepts of sex to locate homosexuality and subsequently
to ground its negation.[58] Whereas sex and sexual orientation are first
configured together in order to set them apart, the means by which the
wedge between race and sexual identity is driven is distinct. Race enters the discourse of sexual identity only analogically and never deriv-
atively. This suggests that, although race and sex ultimately may share
the same fate, expulsions from the realm of sexual orientation have
been effected differently.

If identificatory difference within the category "homosexual" can
be managed using dissimilar rhetorical means, then efforts to bring on
the collapse of boundaries must pay critical attention to the specificity
of the ways in which those various differences are abridged. Resistance
is a complicated affair about which one cannot and should not be pro-
grammatic. Nonetheless, inasmuch as analyses of the construction of
sexual identities have failed to notice that racial homogenization is as
crucial to their preservation as the strict divide between hetero and
homo, strategies aimed at disrupting that dyad can ill afford to ignore
the centrality of racial erasure. More specifically, if the very production
of the sexual dichotomy itself demands a form of color blindness, its re-
silience may be preserved by strategies that, however unwittingly, concede its racialized borders. Parodic performance of heterosexuality thus
does not necessarily expose it "as an incessant and *panicked* imitation
of its own naturalized idealization."[59] Nor would the suspension of
identity in favor of a dangerous but necessary allegiance with sodomy-
practicing heterosexuals in itself guarantee the revelation of the con-
tingency of heterosexuality.[60] Insofar as these strategic disruptions take
as their point of departure racially unmodified notions of homosexuality and heterosexuality, they isolate only one of the infrastructural
elements in the architecture of dichotomy, continue to operate within
the dyadic mode, and risk reinstallment of its imperative.[61] Re-racial-
izing the homosexual is thus not only a matter of the feel-good politics
of inclusivity, it is crucial to the deconstruction of the category "homosexual."

Epilogue

The purpose of bringing a law suit, most would say, is to secure greater
access to jobs, housing, and the like, and it is most celebrated as a form
of effective social struggle when it succeeds in delivering such things to
those who do not presently enjoy them. However, the redistribution of
material goods and resources is not now, if it ever was, the only purpose behind litigation. There have been times, for instance, when the

legal struggle for gay rights has yielded little in the way of tangible benefits. This was not because such claims lost, but rather because material gain was not their aim. Securing what is referred to as a symbolic victory has more than once been the object of courtroom contests. The search for legal recognition and the effort to redistribute material goods and resources serve two very different (although not incompatible) purposes, but parties pursuing both tend to view the aim of legal engagement in terms of winning and losing, and to regard litigation as a zero-sum game.

Behind both these versions of the object of legal struggle lurks an identifiable "we" who, in the quest to wrest from law rights long overdue or the recognition we so crave, may be pleased or disappointed with the final result, but who remain essentially unchanged in the process. To return to the discussion with which this essay began, law can be reconceptualized, in Foucauldian terms, as productive and not simply repressive, and the legal can therefore be conceived as a sphere in which identity is constituted rather than reflected. Law, in other words, is not or not only a repository of power effects articulated elsewhere, but forms part of the matrix in which human beings are transformed into subjects. If law is recharacterized in this way, the notion that legal struggle is a purely resistive exercise must be relinquished, as must the notion that legal victory can be exclusively gauged in terms of how well or how often we succeed in securing rights or recognition. Instead, we might understand litigation as a kind of technique of the self in a repertoire of identificatory practices in which, paraphrasing Foucault, the "we" is not previous to the process but rather its result.[62] It is quite probable that an attempt to alter the racial contours of homosexuality through litigation will be resisted by the courts (and perhaps from the queer legal community as well), but there is more at stake in insisting upon this project of re-racialization than litigative success, either in the classic or in the symbolic sense. If the very notion of homosexuals as an outsider class requires the erasure of race, then to attempt to re-racialize homosexuality is to call into question homosexuality's own conception of *itself* in perhaps the most productive of ways.

NOTES

1. I use the words "gay," "lesbian," "homosexual," and "queer" rather indiscriminately throughout this essay. My unsystematic language is not a reflection either of my ignorance or of my sloppiness: I fully appreciate that because each of these terms, in its own way, has been considered to convey particular and intended meanings useful to the achievement of various political

purposes, each has had its own advocates. In the past, I myself have made such arguments concerning the appropriate/productive use of the "name," even passionately, but now I am less than convinced that any one of these words, standing alone, can do the work imagined or hoped for them. For example, inasmuch as "queer" appears to me to be a racially unmarked word, it probably ought not to be overly invested with the transformatory potential ascribed to it by some.

2. See, e.g., Anita Cornwell, *Black Lesbian in White America* (Tallahassee: Naiad Press, 1983); The Combahee River Collective, "A Black Feminist Statement," in Gloria Hull et al., eds., *But Some of Us Are Brave* (New York: The Feminist Press, 1982), p. 13; Makeda Silvera, ed., *Piece of My Heart: A Lesbian of Color Anthology* (Toronto: Sister Vision Press, 1991); and Essex Hemphill, ed., *Brother to Brother: New Writings by Black Gay Men* (Boston: Alyson Publications, 1991).

3. A few examples should suffice to demonstrate that there has long been considered a connection between the two. At times, inversion seems to have been regarded as a degenerate condition experienced by peoples at advanced levels of civilization. Freud himself, for instance, saw that this view carried enough currency to warrant its mention. Sigmund Freud, *Three Essays on the Theory of Sexuality*, trans. James Strachey (New York: Basic Books, 1975), p. 5. At other times, homosexuality appears to have been figured as a problem peculiar to the inferior races. In his *Studies in the Psychology of Sex* (New York: Random House, 1905), p. 19, Ellis quotes correspondence he received from a resident of the United States commenting on the sexual practices of American blacks: "Inversion is extremely prevalent among American negroes. . . . [I]t is far more prevalent among them than among white people of any nation." It would be very interesting to track and analyze the shifting role race has played in various discourses about homosexuality at different historical moments, but unfortunately, I know of no one who has made such an attempt.

4. See, e.g., Cindy Patton, "From Nation to Family: Containing African AIDS," in Henry Abelove et al., eds., *The Lesbian and Gay Studies Reader* (New York: Routledge, 1993), p. 127.

5. 876 F.2d 56 (8th Cir. 1989).

6. 847 F.2d 1329 (9th Cir. 1987) (hereinafter cited as *Watkins*).

7. Michel Foucault, *The History of Sexuality, vol. 1, An Introduction*, trans. Robert Hurley (New York: Vintage Books, 1978).

8. Ibid., p. 17.

9. Ibid., p. 43: "The nineteenth-century homosexual became a personage, a past, a case history, and a childhood, in addition to being a type of life, a life form, and a morphology, with an indiscreet anatomy and possibly a mysterious physiology."

10. Ibid., p. 32.

11. Ibid., p. 68.

12. Ibid., p. 103.

13. Likewise, although he did make the occasional reference to race (see, e.g., ibid., pp. 26, 54, 125, and 149) and appeared to recognize that the deployment of sexuality was linked to racism, Foucault made no mention of race or racism in his discussion of homosexuality. The omission is somewhat

odd given the apparent preoccupation of nineteenth-century sexologists with the relation between race and inversion. See, e.g., Ellis, *Psychology of Sex*, pp. 8–64 (summarizing the literature on homosexuality "among the lower human races").

14. Foucault, *History of Sexuality*, p. 94.

15. Ibid., p. 92.

16. Alan Hunt, "Foucault's Expulsion of Law: Toward a Retrieval," *Law & Social Inquiry* 17(1992): 11.

17. Michael Walzer, "The Politics of Michel Foucault," in David Couzens Hoy, ed., *Foucault: A Critical Reader* (Oxford: Basil Blackwell, 1986), p. 62.

18. *Ibid.*, p. 66.

19. I think this is partly, although not entirely, what Edward Said was alluding to when he noted that "the relationship between subjectivity and ideas of justice" was one problematic neglected in Foucault's notions of power. See Said, "Foucault and the Imagination of Power," in Hoy, ed., *Foucault: A Critical Reader*, p. 155.

20. Foucault, *History of Sexuality*, p. 68.

21. Empiricists will no doubt find fault with my conclusions, based as they are on an admittedly skimpy sample. One can answer such challenges, of course, although I will refrain from doing so here. I nonetheless do regard my analysis as purely initiatory and tentative but for other, more important, reasons. The two judicial decisions that constitute my archive both concerned African-American gay men. Consequently, my use of race does not contemplate differences across genders or races.

22. This subtitle is borrowed from Isaac Julien's film on the life of Langston Hughes. Julien discusses the film's project in an interview published in Essex Hemphill, *"Looking for Langston:* An Interview with Isaac Julian," in Hemphill, ed., *Brother to Brother*, p. 174.

23. *DeGraffenreid v. General Motors*, 413 F. Supp. 142 (E.D. Mo. 1976).

24. 42 U.S.C. § 2000e et seq.

25. Not all courts have responded to intersectional claims in the same way. Recognizing the absurdity of the decision, the Fifth Circuit in *Jeffries v. Harris Cty. Community Action Ass'n*, 615 F.2d 1025 (1980), permitted a similar claim to go forward under the "sex plus" doctrine developed by the Supreme Court in *Phillips v. Martin Marietta Corp.*, 400 U.S. 542 (1971). Distancing itself from *DeGraffenreid*, the *Jeffries* court thought it "beyond belief" that an employer "could be allowed to discriminate against black females as a class" (p. 1034). It permitted the plaintiffs to sue as "a distinct protected subgroup" (ibid.), but under the rubric of sex.

26. *DeGraffenreid*, pp. 142, 143.

27. Ibid.

28. Ibid., p. 144.

29. Kimberlé Crenshaw, "Demarginalizing the Intersection of Race and Sex: A Black Feminist Critique of Antidiscrimination Doctrine, Feminist Theory, and Antiracist Politics," *University of Chicago Legal Forum* (1989): 139. As well, despite the obvious improvement made by *Jeffries*, the criticism of its relegation of race to secondary status is well founded. See Cathy Scarborough,

"Conceptualizing Black Women's Employment Experiences," *Yale Law Journal* 98(1989):1457; and Peggie R. Smith, "Separate Identities: Black Women, Work, and Title VII," *Harvard Women's Law Journal* 14(1991):21.

30. 42 U.S.C. § 1981.

31. *Williamson,* p. 70.

32. Ibid.

33. Ibid.

34. Gender norms were also operative here in the sense that, by wearing makeup, Williamson failed to comply with the aesthetic requirements of masculinity. Acknowledgment of this social truism does not necessarily result in a conceptual antagonism, as if raced and gendered readings of the transaction between the plaintiff and his employer were in conflict. White supremacy and gender domination are, of course, tangled up with one another and in complex ways.

35. *Bowers v. Hardwick,* 478 U.S. 186 (1986).

36. *BenShalom v. Marsh,* 881 F. 2d 454 (7th Cir. 1989).

37. This evidence is detailed in an earlier decision, *Watkins v. U.S. Army,* 541 F. Supp. 249, 257, 259 (W.D. Wash. 1982). Another enlisted man, Valley, maintained that Watkins had asked him to move into his apartment and that he used to come by the mailroom and stare at him. His evidence was not credited, however, when he admitted to "being prejudiced against black people and against homosexuals."

38. I have not gathered the necessary statistical evidence to support such a claim, but scattered accounts suggest that the military's discharge practices may follow a racial pattern. Shilts, for example, reports that, in the lesbian purge of the *Norton Sound,* which began in 1980, all but one of the ship's 9 African-American female members were named among the 19 women accused of lesbianism and questioned by the Naval Investigative Service. See Randy Shilts, *Conduct Unbecoming* (New York: St. Martin's Press, 1993), p. 337. Eight women in total were actually indicted, 3 of whom were African-American (ibid., p. 352).

39. *Watkins,* p. 1340.

40. Ibid., p. 1347.

41. Ibid., p. 1357.

42. Ibid., p. 1354.

43. 163 U.S. 537 (1896).

44. *Watkins,* p. 1358.

45. Ibid., p. 1360.

46. Trina Grillo and Stephanie Wildman, "Obscuring the Importance of Race: The Implications of Making Comparisons Between Racism and Sexism (or Other -Isms)," *Duke Law Journal* (1991): 397. I agree with the authors that, although there are problems with analogical reasoning, it may nevertheless be necessary or at least useful for teaching, explaining, and understanding the lives of others. Like them, I am not suggesting that analogical reasoning is per se falsifying, but rather that it should be used "ethically and with care" (ibid., p. 410).

47. *Watkins,* p. 1357.

48. *Plessy*, p. 537.

49. There is always a danger in drawing conclusions from comparisons, since the very operation of comparing is by nature somewhat scientistic, reductive, and simplistic. That risk is especially real in my analysis here, inasmuch as the effect of gender has been theoretically suspended in order to contrast the legal construction of the black woman and the black gay man. I acknowledge this imperfection and wish to make clear that the deductions I make are not intended to be definitive but merely suggestive.

50. Janet E. Halley, "Reasoning About Sodomy: Act and Identity in and After *Bowers v. Hardwick*," *Virginia Law Review* 79(1993): 1721.

51. Ibid., p. 1734.

52. Ibid., p. 1770.

53. Ibid.

54. Diana Fuss, "Introduction," in Diana Fuss, ed., *Inside/Out: Lesbian Theories, Gay Theories* (New York: Routledge, 1991), p. 2.

55. David M. Halperin, "Sex Before Sexuality: Pederasty, Politics, and Power in Classical Athens," in Martin Duberman et al., eds., *Hidden from History* (New York: Meridian, 1990), p. 40.

56. Fuss, "Introduction," p. 6.

57. I am concentrating here on the elision of race from social constructionist theories of sexual identity, but biologistic accounts of sexual origins are not immune from similar criticism. To a large extent, the appeal of the immutability thesis hinges on an analogy between sexual orientation and other ostensibly enduring features of personhood, especially race. If protections against racial discrimination were secured and retain their utility on the footing that race is a characteristic over which one can exercise no meaningful control, so the argument goes, then to the extent homosexuality is likewise beyond personal volition, it too should be protected and to the same degree. But race, on my analysis, seems not to be the signifier of a transcendental signified, but itself is afforded shifting significance in different sexual contexts. Race, that is to say, is socially constructed, too. See Lucius Outlaw, "Toward a Critical Theory of 'Race,' " in D. Goldberg, ed., *Anatomy of Racism* (Minneapolis: University of Minnesota Press, 1990), p. 58.

58. The courts are, of course, not far off the mark in recognizing that sex cannot be easily divorced from sexuality.

59. Judith Butler, "Imitation and Gender Insubordination," in Fuss, ed., *Inside/Out*, pp. 13, 23.

60. Halley, "Reasoning About Sodomy," pp. 1771–72.

61. To be fair to Butler and Halley, neither insisted that the strategies they proposed would necessarily bear fruit, so to speak. My point is only that if such attempts should fail, the reasons may partly reside in their neglect to take race into account.

62. Michel Foucault, "Polemics, Politics, and Problemizations: An Interview with Michel Foucault," in Rabinow, ed., *The Foucault Reader*, p. 385.

PART II

THE IMPLICATIONS OF STRATEGY

An increasing conflict in lesbian and gay politics involves potential custody and access battles between lesbian mothers and gay sperm donors. These cases raise fundamental questions about the nature of parenthood, the meaning of family, and the role of the law and legal processes in regulating arrangements within lesbian and gay communities. In the following essay, Katherine Arnup and Susan Boyd address these issues in the context of a major American case—Thomas S. v. Robin Y. The authors are particularly concerned about the ways in which a gay donor's resort to law can serve to entrench and reinforce traditional notions of the family. They situate their discussion in a feminist analysis of the fathers' rights movement and the problematic history of the "best interests of the child" principle.

Familial Disputes? Sperm Donors, Lesbian Mothers, and Legal Parenthood

Katherine Arnup and Susan Boyd

Ry . . . considers Sandra R. and Robin Y. to be her parents and Cade to be her full sister. She understands the underlying biological relationships, but they are not the reality of her life. The reality of her life is having two mothers, Robin Y. and Sandra R., working together to raise her and her sister. Ry does not now and has never viewed Thomas S. as a functional third parent. To Ry, a parent is a person who a child depends on to care for her needs. To Ry, Thomas S. has never been a parent since he never took care of her on a daily basis.[1]

THESE are the words of Judge Edward M. Kaufmann in *Thomas S. v. Robin Y.*, a case in which a gay sperm donor (Thomas S.) sought an order of filiation and visitation, a challenge successfully resisted by the

© Katherine Arnup and Susan Boyd. Research for this essay was supported by a grant from the Social Sciences and Humanities Research Council of Canada. An early draft was presented by Susan Boyd at Columbia Law School, Feminist Legal Theory Workshop on Parents and Children, New York City, March 26, 1994. A revised version was presented at the Canadian Law and Society Association, Learned Societies Conference, Calgary, June 13, 1994. Thanks to Susan Ursel for comments, and Jenni Millbank, LL.M. 1994 (University of British Columbia), for research assistance and computer help in the face of technological failure.

biological mother and her lesbian partner, the child's co-mother. Judge Kaufmann's characterization of how Ry, the child at issue in the case, identified her parents and sibling laid much of the groundwork for his decision that Thomas S. should be prevented from obtaining a declaration of paternity. His words demonstrate the potential that lesbian motherhood holds for challenging the biological ties that underlie the dominant heterosexual model of family. The resulting exclusion of the sperm donor from Ry's legally constituted family raises difficult questions for the lesbian and gay communities. Does legal affirmation of this lesbian family assist or impede the recognition of diverse lesbian and gay relationships and various caring connections? In the absence of legislation recognizing our parental relationships, can we rely on courts to recognize and affirm our families? What are the risks and the benefits? Is it possible to articulate alternative forms of relationship structures in the current highly gendered sociolegal context? Can lesbians and gay men develop a collective political strategy on legal parenthood? Finally, what role can law play in transforming the structure of familial relationships?

Much of the body of laws called family law can be read as a history of the regulation and reinforcement of heterosexual familial relations. Marriage, the center point of family law, is clearly heterosexual in its "opposite sex" requirement, although litigation is challenging this imperative. Only recently has the existence of lesbian and gay familial relations been acknowledged in family law discourse in anything other than a negative or sometimes invisible manner. Until the late twentieth century, the equation of marriage and heterosexuality with economic survival was arguably the best guarantor of the observance of patriarchal rules. Increasingly, however, marriage and economic survival have become somewhat disentangled, creating a need for a more overt legislation of heterosexuality as the material imperative to heterosexuality is eroded.[2] Indeed Davina Cooper and Didi Herman argue in this volume that it is precisely because the ideology of the (heterosexual) family has lost some of its force that legislative intervention to enforce it has become more prevalent (see Chapter 8).

At the same time, the lesbian and gay movements have confronted the legal system with challenges to the traditional image of family. In response, the legal system has begun to acknowledge, albeit in a partial fashion, the existence of private economic relations between two people of the same sex.[3] In the realm of reproduction, such recognition has been considerably more hesitant. As debates over the legalization of same-sex adoption dramatically reveal, children are viewed as having a more public dimension that requires heightened societal scrutiny. In Denmark and Sweden, for example, the existence of registered same-sex domestic partnerships analogous to marriages has not led to the right of lesbians and gay men to develop parental relationships through adoption. Although a limited number of courts have permitted second-parent adoption by a lesbian co-mother, law reforms regulating relationships between same-sex partners usually stop short of facilitating the ability of lesbians and gay men either to procreate or to create legally a parental relationship.

A number of recent legal, political, and social trends thus converge to make *Thomas S. v. Robin Y.* a particularly important case. In the realm of reproduction, women and men, regardless of their sexual orientation, are undeniably constituted differently.[4] Indeed, for lesbians and gay men, these differences may be even more significant than for heterosexual men and women. Lesbians can and do become pregnant and give birth to children. Gay men, while they can provide some of the necessary genetic material, cannot produce offspring. These differences, we will argue, assume crucial significance in the cases involving sperm donors and lesbian mothers. We will argue as well that parenting for lesbians and gay men occurs in a highly gendered context. In particular, the recent reassertion of fathers' rights coupled with the continued undervaluing of women's roles as mothers forms the backdrop for this dispute. The issues raised by this case concern not only biological claims and lesbian and gay parenting, but also the broader issues of women's care-giving role and their ability to raise children autonomously from men. To understand these issues, we describe the *Thomas S. v. Robin Y.* case and then discuss it in the context of the relationship between biological relations, gender relations, economic relations, heterosexism, and parenthood in Western industrialized states. We argue that despite the limits of legal imagination in the trial judgment, which many have pointed out, this case does represent an important departure from earlier jurisprudence on lesbian mothering.[5]

Thomas S. v. Robin Y.

In a 1993 proceeding before the Family Court of the City of New York, a sperm donor sought a declaration of paternity over the objections of the child's biological mother and her partner, the child's co-mother. Robin and Sandra, the co-mothers, had had an exclusive lesbian relationship since 1979. Each had a daughter born into that relationship as a result of assisted insemination with the semen of known donors who are gay. In both instances, the mothers and the donors verbally agreed that the women would co-parent the children and that the donor would have no parental rights or obligations. Each donor agreed that he would make himself known to the child should she inquire about her biological origin, an undertaking that is not unusual in written contracts that otherwise define only the co-mothers as parents. In this instance, however, no contract was signed. It was the second donor, Thomas S., who eventually challenged this agreement. The circumstances leading to his challenge are important.

Although Robin, her partner, and their daughters, Ry and Cade, lived in San Francisco for much of the first year of Ry's life (1981–82), they had little contact with Thomas S., who also lived there. Ry and Cade were given the last names of Robin and Sandra jointly. The co-mothers paid for all the expenses of Ry's birth and jointly supported her. They moved back to New York (their original home) in 1982 and until 1985 had virtually no contact with Thomas S. Both daughters regard each other as sisters and call each co-mother "Mommy."

In 1985 Cade inquired about her biological origins, and the co-mothers contacted both sperm donors to arrange a meeting. They made it clear that they still expected Thomas S. to honor his agreement to treat them as co-mothers to both girls. They also asked that he treat both daughters equally. He agreed to both requests. A continuing relationship of visits several times a year then developed, at the discretion of the co-mothers. However, Thomas S. eventually began to find this arrangement burdensome. Finding it increasingly difficult to treat Ry as Cade's equal, he was, in Judge Kaufmann's words, "not able to put biology aside, as Robin Y. and Sandra R. demanded."[6] In particular, because he wanted to introduce Ry, without her co-mothers, to his own biological relatives, in late 1990 or early 1991 he asked for visitation with Ry without the co-mothers' presence. When the women refused, he brought a proceeding for a filiation order and visitation. At this point, the mothers severed all contact with Thomas S. Ry told a psychiatrist that she did not want to visit Thomas S. and that her "sense of family security" was threatened by his demands.

Drawing in part on the recommendations of the psychiatrist, Judge Kaufmann decided that Thomas S. should be equitably estopped from a declaration of paternity, despite the clear evidence that he was Ry's biological father and that he had a social relationship with Ry. The judge felt that, although in his view Thomas S. was closer to Ry than were many family friends, that did not mean that she viewed him as a "parental figure." As well, he decided that the fact that Thomas S. had shown no interest at the outset in exercising parental rights (a key factor in Robin Y.'s choice of him as a sperm donor), had not paid expenses or support, had not tried to establish paternity earlier, had not seen Ry for the first three years of her life, and had supported the "functional family relationships" of Robin Y., her partner, and their daughters, estopped him from claiming paternity. Furthermore, Judge Kaufmann decided that a paternal declaration would not be in the best interests of Ry, since

> a declaration of paternity would be a statement that her family is other than what she knows it to be and needs it to be. To Ry, Thomas S. is an outsider attacking her family, refusing to give it respect, and seeking to force her to spend time with him and his biological relatives, who are all complete strangers to her, for his own selfish reasons.[1]

He added that even if he were to make a declaration of paternity, visitation would be denied.

The trial decision in *Thomas S. v. Robin Y.* was a significant development for lesbian mothers. For the first time a family consisting of a lesbian couple and their two daughters was affirmed by the courts, and a sperm donor was estopped from claiming paternal status and visitation rights. In marked contrast to previous sperm donor versus lesbian or unmarried mother cases,[8] in which judges went to great lengths to "find a father," Judge Kaufmann declared that "in [Ry's] family, there has been no father".[9] In deciding against a declaration of paternity, he was by implication stating that her family did not *need* a father. Such a decision represents an important step in the struggle for women's reproductive autonomy and in particular in the struggle for lesbian mothers to be recognized in law and society.

Lesbian Mothers and Custody Struggles

An examination of the ways in which the legal system has dealt with lesbian motherhood reveals a profound resistance to parenting outside the institutions of heterosexuality and patriarchy. Prior to the 1970s, few lesbian mothers contested custody against former male partners in court. Until recently in Canada, and still in some jurisdictions in the United States and elsewhere, parental fitness and conduct represented key elements in child custody determination. Judges relied on a variety of factors for determining the fitness of each parent, such as past and present sexual conduct and the quality of the home, which were used to brand virtually every lesbian who attempted to gain custody as an unfit mother. Fearing the implications of open court battles for their daily lives and jobs, and recognizing that they were almost assured of defeat at the hands of a decidedly homophobic legal system, some women "voluntarily" relinquished custody, in exchange for liberal access to their children. Countless others made private arrangements with former husbands, often concealing their sexual orientation to retain custody of the children. Such arrangements are still common to-

day, although the numbers are impossible to estimate given the necessarily private nature of the agreements.

During the 1970s and 1980s, with the support of the gay and lesbian movements and of feminist lawyers and friends, lesbians began to
contest and, in a limited number of cases, win the custody of children
conceived within heterosexual marriages. Concurrently, family law reforms in many jurisdictions increasingly made the best interests of the
child the paramount factor in custody decisions, and rendered parental
behavior, such as lesbianism, *in and of itself* no longer a bar to custody.
Only conduct that is deemed to be relevant to the ability of the person
to act as a parent should be taken into account in such decisions. Typical legislation directs judges to consider the needs and circumstances
of the child, including such factors as the permanence and stability of
the family unit with which it is proposed that the child will live, and
the blood or adoptive links between the child and the applicant.[10]

While such legislation, on its face, appears to improve a lesbian
mother's chances for success in custody struggles, these provisions can
still work against her. No precise rule or formula exists, for example,
for determining *which* household or family arrangement operates in a
child's best interests. A judge may refuse to recognize a homosexual
family as a permanent and stable family unit, since lesbians and gays
are not permitted to marry and therefore do not meet this standard
heterosexual measure of stability. The closeted nature of many gay and
lesbian relationships, and the absence of any census category to capture same-sex partnerships, also make it difficult to offer statistical evidence of the longevity of same-sex relationships. Finally, a lesbian life
style may be viewed as rendering a lesbian mother unfit to provide a
suitable home for her child. Thus, despite the apparently fair-minded
language of family law reform and the liberal pronouncements of
members of the judiciary, judges can and do find ways within the law
to deny lesbian mothers custody.

In the absence of a precise formula, judges examine closely aspects of each applicant's life style in an effort to determine what effect,
if any, the mother's lesbianism will have on the well-being of the child.
In making this assessment, judges have, at least in the reported cases,
attempted to distinguish between "good" and "bad" lesbian mothers.[11]
"Good" lesbian mothers—women who live quiet, discreet lives, who
promise that they will raise their children to be heterosexual, and who
appear to the outside world to be heterosexual single parents—have in
recent years increasingly succeeded in winning custody of their children. "Bad" lesbian mothers—women who are open about their sexual orientation, who attend gay and lesbian demonstrations and other

public events, and who view their lesbianism positively—are almost certain to lose custody of their children to their ex-husbands. Within this legal context, most lesbian mothers seeking court-ordered custody choose to act as "straight" as possible. Such strategies tell us far less about the actual views or practices of lesbian mothers than about the attitudes and prejudices of the courts. Lawyers acting for lesbian mothers in child custody disputes attempt to construct the best possible set of facts in order to secure custody for their clients. Whether achieving victories using such best-case scenarios improves the chances for success for other lesbian mothers or restricts custody rights to those women whose lives mirror the facts of the "best" cases remains a hotly contested issue within lesbian academic and legal circles. It is clear, however, that while a lesbian mother's chances of securing custody and access rights to her children have improved considerably during the past two decades, the threat of a custody battle over the issue of sexual orientation remains a powerful one in the lives of *all* lesbian mothers.[12]

The "Lesbian Baby Boom"

While initially most lesbian mothers who came to public attention had conceived and given birth within heterosexual partnerships or marriages, in the past fifteen years increasing numbers of lesbians have chosen to conceive and bear children either on their own or with a lesbian partner. Relying primarily on donor insemination, these women have produced a "lesbian baby boom."[13] The problems they have faced in their efforts to establish lesbian families that are autonomous from men reveal the strength and persistence of heterosexual hegemony and patriarchal power.

Since the late 1970s, an undetermined number of lesbians have requested assisted insemination services at infertility clinics and sperm banks across North America. Many of these requests were denied once the applicant's sexual orientation was revealed. In some instances clinics declared that they would not inseminate *any* single woman, claiming that they feared a child support suit should the insemination be successful.[14] In a recent study conducted for the Canadian Royal Commission on New Reproductive Technologies, 76 percent of practitioners surveyed said that they would refuse donor insemination "to a woman in a stable lesbian relationship."[15] To date, no legal decisions have been issued concerning infertility clinics or physicians who discriminate against single women or lesbians. In the only documented American case, a woman launched a legal action against Wayne State

University when its medical center rejected her application for assisted insemination. Wishing to avoid a protracted legal battle, the clinic abandoned its restrictive policy, granting her application before the case could be heard.[16] To prevent such legal actions, legislative initiatives in a number of jurisdictions have restricted access to insemination services to married women. Robert H. Blank notes that "the question of allowing single or lesbian women access to AID [artificial insemination by donor] has been approached explicitly in few jurisdictions and rejected in virtually all."[17]

In the absence of legislation securing their access to clinical services, many lesbians have chosen private insemination arrangements, finding a donor through a woman-controlled sperm bank or a circle of friends. Kath Weston found that before AIDS surfaced, "the preferred means of facilitating lesbian motherhood had been to ask gay men to contribute sperm," at least in the San Francisco area.[18] On occasion, the use of a go-between can offer the prospect of anonymity, coupled with the possibility of later identifying the paternity of the child. In most cases, however, women choosing a private insemination know the donor's identity. Indeed, many women prefer to use a known donor, since it provides the possibility of an answer to the "Who is my daddy?" question that often arises. Although that answer is not always easy, the use of a known donor enables a lesbian to demystify to a degree the otherwise mythic proportions that an unknown father can assume. While private inseminations can afford certain advantages, legal measures designed to medicalize the practice of assisted insemination present yet another roadblock. Recently, many jurisdictions in the United States and elsewhere have passed legislation declaring assisted insemination to be a practice of medicine, thereby legally restricting its use to licensed practitioners.[19] In 1985 the Ontario Law Reform Commission recommended the passage of similar legislation.[20] Such measures force women engaged in private insemination arrangements to remain clandestine about their activities to avoid legal sanctions.

Regardless of the legality of the insemination process itself, the parental status of the sperm donor remains at issue. While assisted insemination initially was treated as the legal equivalent to adultery against the woman's husband, gradually courts moved to a position that recognizes the resulting child as the legitimate offspring of the recipient's husband, provided he had consented to the insemination procedure. The husband was thereby legally obligated to support the child. Most legislation now specifies that, in the case of a married couple, the parental rights and obligations of the donor are replaced by the paternal rights of the husband.[21] Thus, assisted insemination becomes a means to support the traditional heterosexual nuclear family structure, assisting in reproduction in cases of male infertility. As Carol Smart has noted, we have witnessed a dramatic shift away from a view of assisted insemination as a "threat to marriage and society" and toward a view of it "as a way of enhancing family life for the childless."[22] Such a shift appears to be true, however, mainly for the heterosexual childless.

The issues are considerably more complex in the case of a lesbian or unmarried heterosexual woman and a known donor, given that most of the statutes are premised on heterosexuality. In such instances, women who arrange a private insemination—most of whom are lesbians—face the risk of paternity claims by sperm donors. To date, no Canadian cases have been reported, but in all American cases before *Thomas S. v. Robin Y.*, sperm donors seeking a declaration of paternity have had their claims upheld by the courts.[23] The decisions have ranged from placing the sperm donor's name on the child's birth certificate to granting the donor access rights.[24] Such decisions have been made even in jurisdictions where relevant legislation can extinguish the rights and obligations of donors. In a 1989 case, for example, the Oregon Appeals Court concluded that, despite a relevant statute, the donor had shown himself interested in performing the duties of a father and was therefore entitled to seek paternity rights similar to those of an unwed father.[25] In a similar case, the Colorado Supreme Court ruled in favor of the donor, crediting his claims of having purchased toys, clothing, and books and of establishing a trust fund for the child as evidence of his desire to parent.[26]

While all cases to date have involved only the legal issues of access and a declaration of paternity, they are by no means limited to those claims. On the contrary, a declaration of paternity can accord any and all of the following: sole or joint physical or legal custody, visitation, decision making in such areas as education, religion, and health care, custody in the event of the mother's death, denial of permission to change residence or to adopt, obligation to provide child support, and inclusion of the donor's name as father on the child's birth certificate.[27] As the U.S. National Center for Lesbian Rights has noted,

> in our system of law there are only two options. Either the donor is merely a donor, with no parental rights or relationship with the child whatsoever, or he is a father, with all of his parental rights intact. There are no gray areas in the law here, and, when in doubt, the courts tend to grant donors full parental rights in cases involving single mothers.[28]

Clearly, then, these cases have far-reaching effects on the lives of lesbian mothers and their children. Given the historical support within the lesbian and gay movements for the custodial rights of lesbian mothers, it might be expected that lesbians and gay men would have applauded the decision in *Thomas S. v. Robin Y.* As always, the situation is more complex, particularly since in this case the sperm donor was a gay man.

What If the Sperm Donor Is Gay?

Despite the initial victory for lesbian mothers in *Thomas S. v. Robin Y.*, the case was not embraced unanimously by the lesbian and gay communities in the United States. A series of letters to *Lesbian/Gay Law Notes*[29] in response to Art Leonard's initial report on *Thomas S. v. Robin Y.* reveals an important division of opinion concerning the ruling that this lesbian family did not include the gay sperm donor. Some argue that if two lesbian co-mothers affirm their parental rights by showing that they are family and that the sperm donor is not, regardless of the relationship that he may have developed with the child, a traditional, insular, and couple-based nuclear model of family is endorsed. Thus, despite this case's affirmation of lesbian families, which offers radical potential in the context of homophobic middle America, some critics argue that this familial stance is neither radical nor progressive, since in their view it invokes the nuclear family, an institution that is arguably central to heterosexist middle America.

Some letter writers argued that before the breakdown of Thomas S.'s relationship with Robin Y. and her family, they broke new ground "as a gay extended family."[30] Others were "shocked at the gay press for not coming to the defense of a gay, HIV-positive man who functioned as the child's father from the time the child was three years old."[31] Some concern was expressed that since Thomas S. was gay and HIV-positive, he was less likely to be affirmed in his paternity claim than a heterosexual sperm donor would have been.[32]

An equal number of respondents maintained that the decision was a victory for the rights of lesbian and gay families. "The decision is a victory for diverse families of all kinds," wrote Kathleen Conkey on behalf of Lesbians at Law, "because it recognizes that a family is built upon emotional and relational bonds rather than biology."[33] She argued that "the case marks an important step forward toward full recognition of lesbian and gay families, whatever their *chosen* form." In the face of continued loss of custody by lesbian mothers and of refusals to recognize the rights of nonbiological mothers, the decision represented for many an affirmation of lesbian families.

The reported case assists in assessing the merits of these arguments. Thomas S. wanted to introduce Ry to his own family without her mothers, a decision that was a denial of the lesbian family as it had been carefully constituted by Robin Y. and her partner. The lawsuit arose not merely because of a "family quarrel," as letter writers such as

Nanci L. Clarence characterized it, but rather a challenge by Thomas S. to this lesbian family's definition of itself, to its autonomy, and to the terms of reference that had always operated between him and the women. As Judge Kaufmann said, the women worried that if Thomas S. were declared to be a father, and if Robin Y., the biological mother, were to die, then Thomas S. or his biological family might seek custody of Ry. "They worried too, that Ry might be exposed to people who might question and undermine the concept of family they had worked to instill in the children—two lesbian mothers raising two children, equally, and two children responding to each other as sisters and responding to two mothers, equally, without regard to biological ties."[34] Their worries were not exaggerated, in our view, when one takes into account the dominant social and legal construction of relations between parents and children. As well, Robin Y.'s appellate brief indicates that in a discussion with the court-appointed psychiatrist Thomas S. contemplated a custody suit and that his parents were homophobic.

It is of note that just as lesbian co-mothers finally were affirmed in their claim to be a family on their own with their children in *Thomas S. v. Robin Y.*, the right of a father (in this case a gay man) to parental status is being put forward. Throughout the history of Western family law, it has been difficult for mothers to assert legally their ability to parent a child without a man. Although in some periods the legal system took little interest in interfering with (or providing support for) a single mother's relationship with her illegitimate child, in recent years, if a father demonstrates interest in a child, it is more common for him to be given some form of parental status.[35] Is it coincidental that in this period of the (re)assertion of heterosexual fathers' rights to children, sperm donors have been granted rights to children with whom they initially had no intention of forming a relationship? We do not believe that the position of the gay sperm donor in *Thomas S. v. Robin Y.* can be separated from general trends to diminish women's ability to mother independently from men.

Legal Parenthood, Marriage, and Fathers' Rights

Child custody law and laws defining parenthood have a long and varied history of reinforcing the ideology of the patriarchal heterosexual family in western democratic states.[36] The technique has ranged from the establishment of paternal custody rights over legitimate children, to the emerging but limited and conditional granting of maternal rights of the late nineteenth and early twentieth centuries, to the current focus on the "best interests of the child" principle. In all periods, a normative model of family based on male power and heterosexuality has prevailed. Biological relations have played an ambiguous and some-times mythical role in defining paternity, with marriage relations being a central mechanism used to link a father with a woman and her child, often *regardless* of an actual biological paternal connection.[37] In contrast, the biological relationship between mother and child has been taken for granted in its naturalness, so much so that it is almost invisible.[38] Oddly and perversely, this phenomenon may account for the legal propensity to limit maternal rights to ensure the rights of fathers.

Marriage has been the main mechanism by which law recognizes the relationship between men and children, and the concept of legitimacy—being born within marriage—has been key. In the context of custody, prior to the twentieth century only legitimate children were viewed as properly belonging with their father upon marriage breakdown. Illegitimate children who were largely excluded from familial property transfers and inheritance could be left with their (usually poor) mothers. As the welfare state expanded in the early twentieth century, mothers of illegitimate children were urged to file filiation suits and obtain support from men defined as fathers.[39]

More recently, as unmarried (heterosexual) cohabitation has been accorded legitimacy (as have children born into such a relationship), and as women have begun to find ways to bear and raise children independently from men (including the biological fathers of their children), the paternal biological link has been reasserted in its own right. The concept of the illegitimacy of children has gradually been eradicated by using ways other than marriage to find a father for children. Often these ways are analogous to marriage—and make similar assumptions about biology—because they stress the significance of the person with whom a woman was living when she conceived a child.[40] In addition, however, paternity has been recognized apart from live-in relationships: Unwed biological fathers have claimed the right to veto a mother's decision to put a child up for adoption, sometimes regardless of whether he knew she was pregnant.[41] Some courts have affirmed this right, which is somewhat ironic in these days of emphasis on parents' psychological bonding with children. Or perhaps it is not ironic that fathers are asserting biological claims and the importance of fathering per se, given that they rarely can assert that they have been primary care givers for children. Smart argues that "the importance of paternity seems to be in an *inverse relationship* to the amount of physical and emotional care provided by fathers."[42] Meanwhile in issues such as surrogate motherhood, mothers' biological or genetic link with children has been rendered largely invisible.[43] This trend to diminish maternal biological/genetic connections with children has been accompanied by a tendency to undervalue the primary care-giving labor for children that women still overwhelmingly perform even in supposedly liberated Western capitalist societies.[44]

The sometimes contradictory legal treatment of biology shows underlying support for a particular family structure, that is, "a heterosexual couple living together in a stable relationship, whether married or not."[45] This dominant normative model of the heterosexual nuclear family, reinforced by laws related to parenthood and family, has been convenient to capitalist relations, not least because of its delivery of "free" reproductive labor performed by women and its ability to reproduce dominant social values in children.[46] Many of the historical shifts outlined above can be traced to the perceived need to ascribe economic responsibility for children to an individual man who can be viewed as responsible for woman and child. The heterosexual nuclear family emerges as a privatizing and cost-saving measure for societies that do not want to confront the social costs of reproduction.[47] Such developments have been cloaked in the rhetoric of the welfare of the child and presented as a means of protecting children, best raised in the two-parent (read "heterosexual") nuclear family, preferably united by marriage.[48]

The paternity claim of Thomas S. must be seen in this larger picture of the difficulties that both heterosexual women and lesbians have experienced in exercising reproductive autonomy. This is particularly true given that Thomas S. denigrated the financial stability of Robin Y. and Sandra R., and argued that he was Ry's only reliable source of financial security.

Gay Men and Fathers' Rights

In her letter to *Lesbian/Gay Law Notes,* Rebecca Westerfield asked, "Would the court have better served the child by permitting more love and support in her life? Is it possible for a child to have too many devoted and supportive parents or too much love?"[49] While these important questions challenge dominant models of individualized, couple-based childrearing, the timing of these claims is key. It remains very difficult for women to affirm the role of a man in their children's lives without becoming subject to legal threats to their own definition of family. Furthermore, these threats increasingly emanate not only from heterosexual men with paternity claims but also from gay men, as in *Thomas S. v. Robin Y.* and at least one earlier American case (see note 8). As well, when the interests and concerns of these supportive parents come into conflict, it may well be possible to have too many parents.

Ellen Lewin and Kath Weston both have observed that the interest of gay men in children and family has intensified during the AIDS

era: "The coincidence of these developments with the AIDS epidemic
and its devastating impact on the gay community . . . cannot be ignored; synagogue members suggested to me that the enthusiasm for
activities involving children now evidenced by the men in the congre-
gation seems to parallel their weariness with disease and death."[50]
While this interest holds progressive potential in the old feminist sense
of hoping that men would assume some responsibility for child care in
Western societies, the assertion in Thomas S.'s case, as in the other
sperm donor cases, was primarily for rights and not ongoing responsibility—and it is responsibility for children that feminists have been demanding that men begin to take. Even in cases where men wish to assume greater responsibility, in the context of the still fragile efforts by
women to raise children autonomously from men, this progressive potential simultaneously holds a threat.

In the process of asserting his parental claim to Ry, Thomas S. apparently wished to deny the existence of the co-mothers and presumably the reality of family in Ry's life. One can sympathize with the fact
that HIV-positive gay men might have strong desires to introduce their
progeny to their own parents. One can also imagine that they might
have conservative or homophobic parents and feel uncomfortable
telling the full story of how the child was conceived. Nonetheless
Thomas S.'s denial of Robin Y. and Sandra R. is difficult to reconcile
with the argument of those who feel that he should have been regarded as part of Ry's family. At trial, he presented evidence about
the insularity of Ry's family, which, according to one letter writer,
amounted to "a blatant attack on lesbian families."

> Drawing on negative assumptions about women's emotional rather than
> rational tendencies, the donor's expert basically pathologized lesbian re-
> lationships as inappropriately "merged," testified to the necessity of fa-
> ther figures in this child's life, advanced a hierarchical model of family
> organization, and criticized attempts at mutual equality as parents that
> the mothers have worked out between themselves.[51]

While this argument was dropped on appeal, it remains a disturbing re-
minder of the depths of the divisions that this case revealed.

It is significant that at trial Thomas S. affirmed his biological connection with Ry as the key to his case, and it is even more notable that
he argued at trial and on appeal that equitable estoppel applied only
where a declaration of paternity would brand a child illegitimate.
Thomas S. thereby invoked the patriarchal history of (il)legitimacy and
paternal relationships with children, not to mention the denial of the
particular context of this family, which rendered the concept of illegitimacy irrelevant. Given the evidence, of course, he could not argue
that a consensual agreement had been reached that he was "family."

Neither could he argue that he had cared for Ry on a daily, weekly, or even regular basis, thereby developing a relationship akin to social fatherhood. He could only resort to his claims of biological paternity.

We may well wish in our own communities to enhance connections between various adults and children, but invoking the legal system in litigation like this to enforce these connections against the wishes of the primary care giver(s) is another issue altogether. The context and form of these cases are not conducive to efforts to create and recognize noncouple-based familial relations. In these cases lesbian mothers are cast in a defensive legal position, much as heterosexual mothers often are when trying to extricate themselves from a family that includes the father of their children. This defensive posture in turn limits the discourse that can be used by lesbian mothers, particularly at a time when greater credit is accorded to men's voices in parental claims and when the fear of women living autonomously is widespread. It is not at all clear that legally recognizing men's social relationships with children, as some letter writers advocated, is much less threatening to women's autonomy than recognizing the biological connection in Western patriarchal systems.

The Limits and the Power of the Law

Westerfield pointed out in her letter to *Lesbian/Gay Law Notes* that Judge Kaufmann felt bound by a restrictive either/or choice that the law tends to encourage: "The court seemed to believe it had to reject either the biological father completely or the legitimate parental claims of the non-biological mother. It thus never created the opportunity to devise an equitable solution that could accord contact between the child and father and at the same time recognize and respect the primary custodial rights of the mothers."[52] Clarence wrote that "the premise that exactly two and only two people can claim parental rights is as arbitrary and unreflective of social reality as the requirement in two parent families, that parents must be different genders. There would be no terrible fear of calling a father a father, if one mother did not automatically have to lose."[53] These women point toward interesting models, but more pertinently raise a key strategic issue: At what stage is it viable to ask the law to recognize noncouple-based family forms? Westerfield and Clarence think that that time is now. Before we reach a political/legal position where one mother does not have to lose, however, we must determine how to work politically with the current legal discourse, which is so embedded in the ideology of the patriarchal nuclear family, to transform it.

Asking the law to recognize alternative family forms is not a neutral exercise. At present, it occurs in the context of an apparent judicial

(and societal) desire to (re)-create heterosexual family forms even after family breakdown.[54] The way in which lesbian family constellations
will be recognized will reflect this desire and quite possibly give greater
credence to the male voices of potential fathers than to those of mothers. Had Thomas S.'s paternal status been recognized, the efforts of the
lesbian co-mothers to develop their own family definition through
careful consensual agreement would have been eradicated. Even if
there had been a written contract, the logic of Judge Kaufmann left the
door open for a father who assertively pursued paternal status to be so
declared if he had indicated interest sooner, tried to pay expenses related to the pregnancy or the child, took the initiative to see the child
regardless of the mothers' desire, and so on. The outcome of all the
sperm donor cases suggests that we are stuck in an either/or dilemma
where we can only recognize one package of parental rights or the
other. This dilemma, though, may tell us something important about
current gender-based dynamics in the way we determine legal relationships between adults and children. It may not be as easy to ask the
law to recognize noncouple-based family constellations as some may
think, particularly not at the time of breakdown of relationships. As
Julia Brophy has noted, "A custody dispute is not the forum in which
to mount a feminist critique of the family."[55]

Determining a strategy for defining lesbian and gay familial relations requires consideration of the complex relationship between
law and social change. Several feminist authors working on family law
have pointed out that it is probably "beyond the scope of family law
radically to transform structural differences in child care."[56] Mary Ann
Glendon has observed that "when the law is in harmony with other social forces, it will synergistically produce a greater effect in combination with them than it could on its own. But when the messages com-
municated through law run counter to those prevailing elsewhere in
the culture, the effect of law on ideas and behaviour must be small."[57]
The best strategy may be to use the law to *recognize* dominant and gendered power-based patterns, such as women's primary care-giving
labor and the excessive attention paid to men's parental claims, and
to avoid the disempowering of women that results from a gender-
neutrality that obscures these patterns. The law may reinforce existing
socioeconomic structures of patriarchy and heterosexism more often
and more readily than it can change them.

Where Do We Go from Here?

Given all the questions that have been raised above, strategies for
defining the status of lesbian co-mothers vis-à-vis sperm donors must
be developed carefully. It is difficult to do so in any conclusive way

based on the cases reviewed in this essay, which appear to involve mainly white, middle-class individuals. We must also keep in mind the role that custody and access disputes play in the lives of a variety of women who sometimes need to resist men's legal claims to children in order to obtain autonomy over their lives and often over their bodies. One feminist strategy in addressing the difficulties that heterosexual women have had in obtaining custody in recent years has been to argue that past primary care giving should be the key factor in determining the best interests of the child. Under a primary care-giver presumption, custody normally should be given to the parent who has been primary care giver in the past. In heterosexual relationships, this would usually be the woman, thereby recognizing the sexual division of labor that persists in most heterosexual households and valuing women's labor in this context. The gender neutrality of the presumption, however, would permit those men who have been primary care givers to claim its benefit, thereby not hindering shifts in the sexual division of labor in heterosexual relationships.[58]

In *Thomas S. v. Robin Y.*, Ry's definition of "parent" relied on a concept of who provided her daily care. This stood in contrast to the visiting relationship she had with Thomas S. She was affirming the primary care-giving relationships she had with her co-mothers and distinguishing Thomas S.'s role from that relationship. The primary care-giver presumption, though, may not ultimately assist in the sperm donor versus lesbian mother cases, where the sperm donor is usually asking for access, not custody.[59] Under a strict application of the primary care-giver presumption as it is usually enunciated, Thomas S. would not have had a chance of obtaining custody, but he would have had a chance—a very good chance—of obtaining generous visitation rights. To the extent that access is now a key site for struggle over children, and that its definition has steadily expanded so that custody and access are not as distinct as they once were,[60] the primary care-giver presumption cannot assist women who wish to mother autonomously from men unless certain primary care-giver rights to sometimes exclude other adults from their children's lives are developed along with it.

As well, given that one of the issues for lesbian co-mothers in many of these cases is how to gain recognition of the nonbiological co-mother's parental status,[61] the primary care-giver presumption may not help. If she is not the primary care giver, she may be rendered invisible entirely if a dispute develops between the biological mother and the donor. Furthermore, if the nonbiological co-mother were indeed the primary care-giver mother, a sperm donor may well be able to trump the primary care-giver presumption by his biological link, just as biological fathers have been able to some degree to trump "social (step)fathers" living with a biological mother.[62] The limits of the pre-

sumption that have been revealed in terms of its ability to accommodate the realities of lives of women with disabilities, women who parent in an extended family context, women employed in demanding
jobs, and so on, are thus further revealed by the sperm donor/lesbian
mother cases.[63] It was suggested in a recent submission to the Canadian government by the National Association of Women and the Law
that both women in lesbian couples might be considered primary care-
givers, but the exact implications of this recommendation were not
spelled out.[64]

In this light, Martha Fineman's suggestion of defining the core familial unit as the mother–child dyad[65] is intriguing, perhaps used in conjunction with a contract that would permit the mother to define the con-
stellation of people who will have special relationships with her child.
This proposal is attractive insofar as it undermines the husband–wife/
mother–father dyad of the heterosexual nuclear family, while simultaneously redressing the invisibility of women's primary care giving. Its biological underpinnings are problematic, however, particularly in the inherent assumption that biological mothers necessarily are good. We
might rearticulate Fineman's proposal into an argument for social and
legal policies that prioritize and support a child's primary care-giving re-
lationship(s) with adult(s) (in our society more often women), and develop mechanisms that allow for the recognition of nonprimary caring
relationships for children without undermining the autonomy of the primary relationship.

Within this context, what rights and responsibilities should ac-
crue to a sperm donor? In the heterosexual context, courts and legislators have increasingly moved to deny any rights to sperm donors, in
recognition of the importance of the autonomy of the family unit to
which the child was born. It is almost entirely within the context of lesbian and/or single motherhood that judges have felt compelled to "find
a father." It is imperative that in our rush to create alternative families
we do not ignore the homophobic and patriarchal implications of those
decisions. We should support the continued resistance to force either
rights or responsibilities upon sperm donors. In addition, we should
urge lesbians and gay men entering into such arrangements to formal-
ize their agreement via contracts. While subject to amendment upon
agreement of both parties as a result of changed circumstances, such
contracts would afford protection for both the lesbian mother(s) and
the sperm donor.[66]

Although it has been suggested that an analogy can be drawn between sperm donors and surrogate mothers, such a comparison ignores crucial aspects of gender. The reproductive labor engaged in by
the surrogate mother through the processes of pregnancy and birth is

hardly comparable to the effort of depositing a semen donation in a vial. Asserting sperm donor rights on the basis of biological connection is somewhat akin to asserting rights based upon a donation of blood or a vital organ, or perhaps ova rights, which to date, have been neither proposed nor affirmed. In the final analysis, men and women have radically different reproductive capacities, and it is perhaps this difference, above all else, that causes such deep division on this issue.

Ruthann Robson argues for preserving "lesbian choice," not the legal category "family" and certainly not "father right."[67] How to avoid the invocation of family or father right in a society so entrenched in these images is, however, a complex question. Determining what it means to talk about lesbian choice, when choices are socially constructed both materially and ideologically, is difficult. A key strategy for lesbian mothers has been to affirm the ability of lesbian mothers to provide for the best interests of their children. While this strategy was framed initially within the context of a closeted lesbian household, an emerging argument has been that lesbian households can constitute a family in their own right. This argument was accepted in *Thomas S. v. Robin Y.* but is clearly controversial in the lesbian and gay communities. In our view, keeping in mind the highly gendered power relations that have thus far determined familial legal disputes is a start in finding a way through these debates, and cautions us to look before we leap into an ungendered strategy for defining lesbian and gay parenthood.

Afterword

In a three-to-two decision entered on November 17, 1994, the appellate division of the New York Supreme Court overturned Judge Kaufmann's decision and ruled that an order of filiation be entered in favor of Thomas S.[68] The issue of visitation was remanded for a further hearing. Noting that the effect of the family court's order was to "cut off the parental rights of a man who is conceded by all concerned . . . to be the biological father," the majority affirmed that the issue in the case is not "whether an established family unit is to be broken up" but "whether the rights of a biological parent are to be terminated." The termination of Thomas S.'s parental rights would be "in violation of well established standards of due process" and therefore could not be allowed to stand. A false analogy is thereby drawn with "the typical case of divorce and remarriage of a mother," where, it is said, no one would suggest that a father's parental rights should be terminated.

Two aspects of the appellate division's decision are worthy of comment. First, in describing the relationship between Ry and Thomas S., the majority repeatedly refers to Thomas S. as "her father." In marked contrast, the dissenting judges variously refer to Thomas S. as the "petitioner sperm donor," the "biological progenitor," and the "sperm donor and paternal biological progenitor of the child Ry," but never as Ry's father. The terminology employed in the dissent is consistent with Judge Kaufmann's observation that "in her family, there has been no father."

Second, while the dissent notes that the fact that the "petitioner is a gay man is wholly irrelevant," the majority makes the following disturbing observation: "The notion that a lesbian mother should enjoy a parental relationship with her daughter but a gay father should not is so innately discriminatory as to be unworthy of comment." The contrast between the rights of lesbian mothers and gay "fathers" was highlighted by a number of American newspapers in commentary on the case. This false analogy fails to consider the fundamentally different relationships that the lesbian mothers and Thomas S. had to Ry, especially in terms of care giving. As a result, it simplistically invokes biology as the key determinant of legal paternity, demonstrating that it may be some time before it is possible to eliminate the longstanding judicial determination to "find fathers" for children, even where lesbian families are concerned.

NOTES

1. *Thomas S. v. Robin Y.*, 599 N.Y.S. 2d 377, 380 (Fam. Ct. 1993).

2. Jane Ursel, *Private Lives, Public Policy: 100 Years of State Intervention in the Family* (Toronto: Women's Press, 1992), p. 46.

3. For example, in Canada, the unjust enrichment doctrine has been used to provide a mechanism for settling property disputes between partners of the same sex. See, e.g., *Anderson v. Luoma* [1984] 42 R.F.L. (2d) 444 (B.C.S.C.). In Ontario in 1994, a bill was introduced, and defeated, that would have treated lesbian and gay couples like unmarried heterosexual cohabitants. See Susan Boyd, "Expanding the 'Family' in Family Law: Recent Ontario Proposals on Same Sex Relationships," *Canadian Journal of Women and the Law*, 7(2)(1994): 545.

4. Jenni Millbank looks at the similarities and differences between gay men and lesbians in the context of custody in "Lesbian Mothers, Gay Fathers: Sameness and Difference," *Australian Gay and Lesbian Law Journal* 2(1992): 21.

5. Litigation in this area appears to have been chiefly between white, mainly middle-class individuals, so that to the extent that it rests on cases, our analysis represents a partial view of the nature of parenting and parenting disputes involving lesbians and gay men.

6. *Thomas S. v. Robin Y.*, p. 379.

7. Ibid., p. 382.

8. *C.M. v. C.C.*, 377 A. 2d 821 (N.J. Super. 1977); *Jhordan C. v. Mary K.*, 224 Cal. Rptr. 530 (Ct. App. 1986); *McIntyre v. Crouch*, 780 P. 2d 239 (Or. App.

1989); *Interest of R.C.*, 775 P. 2d 27 (Colo. 1989). Another case was described in "Sperm Donor Wins Fight with Lesbians," *Toronto Star*, July 26, 1991, p. F1. (We were unable to locate a report of this case.)

9. *Thomas S. v. Robin Y.*, p.380.

10. See, e.g., Ontario Children's Law Reform Act, R.S.O. 1990, c. 68, s. 24.

11. For a discussion of these cases, see Wendy Gross, "Judging the Best Interests of the Child: Child Custody and the Homosexual Parent," *Canadian Journal of Women and the Law* 1(2)(1986): 505; Katherine Arnup, " 'Mothers Just Like Others': Lesbians, Divorce, and Child Custody in Canada," *Canadian Journal of Women and the Law* 3(1)(1989):18. For a recent comprehensive review of cases from England, Canada, the United States, and Australia, see Jenni Millbank, "What Do Lesbians Do? Motherhood Ideology, Lesbian Mothers, and Family Law," LL.M. thesis, University of British Columbia, 1994.

12. See Millbank, "What Do Lesbians Do?" A U.S. article estimated that 1% of lesbian mothers won custody in 1970; that figure had risen to 15% by 1986. See Diane Raymond, " 'In the Best Interests of the Child': Thoughts on Homophobia and Parenting," in Warren J. Blumenfeld, ed., *Homophobia: How We All Pay the Price* (Boston: Beacon Press, 1992), p. 116. Given the number of private arrangements and the tendency to seal records and for such cases to go unreported, it is impossible to provide accurate statistics on the number of lesbian mothers who secure custody rights.

13. See Kath Weston, *Families We Choose* (New York: Columbia University Press, 1991), chap. 7.

14. For a discussion of such arguments, see Katherine Arnup, "Finding Fathers: Artificial Insemination, Lesbians, and the Law," *Canadian Journal of Women and the Law* 7(1)(1994): 97.

15. See Rona Achilles, *Donor Insemination: An Overview* (Ottawa: Royal Commission on New Reproductive Technologies, 1992), p. 23.

16. *Smedes v. Wayne State University*, No. 80-725-83 (E.D. Mich., filed July 15, 1980). The case was widely reported in the American press; see, e.g., "Woman Sues to Be Mother," *Philadelphia Bulletin*, July 17, 1980; and "A Single Sues for Artificial Insemination," *Seattle Times* July 17, 1980, p. A5.

17. Robert H. Blank, *Regulating Reproduction* (New York: Columbia University Press, 1990), p. 151. No Canadian legislation yet exists, although recommendations to this effect have been made by a number of commissions. Most recently, the Royal Commission on New Reproductive Technologies, in its 1993 final report, supported the right to assisted insemination (including private insemination) for single women, and argued explicitly that lesbians should not be discriminated against. See Recommendations 94(f) and 99 (d), *Proceed with Care: Final Report of the Royal Commission on New Reproductive Technologies* (Ottawa: Government of Canada, 1993), p. 485. This position stands in marked contrast to the relevant British legislation, the *Human Fertilization and Embryology Act 1990*, c.37, which states in s. 13(5) that: "A woman shall not be provided with treatment services unless account has been taken of the welfare of any child who may be born as a result of the treatment (including the need of that child for a father), and of any other child who may be affected by the

birth." Whether the recommendations of the Canadian report will be enacted remains to be seen, particularly given that the report was commissioned under a Conservative government, now no longer in power.

18. Weston, *Families We Choose,* p. 177.

19. Cooper and Herman (see Chapter 8) note that self-insemination was criminalized in Victoria, Australia, under the *Medical Procedures Act of 1984.*

20. Ontario Law Reform Commission, *Report on Artificial Reproduction and Related Matters* (Ontario: Ministry of the Attorney General, 1985).

21. Section 5 of the Uniform Parentage Act, the model legislation drafted in the United States by the National Conference of Commissioners on Uniform State Laws in 1973, states:
(a) If, under the supervision of a licensed physician and with the consent of her husband, a wife is inseminated artificially with semen donated by a man not her husband, the husband is treated in law as if he were the natural father of a child thereby conceived. . . .
(b) The donor of semen provided to a licensed physician for use in artificial insemination of a married woman other than the donor's wife is treated in law as if he were not the natural father of a child thereby conceived.
Cited in Dominick Vetri, "Reproductive Technologies and United States Law," *International and Comparative Law Quarterly* 37(1988): 510.
    Section 13(6) of the Yukon statute dealing with this issue is typical of legislation regarding donor rights: "A man whose semen is used to artificially inseminate a woman to whom he is not married or with whom he is not cohabiting at the time of the insemination is not in law the father of the resulting child." Children's Act, S.Y.T. 1986, c. 22, s. 13 (6). To date, in Canada only Quebec, Newfoundland, and Yukon have enacted legislation explicitly dealing with donor insemination.

22. Carol Smart, " 'There is of Course the Distinction Dictated by Nature': Law and the Problem of Paternity," in Michelle Stanworth, ed., *Reproductive Technologies: Gender, Motherhood, and Medicine* (Minneapolis: University of Minnesota Press, 1987), p. 107.

23. But see *Leckie v. Voorhies,* No. 60-92-06326 (Or. Cir., April 5, 1993), decided after the trial decision in *Thomas S. v. Robin Y.* This decision was affirmed by the Oregon Court of Appeals (128 Or. App. 289 (1994)), on the grounds that the donor had explicitly waived in a written contract any entitlement to assert parental rights.

24. See "Sperm Donor Wins Fight with Lesbians." For a discussion of these cases, see Arnup, "Finding Fathers."

25. In *McIntyre v. Crouch,* the court remanded the matter to the lower court to allow the donor to make arguments that the statute violated his constitutional rights of Due Process. If the donor could establish that he and the mother had agreed that he should have the rights and responsibilities of a father, and in reliance on that contract he donated his sperm, the statute as applied would violate his federal constitiutional rights.

26. *Interest of R.C.,* 775 P. 2d 27 (Col. 1989). In her appellate brief, Robin Y. distinguishes her case from the earlier ones on the ground that, in those, courts had been able to determine that the parties agreed that the sperm donor

would be a parent and the donor asserted those rights promptly, within months of the birth.

27. For a discussion of the implications of donor rights, see National Center for Lesbian Rights, "Lesbians Choosing Motherhood: Legal Implications of Donor Insemination and Co-Parenting," reprinted in William B. Rubenstein, ed., *Lesbians, Gay Men, and the Law* (New York: New Press, 1993), p. 543.

28. Ibid., p. 546.

29. We will quote frequently from these letters, which were published in the June 1993 issue of *Lesbian/Gay Law Notes*, 33:1–4.

30. Tanya Neiman, ibid., p. 1.

31. Lia Brigante, ibid., p. 2.

32. There is no indication in the report to suggest that his HIV status was a factor in the decision. Judicial attitudes toward gay men generally may, however, be affected by even the possibility that they may be HIV-positive, in particular when parenting is involved.

33. Kathleen Conkey, Steering Committee, Lesbians at Law, New York, *Lesbian/Gay Law Notes*, p. 4.

34. *Thomas S. v. Robin Y.*, pp. 379–80.

35. Selma Sevenhuijsen, "Fatherhood and the Political Theory of Rights: Theoretical Perspectives of Feminism," *International Journal of Sociology of Law* 14(1986): 329; Smart, "Law and the Problem of Paternity."

36. Feminist scholars have been largely responsible for illuminating the gender dynamics of this history. See, e.g., Carol Smart and Selma Sevenhuijsen, eds., *Child Custody and the Politics of Gender* (London and New York: Routledge, 1989); Martha Albertson Fineman, *The Illusion of Equality: The Rhetoric and Reality of Divorce Reform* (Chicago and London: The University of Chicago Press, 1991); and the special issue on women and custody in the *Canadian Journal of Women and the Law* 3(1)(1989). Some authors argue that, in the current period, mothers have lost a language for expressing the experience of motherhood: see Martha Fineman, "The Neutered Mother," *University of Miami Law Review* 46(1992): 653; and Carol Smart, "The Legal and Moral Ordering of Child Custody," *Journal of Law and Society* 18(1991): 485.

37. Smart, "Law and the Problem of Paternity."

38. In the context of reproductive technology, Mary Anne Coffey refers to this as "sperm idolatry," noting the invisibility of ova. See her "Of Father Born: A Lesbian Feminist Critique of the Artificial Insemination Provisions of the Ontario Law Reform Commission Report on Human Artificial Reproduction and Related Matters," *Canadian Journal of Women and the Law* 1(2)(1986): 424.

39. See Ursel, *Private Lives, Public Policy*, pp. 104–5, 152, 162–63.

40. See, e.g., Ontario Children's Law Reform Act, s. 8(1)4.

41. See Mary L. Shanley, "Unwed Fathers' Rights, Adoption, and Sex Equality: Gender-Neutrality and the Perpetuation of Patriarchy," *Columbia Law Review* 95(1)(1995): 60.

42. Smart, "Law and the Problem of Paternity," p. 117.

43. For an extreme example, where the birth mother was declared to not be the natural mother of the child, see *Johnson v. Calvert*, 5 Cal. 4th 84, 851

P. 2d 776, 19 Cal. Rptr. 2d 494 (S.C. 1993). Cert. denied, 126 L. Ed. 2d 163, 114 S. Ct. 206, 62 *U.S.L.W.* 3249 (U.S. 1993), cert. dismissed, *Baby Boy J. v. Johnson,* 126 L. Ed. 2d 324, 114 S. Ct. 374 (U.S. 1993). This trend is also evident in custody discourse.

44. Pina La Novara, *A Portrait of Families in Canada* (Ottawa: Statistics Canada, Housing, Family, and Social Statistics Division, 1993), cat. no. 89-523E, pp. 49–50.

45. Smart, "Law and the Problem of Paternity," p. 114, citing the Warnock Report (1985), p. 10.

46. Ursel, *Private Lives, Public Policy;* Michèle Barrett and Mary McIntosh, *The Anti-Social Family,* 2nd ed. (London and New York: Verso, 1991).

47. In a recent British case, where two lesbians were declared as having parental responsibility for a child that one of them had borne after insemination, the Child Support Agency almost immediately declared the intention to track down the sperm donor fathers of the children of lesbian couples and hold them liable for child support. See Chris Barton, "Whose Child Is It Anyway?" *The Times* (London), July 19, 1994.

48. Not only women, children, lesbians, and gay men have been disempowered through the ideological and material reinforcing of this dominant form of family, but also poor, black, and First Nations families. See Martha Fineman, "Images of Mothers in Poverty Discourses," *Duke Law Journal* 1991: 274; Marlee Kline, "Complicating the Ideology of Motherhood: Child Welfare Law and First Nation Women," *Queen's Law Journal* 18(1993): 306; and Carrie G. Costello, "Legitimate Bonds and Unnatural Unions: Race, Sexual Orientation, and Control of the American Family," *Harvard Women's Law Journal* 15(1992): 79.

49. *Lesbian/Gay Law Notes,* p. 2.

50. Ellen Lewin, *Lesbian Mothers: Accounts of Gender in American Culture* (Ithaca and London: Cornell University Press, 1993), p. 48; Weston, *Families We Choose,* pp. 180–185.

51. Paula Ettelbrick, *Lesbian/Gay Law Notes,* p. 1.

52. Westerfield, ibid., p. 2.

53. Nanci L. Clarence, ibid., pp. 3–4.

54. Martha Fineman, "Dominant Discourse, Professional Language, and Legal Change in Child Custody Decisionmaking," *Harvard Law Review* 101 (1988): 727.

55. Julia Brophy, "New Families, Judicial Decision-Making, and Children's Welfare," *Canadian Journal of Women and the Law* 5(1992): 496.

56. Julia Brophy, "Custody Law, Child Care, and Inequality in Britain," in Smart and Sevenhuijsen, eds., *Child Custody and the Politics of Gender,* p. 234; Susan B. Boyd, "Potentialities and Perils of the Primary Caregiver Presumption," *Canadian Family Law Quarterly* 7(1990): 1.

57. Mary Ann Glendon, *The Transformation of Family Law: State, Law, and Family in the United States and Western Europe* (Chicago and London: University of Chicago Press, 1989).

58. See Fineman, *The Illusion of Equality;* and Smart and Sevenhuijsen, eds., *Child Custody and the Politics of Gender.*

59. In a 1991 case, a California sperm donor won the right to be listed as the child's father on the birth certificate. The newspaper article indicated that the donor was still seeking an order of joint custody. See "Sperm Donor Wins Fight with Lesbians."

60. In some jurisdictions, such as England and the state of Washington, the distinction between custody and access has been eradicated entirely by eliminating that terminology and talking about "parenting plans" or "parental responsibility" instead.

61. See Shelley A. M. Gavigan's essay in this collection (Chapter 5); and Nancy D. Polikoff, "This Child Does Have Two Mothers: Redefining Parenthood to Meet the Needs of Children in Lesbian-Mother and Other Nontraditional Families," *Georgetown Law Journal* 78(1990): 459.

62. See Smart, "Law and the Problem of Paternity," p. 114.

63. See Judith Mosoff, "Motherhood, Madness, and the Role of the State," LL.M. thesis, University of British Columbia, 1994, for a discussion of women with disabilities and the primary care-giver presumption. See also Kline, "Complicating the Ideology of Motherhood."

64. National Association of Women and the Law, *Response to Custody and Access: Public Discussion Paper* (Ottawa: NAWL, 1994), p. 7.

65. Fineman, "Images of Mothers in Poverty Discourses."

66. For a sample sperm donation agreement, see Laurie Bell, *On Our Own Terms: A Practical Guide for Lesbian and Gay Relationships* (Toronto: Coalition for Lesbian and Gay Rights in Ontario, 1991), pp. 43–44.

67. Ruthann Robson, *Lesbian (Out)Law* (Ithaca, NY: Firebrand Books, 1992), p. 136.

68. 209 AD 2d 298; 618 N.Y.S. 2nd 356, pp. 356–365.

FIVE

Within feminist theorizing, the concept of familial ideology has played an important role. At a basic level, it refers to the ways in which the dominant form of family—the nuclear heterosexual unit—is rendered natural, inevitable, and ideal. Shelley A. M. Gavigan, in this essay, uses the concept to think about legal battles between lesbian mothers. Her interest is in exploring how familial ideology plays out in these conflicts: Who resorts to furthering it and why? Do custody and access fights between lesbian co-parents entrench or undermine dominant notions of family? Ultimately, Gavigan problematizes traditional (within lesbian and gay theorizing) understandings of judges as homophobic and argues that familial ideology informs and shapes the positions of both mothers, long before they come to court.

A Parent(ly) Knot: Can Heather Have Two Mommies?[1]

Shelley A. M. Gavigan

Introduction

There is a children's book entitled *Heather Has Two Mommies*. It is the story of a little girl whose parents are a lesbian couple—Kate and Jane; Kate is a doctor, and Jane is a carpenter. Kate and Jane are blissfully happy, but they want to have a child in their lives. Following a joint decision, Jane becomes pregnant through alternative insemination, and, soon thereafter, Heather is born. Heather regards each woman as her mother: they are called "Mama Kate" and "Mama Jane." However, when she goes to nursery school, she discovers, apparently for the first time, that she is different from other children—she doesn't have a daddy. The story proceeds to illustrate, through the first-person accounts of the other children in Heather's nursery school, that there are many kinds of families. Reassured, Heather greets her two mommies at the end of the day, and she, Kate, and Jane leave together, presum-

I wish to thank Jill Grant for her superb technical assistance and Karen Pearlston for her equally superb research assistance. I also acknowledge with thanks the comments of Didi Herman, Susan Boyd, and Aviva Goldberg on an earlier draft. Karen Andrews, Judy Fudge, Brenda Cossman, and Dorothy Chunn endured many hours of discussions, and I thank them for their insight and stamina. Judy Deverell inspired me, and Amy Deverell decided for herself.

ably to live happily ever after with their ginger cat and black Labrador dog.

For those of us who are students of family law and perhaps of family life, Heather's story raises interesting questions, including interesting legal ones. While the story undoubtedly provides a measure of comfort to lesbian parents and a new generation of children being raised in lesbian households, the extent to which its content is regarded by many as controversial should not be underestimated.[2] This is not simply a story about a little girl being raised by two women, or even two lesbians, who, as refugees from heterosexual relationships, are raising a child from an ended marriage. This little girl does not have and has never had a daddy; she was conceived neither in a bed nor in the back seat of a car. She is a baby whose conception was made possible by a less traditional method. It is this aspect of the story, as well as perhaps the happy and ostensibly normal lives of the lesbians, Kate and Jane, that has given rise to its reception as a controversial book.

In this essay, I take this story as a departure point to interrogate and apply the concept of familial ideology. By "familial ideology," I mean the range of dominant ideas and social practices, discourses and prejudices, common sense and social science, in which relations of gender and generation are held out and generally accepted to be best organized around and through a household comprised of two adults of the opposite sex who (usually) have expressed a primary personal, sexual, and economic commitment to each other and to care for and raise any children they may have. The family is often asserted to be the basic unit of society and is celebrated by religious authorities in quasi-sacred terms. This form of relationship is often crystallized by marriage and supported by the state as well as by a range of nonstate institutions. The naturalized privacy, independence, interdependency, intimacy, security, and domesticity of this form of relationship are also heralded and accepted.[3] In this essay, then, I examine the implications of familial ideology in the context in which family members do not resemble the dominant image of the "normal" family: lesbian parents.[4]

I explore the extent to which dominant, socially shared understandings of biological and social reproduction and the relations expressed by the terms "parent" and "child" in law may be simultaneously challenged and reinforced by the existence (and even attitudes) of lesbian parents. More specifically, however, I challenge the view that the positions and legal struggles of lesbian parents can be deciphered by "centering" lesbians[5] or explained by recourse to the concept of heterosexual privilege. Lesbians do not live outside the law in a kind of legal limbo, nor do they exist in a legal vacuum. They shape and are shaped by the legal and social relations in which they live. I am wary of any analysis that focuses only on lesbians, because it seems to me that the "centered" lesbian can easily become the abstracted, or de-contextualized, lesbian. The relational nature of my inquiry and my argument means that I am unable to isolate the lesbian parent from the dominant familial realm. I begin by arguing for the necessity of ideological analysis and then move on to a discussion of lesbian custody cases.

Lesbian Parents: Is Familial Ideology Still Relevant?

In North America, the meaning of the family until recently enjoyed an unchallenged self-evidence as well as a certain naturalized and universalized quality, thanks in part to the trumpeting of "old-fashioned" family values in the 1992 U.S. presidential campaign. It is important to remember that the celebration of "The Family" was not simply a plank in the campaigns of the official right. The Democratic party's own nominating convention managed to produce more homages to the family than theretofore one might have imagined possible: The Democratic party was family; the gay and lesbian members of the party were family within family; the metaphor extended to presumably the greatest family of all—the American people were family. In the Canadian context, we have seen self-professed profamily politicians from all parties driving stakes into the hearts and hopes of lesbian and gay citizens in a self-aggrandizing defense of the family front.

The terrain of the family is a site of struggle and challenge, a challenge that tests the universality of the family form, rejects its naturalized quality and the denigration of other forms of relationships, and blows the whistle on its claim to reflect social reality. For defenders of the traditional family, the stakes are high. One great fear, it seems, is that a mythical army of mighty homosexuals and antifamily hedonists has set its sights too close to home: gay men and lesbians now want in. They want families—chosen families, social families—they want children; they want the fact acknowledged that some already have children; and they want their relationships recognized and valued. This is understandably traumatic for the defenders of the familial status quo, who thought they had their hands full just holding back the antifamily tide. Imagine their horror: The enemy wants in.

However, the positions taken by both the defenders of the familial fortress and the righteous band hammering at the gates illustrate the tenacity, complexity, and, perhaps even more profoundly, the contradictory nature of familial ideology: This Siren we know as the family attracts and holds almost everyone who encounters it. I am inclined to the view that few of us escape the embrace of familial ideology. As Wendy Clark once observed, "apart from men, one thing which feminists love to hate is the family," and yet they find it the most difficult to leave.[6] And understandably so—because familial ideology is more than just a pretty face. Its appeal also packs a punch, for there are tangible material dimensions to the family. It is almost as impossible to opt out of familial relationships and the familial forms of distribution of scarce resources as it is to opt out of wage labor in a capitalist society.[7]

It is incumbent upon those of us in law to identify and analyze the ways in which law is implicated in the construction, regulation, and reproduction of the dominant notion of family, while remaining alert to the extent that law may not be the dominant site of these processes.[8] It is critical that we analyze both the form of the legal regulation and the ideological content that infuses that form. The utility of ideology as an analytic device is that it helps us understand a concept's appeal and hold on our captured hearts and constrained imaginations, and the fact that one's sense of social reality finds resonance. As Terry Eagleton has argued:

> successful ideologies must be more than imposed illusions, and for all their inconsistencies must communicate to their subjects a version of social reality which is real and recognizable enough not to be rejected out of hand. . . . Any ruling ideology which failed to mesh with its subjects' lived experience would be extremely vulnerable and its exponents would be well advised to trade it in for another. But none of this contradicts the fact that ideologies quite often contain important propositions which are absolutely false.[9]

This then is not a form of false consciousness; the success of an ideology is its resonance with some aspect of experience or aspiration.

As Douglas Hay has illustrated, successful ideologies have an elasticity and cogency that allow the gaps and contradictions to be glossed over.[10] We need to be able to explain, for instance, when and why the law holds an appeal for people. For, if we do not appreciate this important dimension of ideology, we will not be able to explain why people, even courageous, oppressed, and marginalized people, continue to turn to the law, continue "to take their lives to court"[11] and to the legislature to press for redress or change.

If (as I believe) ideology as an analytic concept requires us to look as well to the hearts, minds, and hopes of the subordinate, can we be confident that the hearts and minds of the mothers who lose custody of their children to ex-husbands or of the aboriginal parents whose children are taken from home and community are "held" by the dominant ideology of mother or family? Do these parents turn to the courts for assistance and support? Do they, as condemned felons on eighteenth-century public scaffolds were importuned to do, accept the rightness or justness of the results? Or might they rather offer an instance of the elasticity of familial ideology being stretched to its limits—an instance of resistance?

We must be prepared to do more than analyze the judges and lawyers. We need to look to the litigants, the positions they take, and why (if we can discern this) they take them. And, as academics, we must be prepared to take a hard look at ourselves (as Eagleton has intimated, ideological thought, like halitosis, may be more readily detectable in another[12]). We do not have the luxury of idle critique.[13] In other words, if we are prepared to be rigorous in a decentering project, we will admit that the courts have not been alone nor necessarily even principally implicated in the denial of lesbian families. Surely, some of the lesbian parenting cases discussed below suggest that a fundamental denial occurs long before the lesbian parents/partners find themselves in court.

Here, then, is the paradox that reveals the contradictory nature of family and familial ideology: A commitment to familial ideology, to the dominant notion of family, may be found in the positions of those who go to lengths (and to court) to deny that their relationships are familial as well as those who expressly embrace the family. What must be examined is who turns to the law, who invokes what, and to what end?

Heather and Her Mommies Meet the Law

The circumstances of Heather's conception and birth give rise to a large set of questions, some of which again have been raised and examined in a preliminary way in a few cases and commentaries. At the very least, it is clear that it is increasingly difficult, if not problematic, to apply either common sense or traditional legal definitions of parent and child to new forms of parenting and child-rearing relationships and arrangements. What makes a person a parent? What makes a child one's child? Who is a father: Is the contribution of sperm to a pregnancy enough to qualify?

The legal contexts in which these questions have been touched upon to date vary. In the adoption context, some Canadian judges have offered a less than sympathetic assessment of the right of a male "casual fornicator" to be regarded as a parent whose consent to a child's adoption is required.[14] In a famous Canadian abortion injunction case, a man who attempted to prevent his former girlfriend from terminating her pregnancy was told by the Supreme Court of Canada that his was not a "father's rights" case: his "semenal" contribution to pregnancy did not make him a father, only a *potential* father.[15] A small line of American cases is suggestive that a sperm donor may well be able to press a claim for access to any child born as a result of an alternative method of conception[16] (*quare* whether this may suggest that the casual ejaculator tends to enjoy a more protected legal position than the casual fornicator). If a man enters into a preconception agreement with a woman in which he agrees to cover her expenses during a pregnancy if she will be inseminated with his sperm, does that make him a father or a purchaser of the baby eventually born?[17] Does this woman cease to be a mother if she enters into such an agreement or contract?[18]

As Heather's story suggests, the legal definition of parent and mother is challenged even further by a child-rearing lesbian household. What makes a woman a mother? Is biological maternity enough? If a biological mother has not relinquished her child through adoption, is biological maternity a necessary precondition to motherhood or to parenthood? Does the Heather of our story (legally) have two mothers? Can such a Heather ever have two mothers? Could she have more than two mothers? If Jane gave birth to Heather, can Kate be her mother too, or is Kate simply a biological stranger?[19] Could Kate register Heather in day care or school, claim her as a dependent, authorize her medical care, or leave the country on a holiday with her? If Jane and Kate separate, would Kate be able to advance an argument for custody or access to Heather? Should she ever have to? Could they jointly apply for and obtain a court order for joint custody? Should they have to? Could Jane obtain a court order for child support? Should she have to? Could Kate adopt Heather without Jane having to relinquish her parental relationship? If Jane died, could Kate be confident that her relationship with Heather would not be altered or ended? Could Kate under a will specify conditions for Heather's custody in the event of her own death?[20]

The answers to the questions of what makes a man a father and what makes a woman a mother once seemed to be self-evident, just as the answer to the question of what is a family may have seemed self-evident. However, as with the allure of all appearances and the frailty of self-evidence, the image can be altered and may not withstand a body blow. Just as the formal definition of family is under siege, so too are the definitions of parent. And just as the formal definitions are being challenged, so too is the mother/father dyad content that has traditionally infused them.

I raise these questions not to offer conclusive answers nor to illustrate an infinite, if irritating, imaginative capacity. Indeed, some of these questions and issues have been raised already by lesbian litigants,[21] their lawyers,[22] academics,[23] and nonlitigating lesbian parents themselves.[24] We may be able to observe in a preliminary way that a biological father has an easier time establishing his claim to be a parent within the current legal framework than does a lesbian social parent.[25]

To date lesbian parents in dispute have revealed two lines of argument. In one line, the nonbiological parent, seeking to avoid the imposition of parental responsibility, contends that she was never a mother to the child.[26] In the other line, the biological parent, seeking to win sole custody, argues that the nonbiological parent was never a mother to the child.[27] I am inclined to characterize these as the "I was just being a good sport" (and hence not a parent) and the "she was just being a good sport" (and hence not a parent) arguments, respectively. It is important to note that they have been advanced by *lesbian* litigants. And happily for them, but not for their former partners, the courts have been receptive to the argument that the nonbiological lesbian parent is not a parent.

I hope that a close examination of these lesbian parent/lesbian custody cases, and the issues raised therein, may assist in elucidating some of the problems raised in other lesbian and gay legal contexts. For instance, the debates surrounding legal rights for same-sex couples and for lesbian and gay families have centered upon the benefits and equality dimensions. An apparent polarization, noted by others writing in this field,[28] has emerged around the question of family status. This division, or polarization, is sometimes characterized as either assimilationist or anti-assimilationist.[29] This language however, implies that one position is a form of false consciousness, one that involves a denial of lesbian or gay life, and a desire to imitate or mimic the more conventional heterosexual relationship—to live "white"—while the other embodies a fervent desire to resist this impulse.

The lesbian custody cases discussed here focus not on the issue of whether to extend the definition of family, but rather on how to resolve or address a situation that lesbians themselves have created through their relationships. And here, the language of assimilation versus anti-assimilation seems inapt. It is my argument that the positions taken by both the lesbian parents asserting parental claims and those resisting the claims are informed and framed by the dominant ideological construction of the family. In other words, I hope to illustrate that the two apparently countervailing positions are derived from the same ideological framework.

Lesbians Take Each Other to Family Court

There is clearly no singular form of lesbian custody case. Custody litigation involving lesbians who leave straight relationships or who run afoul of parental expectations illustrate what others have noted elsewhere: lesbian and gay parents are at risk in the courtroom if they do not conform to dominant notions of appropriate lesbian or gay sexual behavior, which is preferably invisible and apolitical. And even that may not be enough. Cases in which straight former spouses use sexual orientation as a weapon tend to reveal much about the social and, in particular, the gendered nature of dominant notions of appropriate parenting. The ability of lesbians to be "good" mothers is always suspect, always subject to scrutiny, but while they may be assailed as bad mothers, they are still mothers. While they may be found to be poor or unfit (social) parents, they are still (biological and hence legal) parents.

Cases involving child custody, access, or support disputes *between* lesbians seem to reveal that, paradoxically, lesbian litigants may also be using sexual orientation as a weapon when they rely on biological and hence legal definitions of parent and take the position that children born into a lesbian relationship are not children of that relationship. In this section, I shall examine the admittedly few reported cases in which lesbian partners (or former partners) take each other to court, contesting not only each other but the very basis of their relationship to each other and to their children. Here the issue could be fitness to parent, but these lesbian cases suggest a more fundamental challenge: the ability to *be* a (legal) parent.

It has become axiomatic in the literature on lesbian parenting to refer to a "lesbian baby boom."[30] The combination of the availability and use of alternative methods of insemination has opened the possibility for lesbians to conceive and bear children independent of medical and patriarchal relations. And, as adoption has also become increasingly available to single parents, individual lesbians have adopted children who are then raised in a de facto two-(lesbian) parent household. Hard data are elusive; no one knows for sure how many "new" child-rearing lesbian households exist.

It follows that the few custody cases involving lesbians may tell us very little about how lesbian parents deal with the matters of raising children when together, and custody and access upon separation. It is more than possible that most do not litigate; it might be fanciful to think that those who settle the issue between themselves do so based on principles of fairness and generosity. Nor is it true that every lesbian custody case necessarily involves or has to involve a denial of a relationship. There are Canadian cases of lesbian grandmothers[31] and lesbian aunts[32] winning custody of children in their care.

I am interested in revisiting the lesbian parenting cases that to date have elicited the most discussion and most criticism. In the Canadian context, one reported case stands out: *Anderson v. Luoma*.[33] This case involved litigation between a lesbian couple who had lived together for ten years. During their relationship, Anderson gave birth to two children, whose conception was made possible by alternative insemination. The older of the two children was given Luoma's first name as a second name. When the children were four and two years of age, respectively, the relationship unraveled; Luoma took up with another woman. Title to houses and property shared by the two women tended to be in the name of the substantively better-off Luoma. She resisted the claim that she was responsible for spousal or child support and (unsuccessfully[34]) took the position that the property in her name was hers alone. Yet at the same time, Luoma, the nonbiological parent, had shared the lives of the children; when asked, the oldest child said, "I don't have a father, I have an Arlene."[35]

At trial, the judge noted that Luoma downplayed "her involvement [with the children] almost to the point of being a disinterested bystander" who suggested that her former partner had been on a "frolic of her own when she had the children."[36] The trial judge took a different view; in his words, "whatever formula was used, I do not have the slightest doubt the children were given love, care and affection in abundance. My impression is that these four people in the two years following the births worked and played as a 'family-like' unit complete with its trials and tribulations, its joy and laughter and its strengths."[37] Despite the trial judge's conclusion that this lesbian household had lived as a "family-like unit," Luoma was able to invoke the very specific statutory definitions of spouse and parent in the relevant British Columbia legislation to avoid the imposition of any financial responsibility for child and spousal support.

While this case is sometimes characterized as an instance of the judicial denial of lesbian families,[38] it is my view that the denial first occurred out of the mouth of the nonbiological lesbian parent. She decided to invoke the legal definitions available to her, including the sex-specific definition of spouse and the patriarchal definition of child. It is important to note that a man in her situation, at the end of a ten-year relationship with a woman whose children may not have been his biological children, would not have had that argument open to him. Thus Luoma enjoyed the benefits of a legal interpretation that would not have been extended to a common-law husband.

The legal significance of this case may be limited to the jurisdiction in which it was decided. For example, while the definition of spouse is similarly premised upon an opposite-sex requirement in Ontario legislation, the Children's Law Reform Act of 1990 provides that a person other than a parent may apply for an order respecting custody of or access to a child.[39] Similarly, the Family Law Act of 1990 defines parent to include a person "who has demonstrated a settled intention to treat a child as a child of his or her family."[40] While it is not likely that Arlene Luoma would have availed herself of the provisions of the Children's Law Reform Act, had they been available to her, it is the case that a less "disinterested bystander" might well be able to do so. On the other hand, given the findings of fact made by the trial judge, had Luoma found herself dealt with under Ontario law, she likely would have been found to be a parent of the two girls. However, as the legislation now stands, she still would have been able to avoid the spousal hook.

The much discussed U.S. case *Alison D. v. Virginia M.*[41] illustrates essentially the same position, this time being taken by a biological lesbian parent against her former partner. In this case the biological mother relied upon the legal definition of parent in the relevant legislation to deny that her former partner had been a parent. The two women had lived together for two years when, in 1980, they decided together to have a child. The majority of the Court of Appeals for the State of New York accepted that the parties had planned for the conception and pregnancy together and had agreed to share jointly all rights and responsibilities of child rearing. When Virginia gave birth to a baby boy in 1981, he was given Alison's last name as his middle name, and for the next two years the women jointly cared for and made decisions about the child. When Virginia left the relationship late in 1983, she initially agreed to access by Alison. By 1986, however, she had begun to limit access, and in 1987, she terminated all contact between the child and Alison, notwithstanding, as the court noted, that a "close and loving relationship" between them had been nurtured. Although the majority of the court was not inimicable to Alison's argument that she was a de facto parent, the fact that she was a "biological stranger" was enough to satisfy them that the legal definition of parent in the governing New York statute did not contemplate her relationship with the child. What is striking about this case, and others like it,[42] is that no issue was raised by either party with respect to fitness. The definition of parent in the legislation allowed the biological mother to trump the other partner.

Again, it is likely that in Ontario the result would have been more favorable to the social parent; at least there the threshold issue of standing, provided in Section 21 of the Children's Law Reform Act, and the statutory extension of the definition of *in loco parentis* to the definition of parent, would have given Alison, the social parent, a running start.

None of this denies the very real risk that lesbians continue to face in the courtroom. My purpose is to illustrate that the litigation postures and strategies of two lesbians in these two important cases have been to deny the relationship and to invoke the dominant construction of family relations as heterosexual and the legal importance of biological parenting to do so.

Conclusion

Heather's story ends where many lesbian parenting stories begin: filled with hope and optimism. The cases discussed above remind us that Heather's story is just that, a story. The endings for children in lesbian legal cases are not so blissfully or naïvely sanguine. Some real-life stories of lesbian households, however, suggest that the children themselves do not buckle or tremble at the prospect of a "daddy-less" life. I know and love a little girl who lived and was loved in a two-parent lesbian household. Her day-care friends coped with this better than did some of her parents' "cool" friends. The day-care kids would call at the end of the day, "Your mom is here," when her (biological) parent arrived, and when her other parent would pick her up at the end of the day, they would call, "Your mom is here, the other one." When she left the sweet comfort of the day care (where her teachers had supported her in her decision to make a Father's Day card for her cat) for the new experience of kindergarten and a new day care, she made no fuss. And, after she had been in kindergarten for a month, one of her parents attended a curriculum night. For the first time, she saw the family chart that had been filled in for each child, with the headings, *mère, père, soeur,* and *frère.* Her little girl's entry was less exhaustive than those of the other children, she having neither siblings nor a father. Squeezed under the heading of mother, however, in her teacher's printed script, were the names of the two women who were her parents. She had said nothing of this to her parents; perhaps it was not a big deal at all for her. After years of matter-of-factly telling each new little friend that, no, she didn't have a daddy, she had two mommies, she had quietly made the leap into the school system. Once again, she had encountered the assumptions of familial ideology. In her quiet and self-assured six-year-old way, she had issued her own challenge to the assumptions of familial ideology, and she declined to be made to fit.

The lesbian parents who deny their children or who deny their former partners access to them have much to learn. In fact, we all do. We must be clear with each other in our relationships with one another and with our children. If we are having children together, making joint decisions, sharing de facto joint custody, we must say this while we are together and not deny it upon separation. We must also be mindful that the children will decide for themselves who their parents are. And they, unlike some of their parents, may have greater courage when confronted by the apparent appeal of familial ideology.

NOTES

1. Taken from the title of the children's book *Heather Has Two Mommies* by Leslea Newman and Diana Souza (illustrator) (Northampton, MA: In Other Words Publishing, 1989). For a Canadian story in which a little girl also has two mothers but in which the lesbian context is muted, see Rosamund Elwin, Michele Paulse, and Dawn Lee (illustrator), *Asha's Mums* (Toronto: Women's Press, 1990).

2. I have been chided for selecting this form of fictive relationship as my focus. Heather's mommies are white, monogamous, and apparently reasonably well-off; the carpenter has landed herself a doctor. They appear to own their own home. They seem to replicate a "Leave It to Beaver" kind of nuclear family, only there are two Mrs. Cleavers, and they both appear to work outside the home. I take the point. To be sure, to the extent that the story suggests that Heather would first learn that she is different from other children is in nursery school, the story is an idealized one. However, criticism of its content needs to be tempered by the fact that this book fueled an antigay, profamily campaign in the United States. As conventionally Eurocentric and class-specific as some readers may find the story, the lesbian content is deeply troubling to the profamily Right. The *New York Times* reported that *Heather Has Two Mommies* was one of the weapons used by a conservative political group in Oregon in its 1992 campaign to force a referendum on the "strongest anti-homosexual measure ever considered by a state"; see Timothy Egan, "Oregon Measure Asks State to Repress Homosexuality," *New York Times*, August 16, 1992, pp. 1, 34.

3. For general discussions of familial ideology see Shelley A. M. Gavigan, "Law Gender and Ideology," in Anne F. Bayefsky, ed., *Legal Theory Meets Legal Practice* (Edmonton: Academic Publishers, 1988); Dorothy E. Chunn, *From Punishment to Doing Good* (Toronto: University of Toronto Press, 1992); Susan B. Boyd, "From Gender Specificity to Gender Neutrality? Ideologies in Canadian Child Custody Law," in Carol Smart and Selma Sevenhuijsen, eds., *Child Custody and the Politics of Gender* (London: Routledge, 1989); Susan B. Boyd, "(Re)Placing the State: Family, Law and Oppression," *Canadian Journal of Law and Society* 9(1994): 39; and Marlee Kline, "Complicating the Ideology of Motherhood: Child Welfare Law and First Nation Women," *Queen's Law Journal* 18(1993): 306.

Informed by the work of feminist and Marxist scholars, I share the view that the concept of ideology makes "reference not only to belief systems, but to questions of power"; see Terry Eagleton, *Ideology: An Introduction* (London: Verso, 1991), p. 5. Eagleton, himself drawing upon the work of other students of ideology, notes that the most widely accepted understanding of the role of ideology is that it legitimates a dominant power. The question of how it does so is particularly important when one considers the family as an ideological form. Again, according to Eagleton, the process of ascendance and dominance may be accomplished through strategies that *promote* particular beliefs and values; *naturalize* and *universalize* such beliefs so as to render them *self-evident* and apparently inevitable; *denigrate* ideas which might challenge it; *exclude* forms of thought process; and which *obscure* social reality (ibid., p. 15 [emphasis in original]). If one considers these strategies with respect to the socially dominant family form, one can readily make the argument that the family is a *quintessential* ideological form.

4. See also Shelley A. M. Gavigan, "Paradise Lost, Paradox Revisited: The Implications of Familial Ideology for Feminist, Lesbian, and Gay Engagement to Law," *Osgoode Hall Law Journal* 31(1993): 589.

5. See, e.g., Ruthann Robson, *Lesbian (Out)Law: Survival Under the Rule of Law* (Ithaca, NY: Firebrand Books, 1992), p.136.

6. Wendy Clark, "Home Thoughts from Not So Far Away: A Personal Look at Family," in Lynne Segal, ed., *What Is to Be Done About the Family?* (Middlesex, England: Penguin, 1983), p. 168.

7. Although, paradoxically, the family has been invoked and used to offer (or force upon) some family members (notably wives and children) a one-way ticket out of wage labor. The work of scholars (feminists, labor historians, social policy analysts, and economists) who have studied the emergence of calls for the "family wage" in the trade union movement has illustrated its gendered and generational implications. See the discussion of this work in Gavigan, "Paradise Lost," pp. 598–600.

8. Postmodernist scholars influenced by the work of Michel Foucault characterize this as decentering law. See Carol Smart, *Feminism and the Power of Law* (London: Routledge, 1990). As Boyd has illustrated recently in "(Re)placing the State," the decentering project is completely compatible with socialist feminist analysis.

9. Eagleton, *Ideology*, p. 15.

10. Douglas Hay, "Property, Authority, and the Criminal Law," in Douglas Hay et al., *Albion's Fatal Tree: Crime and Society in Eighteenth-Century England* (New York: Pantheon, 1975), p. 15.

11. Brenda Cossman, "Family Inside/Out," *University of Toronto Law Journal* 44(1994): 2. See Didi Herman's account of the perspectives of the key litigants in the *Andrews* and *Mossop* cases in her *Rights of Passage: Struggles for Lesbian and Gay Legal Equality* (Toronto: University of Toronto Press, 1994).

12. Eagleton, *Ideology*, p. 2.

13. I am forever indebted to Mary McIntosh's wisdom: "Feminism and Social Policy," *Critical Social Policy* 1(1980): 32.

14. *Re Attorney-General of Ontario and Nevins et al.* [1988] 64 O.R. 311 (Div. Ct.).

15. *Daigle v. Tremblay* [1989] 2 S.C.R. 530, 572. Recently, the British Columbia Supreme Court has rejected a Vancouver man's bid for custody of a fetus prior to birth. He claimed to be the sperm donor, and, with the consent of the pregnant woman, he attempted to obtain a custody order in his favor in an apparent attempt to avoid the baby's apprehension by child welfare authorities at birth: *Re Fink* [1994] B.C.J. No. 485 (S.C.).

16. *Jhordan C. v. Mary K. and Victoria T.*, 179 Cal. App. 3d 386 (1st Dist. 1986). See also Katherine Arnup and Susan Boyd's essay in this volume (Chapter 4).

17. Note that in Ontario, the Child and Family Services Act, R.S.O. 1990, c. 11, s. 175, prohibits payment or reward of any kind in connection with adoption.

18. The American case, *In the Matter of Baby M*, 537 A. 2d 1227 (N.J. 1988), suggests that while the surrogate mother does not cease to be a mother, she is not able to usurp the sperm donor's claim as biological father to custody; they may have to share custody of the child born as a result of their arrangement.

19. In some of the American cases, the nonbiological lesbian parent is described as a "biological stranger." See Elizabeth A. Delaney, "Statutory Protection of the Other Mother: Legally Recognizing the Relationship Between the Nonbiological Lesbian Parent and Her Child," *Hastings Law Journal* 43(1991): 196.

20. The ethnocentrism of these questions needs to be acknowledged. Social parenting, social mothering, and informal adoption practices are all found in the child-rearing practices of many peoples. In other cultures, these questions might well be nonissues. On the role of "other mothers," see Stanlie M. James, "Mothering: A Possible Black Feminist Link to Social Transformation?" in Stanlie M. James and Abena P. A. Busia, eds., *Theorizing Black Feminisms: The Visionary Pragmatism of Black Women* (London: Routledge, 1993), pp. 44–54.

21. See, e.g., *Anderson v. Luoma* [1986] 50 R.F.L. (2d) 127. The most discussed American lesbian parent cases to date seem to be *In the Matter of Alison D. v. Virginia M.*, 77 N.Y.2d 651, 572 N.E. 2d 27 (Ct. App. 1991); *Curiale v. Reagan*, 222 Cal. App. 3d 1597, 272 Cal. Rptr. 520 (3d Dist. 1990); and *Nancy S. v. Michele G.*, 228 Cal. App. 3d 831, 279 Cal. Rptr. 520 (1st Dist. 1991).

22. Paula L. Ettelbrick, "Who Is a Parent?: The Need to Develop a Lesbian Conscious Family Law," *New York Law School Journal of Human Rights* 10(1993): 513. Ettelbrick represented the social lesbian parent, Alison D., in *Alison D. v. Virginia M.*

23. See, e.g., Delaney, "Statutory Protection of the Other Mother"; Nancy D. Polikoff, "This Child Does Have Two Mothers: Redefining Parenthood to Meet the Needs of Children in Lesbian-Mother and Other Nontraditional Families," *Georgetown Law Journal* 78(1990): 459; Martha Minow, "Re-Defining Families: Who's In, and Who's Out?" *University of Colorado Law Review* 62(1991): 511; and Robson, *Lesbian (Out)Law*, pp. 129–39.

24. Rachel Epstein, "Breaking with Tradition," *Healthsharing* 14(1993): 18; Kate Hill, "Mothers by Insemination: Interviews," in Sandra Pollack and Jeanne Vaughan, eds., *Politics of the Heart: A Lesbian Parenting Anthology* (Ithaca, NY: Firebrand Books, 1987), p. 111.

25. See, e.g., *Jhordan C. v. Mary K. and Victoria T.* This case involved a judicial determination that a man who had donated sperm to a lesbian (couple) that resulted in the birth of a little boy was a father and entitled to access. This case also illustrates that the finding of biological paternity was not simply one

of male or heterosexual privilege, as Jhordan had also been ordered to reimburse the county for the public assistance that had been paid for the child's support and to make future support payments. Polikoff, "This Child Does Have Two Mothers"; and Katherine Arnup, "We Are Family: Lesbian Mothers in Canada," *Resources for Feminist Research* 20(1993): 101, have also made this observation. However, note that in the Jhordan case, Victoria T., the social parent, was granted standing as a person with an interest in the child.

26. This is the argument advanced successfully by Arlene Luoma in *Anderson v. Luoma*. Note that the middle name of the first daughter born into this relationship was Luoma's first name: Erin Arlene Anderson. See *Anderson*, p. 134. Thanks to Karen Andrews for drawing this to my attention.

27. This is the argument advanced successfully by the lesbian biological mothers in *Alison D. v. Virginia M.* and *Curiale v. Reagan*. But see *A. C. v. C. B.*, 113 N.M. 581, 829 P. 2d 660 (N.M. App.), cert. denied, 113 N.M. 449, 827 P. 2d 837 (1992), holding that the lesbian co-parent had standing to claim visitation rights under an agreement she had entered with child's mother.

28. See, e.g., Didi Herman, "Are We Family?: Lesbian Rights and Women's Liberation," *Osgoode Hall Law Journal* 28(1990): 789; Cossman, "Family Inside/Out"; and Susan B. Boyd, "Expanding the "Family" in Family Law: Recent Ontario Proposals on Same-Sex Relationships," *Canadian Journal of Women and the Law* 7(1994): 545. Karen Andrews, "Ancient Affections: Gays, Lesbians, and Family Status," paper presented at the Sexual Orientation and the Law Program, Law Society of Upper Canada, Continuing Legal Education, Toronto, June 1994, pp. 31–32, challenges the Ontario Law Reform Commission's expressed concern that the lesbian and gay community is divided deeply, sharply, and significantly on the issue of family status and same-sex spousal benefits.

29. Brenda Cossman and Bruce Ryder, "Gay, Lesbian, and Unmarried Heterosexual Couples and the Family Law Act: Accommodating a Diversity of Family Forms," paper prepared for the Ontario Law Reform Commission, June 1993, pp. 137–39. Cossman and Ryder characterize the positions of some who are critical or wary of family-based strategy (including myself) as "anti-assimilationist." I am inclined to the view that this generalized characterization is overinclusive, and I would characterize the range of positions reflected in the literature in different terms.

30. Arnup, "We Are Family"; Polikoff, "This Child Does Have Two Mothers"; and Ettelbrick, "What Is a Parent?"

31. *Nicholson v. Storey & Nicholson* [1982] B.C.D. 1551–05 (Prov. Ct.). In this case, the lesbian maternal grandmother was awarded custody of her two-and-a-half-year-old granddaughter, who had been in the grandmother's care for most of her life. The trial judge noted that while the grandmother's homosexual relationship was not a bar, "it must be said at the least that a homosexual relationship is a minus factor."

32. *M. (D.) v. D. (M.)* [1991] 94 Sask. R. 315 (Q.B.).

33. [1986] 50 R.F.L. (2d) 127 (B.C.S.C.).

34. The trial judge applied the principle of unjust enrichment to the facts of the case and imposed the remedy of constructive trust: Luoma was required to share the property she and Anderson had acquired and/or lived in together.

In other words, Anderson succeeded in her claim to a significant interest in the property held in Luoma's name.

35. Ibid., p. 134.
36. Ibid., p. 135.
37. Ibid., p. 134.
38. Arnup, "We Are Family," p. 13.
39. R.S.O. 1990, c. C12, s. 21.
40. R.S.O. 1990, c. F.3.
41. Minow, "Re-defining Families"; Ettelbrick, "Who Is a Parent?"
42. See also *Curiale v. Reagan* and *Nancy S. v. Michele G. Curiale v. Reagan* involved two lesbians who had been in a five-year relationship into which a child had been born. When they separated, they initially had an agreement that provided for shared custody; a year later the biological mother informed her former partner that she was not willing to share custody or even allow access. In *Nancy S. v. Michele G.* the women had lived together for 16 years. Two children were born into their relationship; the children were given the non-biological mother's family name, as their last name, and she was listed as their father on their birth certificates. After Nancy and Michele separated, the elder child lived with Michele (the nonbiological mother), and the younger one stayed with Nancy. After several years of this arrangement, Michele would not accede to a request for a change in the arrangement. When mediation failed, Nancy successfully invoked her biological parenthood to obtain sole custody of both children.

SIX

In the following essay, Cynthia Petersen turns her attention to recent developments in lesbian legal theorizing. Her specific focus is upon the work of several theorists who conceptualize sexual orientation discrimination as a form of gender discrimination. Petersen questions this approach, and particularly considers the writings about race and racism in order to do so. She argues that the equation of lesbian oppression with sex discrimination neglects the role that other power relations, especially those based on race and ethnicity, play in lesbian lives. At the same time, Petersen is concerned to show the value in sex discrimination analyses, providing that neither they, nor law itself, becomes the sole focus of strategy.

Envisioning a Lesbian Equality Jurisprudence

Cynthia Petersen

LESBIAN legal theory is appearing in academic literature in Canada, the United States, and Britain. This relatively new area of scholarship includes the work of some legal theorists who are attempting to develop a lesbian equality jurisprudence. This involves an investigation into the nature of lesbian oppression, how it is experienced by lesbians, and how it can and should be framed in legal terms. It also involves a critical examination of the legal instruments and processes that have been used in attempts to redress lesbian oppression, an evaluation of the efficacy of existing legal strategies, and an exploration of the viability of new strategies. In this essay, I engage with the theories of other legal scholars as I endeavor to articulate my own contribution to the emerging lesbian equality jurisprudence.

Legal Approaches to Lesbian Oppression

During the past two decades, one of the primary legal strategies for promoting lesbian equality has been to lobby, in cooperation with gay men, for the inclusion of the expression "sexual orientation" in statutory lists of prohibited grounds of discrimination and in similar lists in other legal documents. This lobby has met with both success and fail-

I thank Wendy Warhaft for providing me with the inspiration to write this article.

ure in various jurisdictions in Canada, the United States, and Britain. Unquestionably, some progress has been made in enacting legal proscriptions against sexual orientation discrimination. Lesbians have subsequently invoked these legal protections, with limited success, in efforts to redress lesbian inequality. Thus, in the legal context, lesbian oppression has largely been conceptualized as sexual orientation discrimination.

This conceptualization of lesbian oppression has recently been criticized, on multiple grounds, by several Canadian and American lesbian legal scholars.[1] One of the primary criticisms is that the sexual orientation discrimination concept fails to capture the specificity of lesbian inequality as distinct from gay male inequality, and to illuminate the intersection between discrimination based on sexual identity and discrimination based on sex. Some scholars have suggested that, in order to appreciate the specific nature of lesbian oppression, it ought to be conceptualized as a manifestation of sex discrimination rather than as sexual orientation discrimination.[2]

The theory that underlies the conceptualization of lesbian oppression as sex discrimination is grounded in a feminist analysis of the social meaning of gender in patriarchal Western cultures. Gender is a construct that is crucial to the perpetuation of patriarchal structures and relations. Patriarchal cultures have developed an elaborate gender script that prescribes appropriate roles for men and women. These roles are dichotomous and hierarchicalized; they are premised upon male domination and female subordination. According to patriarchal myth, men are strong, aggressive, rational, and independent by nature, whereas women are weak, passive, irrational, and dependent by nature. Socially prescribed gender roles require that men and women act according to their respective ostensible natures. All deviations from the gender script are censured either by custom or by law.[3]

As Sylvia Law explains, heterosexuality is a crucial component of the patriarchal gender script:

> A panoply of legal rules and cultural institutions reinforce the assumption that heterosexual intimacy is the only natural and legitimate form of sexual expression. The presumption and prescription that erotic interests are exclusively directed to the opposite sex define an important aspect of masculinity and femininity. Real men are and should be sexually attracted to women, and real women invite and enjoy that attraction.[4]

The construction of heterosexuality as the only natural expression of erotic intimacy provides a framework for the condemnation of same-sex eroticism and love as deviant, perverse, abnormal, and unnatural. Heterosexuality is presented as not only desirable, but also biological and indeed inevitable.[5] It is therefore experienced as compulsory.[6] This compulsory quality of heterosexuality sustains and reinforces patriarchal structures, because heterosexual relationships give men personal power over individual women and direct women's primary energies toward individual men. Heterosexuality is circumscribed by the patriarchal gender script, such that men and women in heterosexual relationships are expected to conform to their prescribed roles. Heterosexual men are supposed to dominate their female partners, and heterosexual women are supposed to defer to them. Heterosexual men are supposed to be sexually aggressive, and heterosexual women are supposed to be ingratiatingly submissive. Heterosexual men are supposed to be indifferent, aloof, and emotionally vapid, while heterosexual women are supposed to be supportive, sentimental, and nurturing.

As Charlotte Bunch explains, lesbians defy the gender script and thereby challenge male supremacist ideology.[7] They expose the patriarchal lie about women's inferiority and their innate need for men, and they disprove the patriarchal myth that heterosex is the only fulfilling expression of women's sexuality. Lesbians challenge the practice as well as the ideology of male supremacy; by resisting heterosex and by refusing to invest their energies in relationships with men, lesbians undermine the practice of male domination "in its most individual and common form."[8] In short, lesbians reject their assigned role as women in patriarchal cultures.

Lesbians are frequently punished for their gender insubordination. Anti-lesbian discrimination and harassment often constitute expressions of contempt for those women who dare to challenge male prerogatives by defying their prescribed (subordinate) gender role.[9] Thus there exists a connection between sexual inequality and lesbian inequality. It is this connection that informs the conceptualization of lesbian oppression as a manifestation of sex discrimination.

Diana Majury is one of the scholars who advocate using legal arguments that characterize anti-lesbian discrimination as sex discrimination.[10] She discusses the practice of lesbian baiting to elucidate her theory that "[d]iscrimination against lesbians is sex discrimination, perhaps in its starkest and most overt form."[11] Lesbian baiting is a common tactic used by men to inhibit solidarity between lesbian and non-lesbian women, to discredit feminist activists, and to silence women's discontent. Women who vocalize their objections to sexist behavior, who actively struggle to improve the material conditions of women's lives, who pursue a feminist agenda for change, or who otherwise challenge their sexual subordination are routinely accused of being lesbians. As Majury explains, "[t]hey are called 'lesbian' or 'dyke', not be-

cause they do, or are even thought to, have 'sex' with women, but because the ostracism and increased inequality that the label 'lesbian'
represents are used to try to bring women back into gender line."[12] Lesbian baiting is an excellent example of how expressions of anti-lesbian
sentiment are sometimes used to enforce and reinforce the patriarchal
gender script. As Majury remarks, "[l]esbian inequality is the warning
to girls and women not to challenge the prescribed meaning of being
female in this society."[13]

This does not, however, mean that lesbian oppression is animated
exclusively, or even primarily, by male supremacist instincts, which is
what the conceptualization of lesbian oppression as sex discrimination
suggests. Law asserts "that contemporary legal and cultural contempt
for lesbian women and gay men serves primarily to preserve and reinforce the social meaning attached to gender."[14] Majury draws upon
Law's work in developing her own thesis that "[l]esbians are discriminated against because they challenge dominant understandings and
meanings of gender in our society."[15] Law's and Majury's theories res-
onate with aspects of my own experience as a lesbian. I agree with
Majury that "[l]esbian oppression functions to reinforce and perpetuate strict notions of gender differentiation"[16]—at times. Yet there are
also times when lesbian oppression functions to reinforce and perpetuate other systems of domination, such as racism and anti-Semitism.

Critique

The history of Vanessa Williams's 1984 abdication of the Miss America
crown, precipitated by the publication of pornographic photographs of
her, provides a useful example of how lesbian oppression sometimes
intersects with racism and reinforces white supremacist ideology. Williams did not surrender her crown merely because it was discovered
that she had posed for sexually explicit photographs and had thereby
defiled the ideology of virtuous womanhood promoted by the pageant.
It was significant that the photographs depicted her in lesbian sex acts;
having been "documented" in lesbian sexual activity contributed to the
disgrace visited upon her.[17] Thus anti-lesbian sentiment was an important element that influenced her abdication of the crown, and since
she was the first Black woman to achieve the Miss America title, her
scandalous fall reinforced what Jackie Goldsby describes as the "racially specific iconography of 'womanhood' promoted not only by the
pageant but by the culture at large."[18]

Lesbian oppression also interconnects with other forms of oppression, such as anti-Semitism, and at times the connection between
oppressions is so profound that it may be undesirable to distinguish be-

tween them. For example, Naomi Dykestein writes as follows about her experience as a Jewish lesbian separatist:

> I resent automatic assumptions about who separatists are and what's behind any of the decisions and choices we make. It's true: separatists are loud, angry, pushy, uncompromising, man-hating, and obnoxious—we do not shut up and we are not "polite" womyn. But those "criticisms" sound uncomfortably familiar—they're the same complaints made about Jews in general and Jewish womyn in particular. No coincidence, I think, considering the large percentage of Lesbian separatists who are Jews.[19]

Systems of domination—whether they are based on race, religion, language, culture, economic class, dis/ability, sexual identity, or gender—often intersect in mutually reinforcing ways. The Black women who formed the Combahee River Collective discuss some of these intersections as follows: "We also often find it difficult to separate race from class from sex oppression because in our lives they are most often experienced simultaneously. We know that there is such a thing as racial-sexual oppression which is neither solely racial nor solely sexual, e.g., the history of rape of Black women by white men as a weapon of political repression."[20] Evidently, it is not always useful (nor possible) to identify a primary source of oppression when analyzing inequalities.

Karin Aguilar–San Juan recounts the following incident of racist-sexist-heterosexist discrimination that, in my opinion, exemplifies the interwoven nature of multiple oppressions: "A group of Asian students at the University of Connecticut in Storrs were on their way to a formal dance. On the bus, a bunch of white students vented their racial hostility by spitting at the women and jeering their boyfriends, 'You want to make something out of this, you Oriental faggots?"[21] Obviously, the heterosexist insult "faggot" was hurled at the Asian men because, in the eyes of their white assailants, they did not conform to their prescribed gender role. Sexism was operating, in conjunction with heterosexism, in so far as the white assailants were attempting to enforce the strict gender code that insists that men behave in an aggressively territorial fashion with respect to "their" women (i.e., that men treat women as objects of possession to be guarded against the encroachment of other men). Yet it was a racist iconography of manhood that influenced the white assailants' perception of the Asian men in the first place (i.e., racist stereotyping typically depicts Asian men as effeminate and passive). Thus this incident demonstrates how oppressions based on race, gender, and sexual identity sometimes coincide and collide in multilayered complexities.

I believe that the conceptualization of lesbian oppression as sex discrimination fails to capture these complexities. In particular, the exclusive focus on gender obscures the significance of race. The lesbian-oppression-as-sex-discrimination theory ignores essential aspects of the experiences of lesbians of color, thus as a legal strategy it cannot adequately redress the inequalities they suffer.[22] It is probably telling that the theory has been articulated by white lesbians, who arguably experience lesbian oppression differently than do lesbians of color; I suspect that my identity as a white lesbian accounts for the fact that the theory resonates with my own personal experience. Despite this resonance, I do not endorse the theory as a legal strategy, for to do so would be "to universalize lesbian experiences as white lesbian experience,"[23] and thereby to contribute to the invisibility (and hence oppression) of lesbians of color.

I want to stress that I am not assuming a position of moral impunity. I do not intend my criticisms of the work of other white lesbian theorists to be interpreted as an assertion that I possess a heightened political consciousness or a more firm commitment to anti-racist scholarship. I know that I am part of a tradition of white middle-class lesbians who occupy privileged positions within academia that enable us to theorize (and publish our theories) about lesbian politics, identities, and experiences. I acknowledge that, as Gloria Anzaldùa asserts, I (like other white lesbian scholars) am prone to "theorize, that is, perceive, organize, classify and name specific chunks of reality by using approaches, styles and methodologies that are Anglo American or European."[24] My criticisms of the work of other white lesbian scholars are offered with the intent to initiate a dialogue with them in the sincere hope that they will return the favor of critical analysis of my work. Of course I do not wish to establish an exclusive dialogue among white lesbian scholars, but I do believe that we (white lesbians) must assume the responsibilities of educating ourselves about the dynamics of racism and of expanding our theories to accommodate our growing understandings.[25] I take seriously Anzaldùa's criticisms about white lesbian scholars like myself: that our theories make abstractions of queer people of color, and although they may "aim to enable and emancipate, they often disempower and neocolonize."[26] In this essay, I am trying to follow the lead of political lesbians of color who, as Barbara Smith remarks,

> have often been the most astute about the necessity for developing understandings of the connections between oppressions. They have also opposed the building of hierarchies and challenged the "easy way out" of choosing a "primary oppression" and downplaying those messy inconsistencies that occur whenever race, sex, class and sexual identity actually mix.[27]

It was Majury's reservations about her own theory that provoked me to question the adequacy of the conceptualization of lesbian oppression as sex discrimination. She questions whether, in her analysis of the limitations of sexual orientation theory and in her articulation of sex discrimination theory, she is "privileging gender and down playing other forms of oppression that give rise to differences and power imbalances among lesbians and gays."[28] Her concerns motivated me to investigate the writings of lesbians of color with the specific goal of trying to understand whether and how their experiences of lesbian oppression differ from mine. Majury writes, "I am not arguing that gender is an oppression that we experience simultaneously with sexual identity oppression and that thereby transforms the experience of both oppressions, but rather, at least for lesbians, sexual identity oppression is gender oppression."[29] The writings of many lesbians of color suggest that not all lesbians experience sexual identity oppression as gender oppression, at least not all of the time.

It has become apparent to me that anti-lesbian discrimination and harassment do not always constitute patriarchal retribution for gender insubordination. Lesbian oppression is sometimes motivated by forces other than mandatory gender conformity. I arrived at this conclusion primarily from the insights that I gained by reading the theories of Black lesbian scholars regarding lesbian oppression within their communities. When heterosexual members of Black communities refuse to acknowledge or to discuss lesbianism, when they condemn lesbianism as a product of the dominant white culture, when they try to enforce lesbian invisibility, or when they ostracize lesbians in their communities, their heterosexist attitudes and behaviors may at times have nothing at all to do with a desire to enforce the patriarchal gender script.

Cheryl Clarke explains that one possible source of heterosexism in Black communities is the desire of Black Americans "to debunk the racist mythology which says [Black] sexuality is depraved."[30] She notes that, in their efforts to destroy this mythology, many Black Americans "have overcompensated and assimilated the Puritan value that sex is for procreation, occurs only between men and women, and is only valid within the confines of heterosexual marriage."[31] Barbara Smith similarly refers to the impact of racist sexual stereotyping as a possible source of lesbophobic attitudes within Black communities. She asserts that "White people don't have a sexual image that another oppressor community has put on them."[32] Although she fails to recognize that white Jews have been subjected to oppressive sexual stereotyping,[33] she nevertheless makes the important point that most white people have not suffered this form of oppression, and I agree that the experience of racist sexual stereotyping may in part explain why "the way most Black women deal with [lesbianism] is to be just as rigid and closed about it as possible."[34] Smith suggests that lesbophobic attitudes among Black women may be animated by a desire to avoid "the whole sexual stereotyping used against all Black people."[35]

Goldsby's analysis of Vanessa Williams's abdication of the Miss America crown provides some additional insights into lesbophobia in Black communities (i.e., it illuminates some of the reasons why Black people may be reluctant to acknowledge or to discuss lesbian sexuality). She asserts that "the historical construction of black sexuality is always already pornographic, if by pornography I mean the writing or technological representation and mass marketing of the body as explicitly sexual."[36] She refers to the history of slavery, in which Black laborers were marketed as assets, and "black bodies were, literally, capital."[37] Since procreation was necessary to perpetuate slavery, the capacity to procreate enhanced a slave's market value, and "black desire was pressed into service to generate wealth." Thus, Goldsby concludes, "slavery constituted a form of sex work."[38] She later posits that the legacy of slavery informs the desire of contemporary Black communities to maintain a silence about sexuality generally (and about the Vanessa Williams scandal in particular). Because of the history of slavery, the right to keep Black sexuality private became an important aspect of Black freedom: "As long as black sexuality was a market commodity, white voyeurism was an always-present threat, as black sex was subject to public inspection ('interventions' made in the name of rape and lynching)."[39] The legacy of slavery (i.e., the desire to keep Black sexuality out of the view of white voyeurs) may contribute to the silencing and enforced invisibility of lesbians in contemporary Black communities.

Jewelle Gomez reaches a similar conclusion about the connection between the history of slavery in America and the presence of heterosexism in contemporary Black communities:

> Given that most black people would rather not talk about sex in public (that is, in front of white people), at all, is it any wonder that the gay rights movement leaves the black community trembling with fear and anger? For a people that has spent its entire modern existence in this country trying to shift its identity away from sex to encounter within itself a sub-group which has been totally defined by its sexual preference is both a shock and a threat.[40]

Valli Kanuha offers yet another explanation for lesbian oppression in communities of color. One of the classic ways that lesbophobia manifests itself in many communities of color is in the prevalent attitude that lesbianism is a deviant sexuality that originated in the dominant white culture and that somehow infiltrated and polluted minority cultures. Kanuha explains that "by relegating lesbians to 'Whiteness,' people of color can protect themselves from further racist attack by dissociating themselves from 'social deviants' that not even White people want to have in their midst."[41] Evidently, anti-lesbian sentiment and discrimination are not always animated by patriarchal retribution for gender insubordination. There are times when lesbian oppression may be, for example, a product of the racism visited upon people of color, rather than (or in addition to) a manifestation of the sexism visited upon women.

Although the theory that conceives of lesbian oppression as sex discrimination is incomplete and hence inadequate, I believe that it nevertheless makes an important (albeit only partial) contribution to our understanding of lesbian inequality. There are instances of anti-lesbian discrimination that are undeniably motivated by male supremacist instincts and that clearly serve to perpetuate the patriarchal gender script that dictates sexual inequality (e.g., lesbian baiting incidents). Thus it is crucial that lesbians learn to identify the intersection between sexual inequality and lesbian inequality, *provided that it does not become the exclusive focus of our theoretical frameworks and legal strategies.* In my opinion, the conceptualization of lesbian inequality as sex discrimination is not by itself an adequate legal strategy, yet to the extent that gender oppression sometimes animates lesbian oppression, it must be critically analyzed, understood, and used to inform our legal strategies.

To that end, Lynne Pearlman's work offers important insights into the role of gender oppression in the dynamics of lesbian oppression.[42] She focuses specifically upon the element of the patriarchal gender script that requires that women engage in heterosexual relationships (i.e., that they be sexually accessible to men and direct their energies toward men). Since male domination is perpetuated by women's participation in heterosexual relationships, and since lesbians expose the myth that women are heterosexual by nature, much patriarchal effort is expended on silencing and obliterating lesbians. As Pearlman explains, "[h]eteropatriarchal dominance flourishes with lesbian erasure."[43] From this premise, she theorizes that the most "conspicuous" lesbians suffer the most severe forms of lesbian oppression.

Pearlman is careful to define what she means by "lesbian conspicuousness" and she stresses that it should not simply be equated with the act of coming out (i.e., "explicitly stating that one is a lesbian, or refusing to remain silent when assumptions of heterosexuality are made"). She writes:

> I have come to understand that being "out" is about a lot more than being public about the fact that one is a lesbian. It is about how lesbian-

identified one is willing to be publicly; it is about how much heterosexual privilege one is willing to renounce; it is about how many traditional vestiges of femininity one chooses to carry; it is about how much energy one invests in males (be they gay or straight friends, ex-lovers, fathers, brothers, uncles, cousins, nephews or sons); it is about how vocal or activist one is about what it means to be lesbian identified; it is about the limited extent to which one is willing to challenge heteropatriarchal norms and principles."[44]

Pearlman describes what she calls "the continuum of outness." At one end of the continuum are those lesbians who make it known that they are lesbians but who "define their aspirations and values as no different than heterosexual aspirations and values." At the other end are those lesbians "who not only make it known that they are lesbians, but who also most reject stereotypically feminine behaviours, priorities, appearances, and values (particularly the focus on men), and speak out about why they do so."[45] It is the lesbians at the latter end of the continuum who are most "conspicuous" in Pearlman's terms. Lesbian conspicuousness is therefore measured by the degree to which lesbians refuse to assimilate to the heteropatriarchal gender script.

Pearlman's notion of a continuum of outness explains why, as she observes, a range of lesbian oppression is commonly experienced by out lesbians who are all in the same environment: some are tolerated, while others are harassed. According to Pearlman's theory, those who are most assimilated are "conditionally rewarded for their assimilation" (i.e., they are tolerated). Those who are the most conspicuously lesbian, "who are the most removed from stereotypical female appearance, behaviour, and values," are the most harassed; according to Pearlman, they "encounter the most severe forms of lesbian oppression."[46]

I am not certain what Pearlman means by "the most severe forms of lesbian oppression." She may be inferring that there are qualitative differences between various acts of discrimination that can be categorized by degrees of severity. Alternatively, she may simply be alluding to the frequency of discrimination. When discrimination is incessant, it is experienced as harassment, and the cumulative effect usually renders the experience worse or more severe than being subjected to a discrete incident of discriminatory treatment. I am more comfortable with the latter interpretation, for although I recognize that some forms of discriminatory treatment (e.g., hate-motivated assaults) are life-threatening and, in that respect, are more severe than others, I am reluctant to hierarchicalize experiences of oppression in terms of severity.

The gravity of any given type of discriminatory treatment will generally depend upon the particular circumstances of the person who experiences it. For example, a working-class single lesbian mother who has not had the privilege of education will likely experience dismissal from employment as an extremely severe form of discrimination, whereas a middle-class educated lesbian with no dependants might not (because she is likely to have greater financial resources and greater access to new employment opportunities). Similarly, ostracization from family members may constitute a more severe form of oppression for Jewish lesbians and lesbians of color than it does for white Christian lesbians. As Aguilar-San Juan explains, "[f]or those of us who are Asian, losing connections to our family represents one of our greatest fears, since in this white society, our cultural identity depends precisely on family links."[47] Based on my assumption that "severe" signifies persistent (rather than more serious) discrimination, I generally agree with Pearlman's theory that unassimilated lesbians suffer the most severe lesbian oppression. Her observations accord with my own, and her theory resonates with my personal experience. Yet I am left with a couple of reservations about the utility of the notion of a continuum of outness in theorizing lesbian oppression.

While Pearlman's theory explains some of the dynamics of anti-lesbian discrimination, it does not fully illuminate lesbian oppression in all of its complexities. I can think of at least two forms of lesbian oppression that seem to be overlooked by the continuum of outness. The first came to mind when I read Pearlman's remark that there are some "lesbians who simply cannot pass as heterosexual females, no matter how hard they may try."[48] Pearlman references Julia Penelope, who writes about her painful experience of living as a lesbian who has never been able to pass for heterosexual.[49] Penelope's account of extreme isolation and lack of validation accords with Pearlman's theory that lesbians who are conspicuous suffer severe oppression. Yet it is also important to recognize that there are some lesbians who simply cannot become conspicuously lesbian, no matter how hard they may try, and they too suffer extreme isolation. This is particularly true of many lesbians of color who are frequently rendered invisible—even within lesbian communities—by the prevailing racist iconography of lesbianism.

Many lesbians of color have written about their experiences of erasure.[50] *Piece of My Heart*, Makeda Silvera's anthology of writings by lesbians of color, includes a conversation between three women (identified only as Joanne, Pramila, and Anu) that is particularly enlightening on this subject. During the conversation, Anu discusses the hiring process at a feminist organization at which she interviewed and at which she was ultimately employed. The other candidate for the job was a white lesbian. Anu eventually learned that she was selected over the other candidate partly because the organizational members felt that they already had enough lesbian employees. She states: "When they hired me, the underlying assumption was that a woman of colour could not be a lesbian. In their minds, these two things were mutually exclusive. They just assumed that I was straight. . . . Even after I started working with the women as a group they overlooked every instance that could point to the fact that I was woman-identified."[51] Later in the conversation, Anu and Pramila engage in the following exchange:

> *Pramila:* I think the problem is that, for example, women in saris and salwar kameez would never be seen as lesbians. One night I was taking a feminist from India to a number of gay bars in Toronto and she was wearing Indian clothes and I was wearing Indian clothes and we were with a Japanese woman . . .
>
> *Anu:* . . . and they figured you walked into the wrong bar, right? (laughter)[52]

Many lesbians of color are unable to attain the kind of conspicuousness enjoyed by white lesbians, even if they are unassimilated in Pearlman's terms, and their invisibility is itself a form of oppression. I suspect that this is also true for many disabled lesbians, whose sexuality is denied by the ableist mentality that prevails in society and whose appearances may not conform to the able-bodied iconography of lesbianism that is promoted by lesbian communities as well as by mainstream culture.[53] Their experience of erasure, of being unable to move along the continuum of outness despite their struggle against heteropatriarchal assimilation, is undoubtedly fraught with frustration, marginalization, isolation, and pain.[54] Although these lesbians (unwillingly) do not occupy the most conspicuous positions on the continuum of outness, they nevertheless suffer severe oppression as invisible lesbians. Their experience is not captured by Pearlman's theory about the politics of outness.

The second kind of lesbian oppression that is obscured by Pearlman's theory is that which is experienced by lesbians who are closeted. They do not fall anywhere on the continuum of outness because they are not out (i.e., they are not known to be lesbian). Given that they pass for heterosexual women, they are most closely aligned with the "tolerable" assimilated lesbians who occupy the "least oppressed" end of the continuum. Yet closeted lesbians do not even have to endure the indignity of being tolerated by dominant society, because no one knows that they are lesbian.[55] They are not simply tolerable but are actually acceptable to mainstream society. Thus the logical extension of the theory of the continuum of outness leads to the conclusion that closeted lesbians suffer even less lesbian oppression than assimilated out lesbians. This conclusion does not, however, accurately reflect the experience of many closeted lesbians.

Closeted lesbians experience unique forms of lesbian oppression that ought not to be overlooked by theorists who are endeavoring to understand the nature of lesbian inequality. I am not referring to the fear, self-hatred, and isolation that usually characterize closeted existence, although these are important aspects of the oppression suffered by closeted lesbians.[56] I am referring instead to the anti-lesbian sentiment to which closeted lesbians are repeatedly exposed *precisely because they pass for heterosexuals* and are therefore assumed to possess a heterosexist perspective. I first recognized this phenomenon when a friend of mine, who was not out as a lesbian to her parents, recounted to me a hurtful conversation that she had with her distraught mother immediately after her brother came out as gay. Her mother telephoned her and expressed extreme disappointment and distress as a result of her brother's revelation. My friend was exposed to a particularly brutal display of her mother's homophobia because her mother, who was unaware of her daughter's lesbian sexuality, assumed that she would sympathize with expressions of heterosexist sentiment. I believe that my friend's mother would not have subjected my friend to such an emotionally damaging conversation had she known that my friend was a lesbian. I do not mean to suggest that parents of lesbians consistently spare their daughters the pain of heterosexist insult, but some parents censor their most visceral and vehement heterosexist comments in the presence of their lesbian daughters, and I believe that my friend's mother would have done so in this instance. The fact that my friend was not out to her mother placed her in a particularly vulnerable position with respect to her mother's heterosexist behavior.

Such vulnerability exists for closeted lesbians in many different circumstances. I know, for example, that I am often shielded from anti-lesbian jokes and remarks because I am out as a lesbian at my place of employment. All of my students and co-workers know that I am a lesbian. Many of them censor themselves in my presence, yet they make hateful and hurtful anti-lesbian comments in the presence of lesbian students and co-workers who they do not know to be lesbians (and who they therefore assume to be like-minded). Thus even though I am very conspicuous[57] as a lesbian in that environment, in certain respects I am subjected to less anti-lesbian discrimination and harassment than those lesbians who are invisible in the same environment. I suspect that this is partially due to my privileged position of relative power and authority as a law professor, but I am convinced that it is also due to the insulation that my lesbian conspicuousness occasionally affords me. The notion of a continuum of outness does not adequately explain this phenomenon. To be fair, I should acknowledge that Pearlman does not purport to address every instance of lesbian oppression with her theory of the politics of outness.[58] That would be an ambitious goal indeed.

Conclusion

I have reached the conclusion that lesbian oppression is so multifaceted and intricate that no single theory will capture its full complexities, particularly not if the theory is constrained by the current model of equality jurisprudence. If we limit our theories to those that will translate into viable strategies within the existing legal framework, then we will probably never arrive at a full understanding of the nature of lesbian inequality. In most Western jurisdictions, the existing legal framework consists of statutes, bills, charters, and other legal documents that contain lists of prohibited grounds of discrimination. As Nitya Iyer explains, "no matter how long or inclusive the list of protected grounds or characteristics, the mechanical, categorical, or category-based approach to equality embedded in such a structure obscures the complexity of social identity in ways that are damaging both to particular rights claimants, and to the larger goal of redressing relations of inequality."[59] I agree that the current legal model is utterly inadequate, not only because (as Iyer explains) it is embedded in categorical thought, but also because it is purely reactionary and therefore does not accommodate affirmative equality-promoting strategies. It endeavors only to redress discrete incidents of discriminatory treatment. Yet inequality is not experienced as a series of discriminatory acts. Inequality is a state of being, a constant, an almost atmospheric condition. For those who live under the oppressive conditions of inequality, equality cannot be achieved by remedying a particular identifiable instance of discriminatory treatment, nor even by remedying multiple identifiable discriminatory acts. Pro-active equality-promoting strategies must be devised in order to transform daily social relations. The existing legal model does not accommodate strategies with such transformative potential.

It is therefore necessary to conceive of an entirely new model of equality jurisprudence, one that does more than endeavor to respond to instances of discrimination and harassment. At minimum, we need legal protections for affirmative action policies that seek to implement equity.[60] We must ensure that the legal instruments that were designed to protect historically disadvantaged groups cannot be appropriated by dominant groups so as to thwart the advancement of true equality.[61] More generally, we must envision a lesbian equality jurisprudence that actively promotes social transformation by endorsing efforts to effect concrete changes in social relations. This is a daunting task that requires tremendous legal ingenuity. Iyer warns that "[a]ttempting to move away from the current legal model of equality is unsettling because it reveals the poverty of our underlying vision of equality."[62] Perhaps she is right, although I am beginning to wonder whether it is our chosen instrument, rather than our vision, that is lacking. It may be that our collective legal imagination has not been sufficiently creative, but it may also be that the law is not an ideal tool for implementing meaningful social change.

We should learn a lesson from the experience of Black political activists who struggled against oppression and inequality long before the emergence of an organized lesbian and gay rights movement. In writing about the civil rights movement in the United States, Jewelle Gomez stresses the limited utility of having obtained legal protections against race discrimination, since the protections did little to alter the daily reality of Black people's lives: "The sanction of law was needed to attack institutionalized racism. However, if we examine the lives of the majority of black Americans and see the poverty and segregation in which they still live, we see that the law has not done much good for them."[63] Gomez expresses her hope that the history of the civil rights movement will endow lesbian and gay activists with an appreciation for the need for multiple and diverse political tactics. I share her conviction that, although we should not abandon our efforts to effect change through the legal system, we also must never cease to investigate and pursue other, non-legal avenues. In particular, we must initiate and sustain public education campaigns as well as private endeavors to enlighten the opinions and beliefs held by our acquaintances, colleagues, friends, families, and foes. It may sound trite, but I genuinely believe that education is the most effective catalyst toward progressive social transformation. Education has the potential to change dominant ideological paradigms, frameworks, and discourses. Law, on the other hand, can govern and regulate social relations and hence can influence the way that people behave, but it cannot alter the way that people perceive, think, and feel. As Gomez writes, "[o]ur survival depends not so much on the laws that are passed, although they are crucial, but on the attitudes we carry in our hearts and pass along to others."[64]

NOTES

1. See, for example, Daphne Budge, "Lesbian Identity, Lesbian History and Lesbian Rights: Does Arguing Sexual Orientation and Family Status Reinforce Labels?" LL.M. thesis, University of Ottawa, April 1990; Mary Eaton, "Theorizing Sexual Orientation," LL.M. thesis, Queen's University, September

1991; Legal Education and Action Fund, "Litigating for Lesbians," Report on Consultations with the Lesbian Community, June 1993; Diana Majury, "Refashioning the Unfashionable: Claiming Lesbian Identities in the Legal Context," *Canadian Journal of Women and the Law* 7:2(1994): 286; and Cynthia Petersen, "Litigating Lesbian Equality Claims: Challenging Heterosexual Privilege," paper presented at the "What Difference Does Difference Make?" conference sponsored by the Institute for Feminist Legal Studies, Osgoode Hall Law School, Toronto, October 1993 (publication forthcoming).

2. The strategy of characterizing lesbian oppression as sex discrimination has already been adopted in at least one Canadian human rights complaint. See the applicant's submissions in *Nielsen v. Canada (HRC)*, [1992] F.C. 561, 573 (T.D.).

3. On the construction and regulation of male and female natures, see Andrea Dworkin, *Intercourse* (New York: Free Press, 1987), pp. 149–51.

4. Sylvia Law, "Homosexuality and the Social Meaning of Gender," *Wisconsin Law Review* (1988): 187, 196.

5. See Marilyn Frye, "Willful Virgin or Do You Have to Be a Lesbian to Be a Feminist?" in *Willful Virgin* (Freedom, CA: Crossing Press, 1992), p. 132.

6. See Adrienne Rich, "Compulsory Heterosexuality and Lesbian Existence," *Signs* 5(1981): 158.

7. See Charlotte Bunch, "Lesbians in Revolt," in *Passionate Politics: Feminist Theory in Action* (New York: St. Martin's Press, 1987).

8. Ibid., p. 164.

9. See Radicalesbians, "The Woman-Identified-Woman," in Karla Jay and Allen Young, eds., *Out of the Closets: Voices of Gay Liberation* (New York: Douglas Books, 1972), p. 173.

10. She recommends that lesbians pursue the explicit inclusion of "lesbian discrimination" in statutory lists of prohibited grounds of discrimination, because she fears that exclusive reliance on the sex discrimination ground may be inadequate, at least in the short term. She insists, however, on the need to present and analyze lesbian discrimination as sex discrimination. See Majury, "Refashioning," pp. 312–314.

11. Ibid., p. 312.

12. Ibid., p. 312. See also "Lesbian is the word, the label, the condition that holds women in line. When a woman hears this word tossed her way, she knows she is stepping out of line. She knows that she has crossed the terrible boundary of her sex role"; Radicalesbians, "Woman-Identified-Woman," p. 173.

13. Majury, "Refashioning," p. 312.

14. Law, "Homosexuality," p. 187.

15. Majury, "Refashioning," p. 311.

16. Ibid., p. 312.

17. Of course, the photographs did not really constitute "documentation." It is remarkable that lesbian activists did not publicly address the fact that, like many other pornographic images, the photographs of Williams did not constitute accurate representations of lesbian sexuality; they were contrived to titillate the heterosexual male voyeurs and consumers of *Penthouse*

magazine. Why were lesbians silent about such a misrepresentation of Black lesbian sexuality? Jackie Goldsby suggests that "[t]he main reason was that none of us knew how to talk about it, and that preemptive assumption resulted from the legacy of nineteenth-century sexual ideologies about race." See Jackie Goldsby, "Queen for 307 days: Looking B(l)ack at Vanessa Williams and the Sex Wars," in Arlene Stein, ed., *Sisters, Sexperts, Queers: Beyond the Lesbian Nation* (New York: Plume, 1993), p. 126.

18. Ibid., p. 119. On the racist iconography of womanhood promoted by the dominant culture, see Patrice Leung, "On Iconography," in Makeda Silvera, ed., *Piece of My Heart: A Lesbian of Colour Anthology* (Toronto: Sister Vision Press, 1991), p. 108.

19. Naomi Dykestein, "One More Contradiction," in Sarah Lucia Hoagland and Julia Penelope, eds., *For Lesbians Only: A Separatist Anthology*, rev. ed. (London: Onlywomen Press, 1988), p. 281.

20. Combahee River Collective, "A Black Feminist Statement," in Cherrie Moraga and Gloria Anzaldùa, eds., *This Bridge Called My Back: Writings by Radical Women of Color* (New York: Kitchen Table Press, 1983), p. 213.

21. Karin Aguilar-San Juan, "Exploding Myths, Creating Consciousness: Some First Steps Toward Pan-Asian Unity," in Silvera, ed., *Piece of My Heart*, p. 189. The account is drawn from Ron Takaki's book *Strangers from a Distant Shore*.

22. One possible legal strategy for overcoming the inadequacy of the lesbian-oppression-as-sex-discrimination argument is to claim multiple grounds of discrimination simultaneously. See Majury, "Refashioning," p. 313–314. This strategy does not, however, escape the problems inherent in the categorical approach to equality (i.e., the categorization of inequality within particular grounds of discrimination that are legally proscribed). See my conclusion for a further discussion of this point.

23. Ekua Omosupe, "Black\Lesbian\Bulldagger," *Differences* 3(1991): 102, 105.

24. Gloria Anzaldùa, "To(o) Queer the Writer—Loca, escritora y chicana," in Betsy Warland, ed., *InVersions: Writing by Dykes, Queers and Lesbians* (Vancouver: Press Gang Publishers, 1991), p. 251.

25. See Audre Lorde, "The Master's Tools Will Never Dismantle the Master's House," in *Sister Outsider* (Freedom, CA: Crossing Press, 1984), p. 113.

26. Anzaldùa, "To(o) Queer the Writer," p. 251.

27. Barbara Smith, "Homophobia: Why Bring It Up?" in Henry Abelove, Michele Aina Barale, and David M. Halperin, eds., *The Lesbian and Gay Studies Reader* (New York: Routledge, 1993), p. 100.

28. Majury, "Refashioning," p. 316. Majury also questions whether her theory inappropriately collapses lesbian inequality into gender inequality. I believe that it does. See Petersen, "Litigating Lesbian Equality," pp. 28–30 (manuscript), where I argue that Majury's theory falsely unifies all women's (lesbians' and non-lesbians') experiences of oppression and obscures the fact that heterosexual women benefit in concrete ways from lesbian oppression.

29. Majury, "Refashioning," p. 316.

30. Cheryl Clarke, "The Failure to Transform: Homophobia in the Black Community," in Barbara Smith, ed., *Home Girls: A Black Feminist Anthology* (New York: Kitchen Table Press, 1983), p. 199.

31. Ibid.

32. Barbara Smith and Beverly Smith, "Across the Kitchen Table: A Sister-to-Sister Dialogue," in Moraga and Anzaldùa, eds., *This Bridge*, p. 124.

33. See Jyl Lynn Felman, "De Vilde Chayes, The Wild Beasts," *Fireweed* 37(1993): 8.

34. Smith and Smith, "Across the Kitchen Table," p. 124.

35. Ibid.

36. Goldsby, "Queen for 307 Days," p. 121.

37. Ibid.

38. Ibid.

39. Ibid., p. 126.

40. Jewelle Gomez, "Repeat After Me: 'We Are Different. We Are the Same,' " *Review of Law and Social Change* 14(1986): 935, 938. On the link between the legacy of slavery and heterosexism in contemporary black communities, see also Makeda Silvera, "Manroyals and Sodomites: Some Thoughts on the Invisibility of Afro-Caribbean Lesbians," in Silvera, ed., *Piece of My Heart*, p. 16.

41. Valli Kanuha, "Compounding the Triple Jeopardy: Battering in Lesbian of Color Relationships," *Women and Therapy: A Feminist Quarterly* 9(1990): 169, 175.

42. Lynne Pearlman, "Theorizing Lesbian Oppression and the Politics of Outness in the Case of *Waterman v. National Life Assurance:* A Beginning in Lesbian Human Rights/Equality Jurisprudence," *Canadian Journal of Women and the Law* 7:2(1994): 454.

43. Ibid., p. 461.

44. Ibid., p. 462.

45. Ibid., p. 463.

46. Ibid., p. 461.

47. Aguilar–San Juan, "Exploding Myths," p. 191. On the importance of family connections to Jewish lesbians, see Irena Klepfisz, "Resisting and Surviving America," in Evelyn Torton Beck, ed., *Nice Jewish Girls: A Lesbian Anthology*, rev. ed. (Boston: Beacon Press, 1989), p. 121; and Melanie Kaye (Kantrowitz, "Some Notes on Jewish Lesbian Identity," in Beck, ed., *Nice Jewish Girls*, p. 36. On the importance of family connections to Black lesbians, see Carmen, Gail, Neena, and Tamara, "Becoming Visible: Black Lesbian Discussions," in Feminist Review, eds., *Sexuality: A Reader* (London: Virago Press, 1987), p. 217; and Gomez, "Repeat After Me," p. 939.

48. Pearlman, "Theorizing Lesbian Oppression," p. 465.

49. See Julia Penelope, "The Mystery of Lesbians I," *Lesbian Ethics* 1(1984): 7, as cited in Pearlman, "Theorizing Lesbian Oppression," p. 465 n. 29.

50. See, for example, Anu, "Who Am I?" in Sharon Lim Hing, ed., *The Very Inside: An Anthology of Writing by Asian and Pacific Islander Lesbian and Bisexual Women* (Toronto: Sister Vision Press, 1994), p. 20.

51. Joanne, Pramila and Anu, "Lesbians of Colour: Loving and Struggling, A Conversation Between Three Lesbians of Colour," in Silvera, ed., *Piece of My Heart*, p. 163.

52. Ibid., p. 164.

53. See Edwina Franchild, " 'You Do So Well': A Blind Lesbian Responds to Her Sighted Sisters," in Jeffner Allen, ed., *Lesbian Philosophies and Cultures* (New York: SUNY Press, 1990), p. 181.

54. Lisa Walker critiques the practice of grounding radical political identity in visible signifiers of difference because it ultimately results in the further marginalization of members of a given marginalized population who do not bear those signifiers or who bear visible signs of another marginalized identity. See Lisa M. Walker, "How to Recognize a Lesbian: The Cultural Politics of Looking Like What You Are," *Signs* 18(1993): 866 (special issue on theorizing lesbian experience).

55. Coming out is an ongoing process. Most lesbians are "out" to some people and in some contexts, yet closeted to other people and in other contexts. For every lesbian, however, there is a moment in her life when she has acknowledged her sexual identity to herself but has not yet begun the process of coming out publicly (i.e., a moment at which no one knows that she is a lesbian). I am using that moment of absolute closetry to make my point, but I think that my analysis applies equally to lesbians who are closeted in limited contexts.

56. See, e.g., Carmen, Gail, Neena, and Tamara, "Becoming Visible," p. 217; Nina Rachel, "On Passing: From One Generation to Another," in Beck, ed., *Nice Jewish Girls*, p. 15; Adrienne J. Smith, "First of All I'm Jewish, The Rest Is Commentary," in Barbara Sang, Joyce Warshow, and Adrienne Smith, eds., *Lesbians at Midlife: The Creative Transition* (San Francisco: Spinsters Book Co., 1991), p. 46; Susan Y. F. Chen, "Slowly but Surely, My Search for Family Acceptance and Community Continues," in Lim Hing, ed., *The Very Inside*, p. 79; and V. K. Aruna, "The Myth of One Closet," in Lim Hing, ed., "The Very Inside," pp.373–74.

57. I use "conspicuous" here in the sense that Pearlman describes. I am not only known to be a lesbian, but I am also outspoken about my lesbian politics, and I try always to challenge the heteropatriarchal norms and assumptions that operate in my work environment.

58. Pearlman's intention is primarily to establish an analytical framework from which she can examine the decision in *Waterman v. National Life Assurance Company of Canada*, (No. 2), (1992) 18 C.H.R.R./176 (Ontario Bd. Inq.). *Waterman* is the first Ontario human rights case to deal with non-benefits–related employment discrimination on the basis of sexual orientation; it is a case in which an out lesbian employee attracted what Pearlman describes as the "discriminatory wrath of management" in a way that other lesbian and gay employees did not. Pearlman's analysis provides important insights into the nature of lesbian oppression, notwithstanding that it fails to explain some forms of anti-lesbian discrimination that were not at issue in the *Waterman* case.

59. Nitya Iyer, "Categorical Denials: Equality Rights and the Shaping of Social Identity," *Queen's Law Journal* 19(1994): 179, 181.

60. The Canadian Charter of Rights and Freedoms includes a provision that is designed to protect affirmative action programs. Subsection 15(2) of the Charter stipulates that the right to equality without discrimination (which is guaranteed in Subsection 15(1)) "does not preclude any law, program or activity that has as its object the amelioration of conditions of disadvantaged individuals or groups." There has been very little litigation involving this constitutional provision; hence its utility has not adequately been tested.

61. It is not uncommon for members of dominant groups to appropriate anti-discrimination protections that were designed to protect the members of historically disadvantaged groups and to restore them to positions of equality in society. During the first three years of equality litigation under the Canadian Charter of Rights and Freedoms, men initiated more than three times as many sex equality challenges as women, and men's successes were more than double those of women. See Gwen Brodsky and Shelagh Day, *Canadian Charter Equality Rights for Women: One Step Forward or Two Steps Back?* (Ottawa: CACSW, 1989), p. 56. Moreover, the pattern of men's sex equality challenges was such that they generally attacked "legislated protections and benefits such as rape law reforms and unemployment insurance pregnancy benefits, which women [had] fought for in the political arena." Ibid., pp. 59, 66. More recently, heterosexuals in the United States have invoked civil rights laws to make sexual orientation discrimination complaints. See, for example, *Green v. Howard*, D.C. Super. Ct., December 4, 1992 (unreported); and "No Straights Allowed?" *The Lawyers Weekly*, February 19, 1993, p. 9.

62. Iyer, "Categorical Denials," p. 207.

63. Gomez, "Repeat After Me," p. 940.

64. Ibid.

PART III

LAW REFORM, STRUGGLE, AND THE STATE

From the 1970s, Western lesbian and gay rights movements began to expand their demands from the decriminalization of same-sex sexual acts to encompass claims for rights to nondiscrimination and legal equality in all spheres of life. Many of these campaigns were highly politicized battles, where lesbians and gay men encountered the increasing vehemence of right-wing opposition. In the following essay, Peter M. Cicchino, Bruce R. Deming, and Katherine M. Nicholson closely examine one such campaign—the fight for a gay civil rights bill in Massachusetts. In addition to tracing the history of these events and offering a nuanced evaluation of the outcome, the authors also challenge prevailing understandings of the role of rights discourse in lesbian and gay legal struggles.

Sex, Lies, and Civil Rights: A Critical History of the Massachusetts Gay Civil Rights Bill

Peter M. Cicchino / Bruce R. Deming /
Katherine M. Nicholson

Whoever enlarges upon the telling of the exodus from Egypt, those persons are praiseworthy.[1]

NO HISTORY is purely descriptive. Even the most committed phenomenologist must make decisions about what will be reported, about what counts as relevant, and about what will be treated as insignificant. Moreover, the very process of compiling information—particularly conducting interviews with participants in the historical processes under investigation—can alter the way in which participants in those processes remember and perceive the events about which they are questioned. Lastly, there is the problem of historical causality—determining the relation of one event to another—and the inescapable, subjective element in determining whether event A did in fact "cause"

This chapter is abridged from "Sex, Lies, and Civil Rights: A Critical History of the Massachusetts Gay Civil Rights Bill," originally published in the *Harvard Civil Rights–Civil Liberties Law Review* 26(2) (1991): 549–631. About half of the original text is composed of footnotes. For this anthology, most notes have been omitted; the reader interested in full source citation should consult the original article.

event B. Despite its aspirations to provide an unbiased and comprehensive account, the historical analysis that follows is no exception to those limits on objectivity.

With that caveat, what follows endeavors to be a historical analysis of a gay civil rights law in one state jurisdiction in the United States. The history concerns the amendment of a state civil rights statute in the state of Massachusetts to prohibit discrimination on the basis of sexual orientation. The history was compiled by an extensive study of the proceedings of the Massachusetts legislature, the media coverage in both the gay and mainstream press over the almost two decades the bill was debated; and the written materials generated by both sides during the public political struggle. Additionally, hours of interviews were conducted with the bill's principal opponents and supporters.

This is not, however, history in the strict sense. Rather, the discussion that follows moves, for want of better terms, from history to jurisprudence to political science. The consistent hypothesis throughout the discussion is that in both the language of the law and the strategy used to achieve its enactment, the Massachusetts Gay Civil Rights Bill is a paradigm of the liberal conception of rights secured through a process of professionalized advocacy that minimized, and even discouraged, both widespread press attention and confrontational tactics of direct action.

The first part of the discussion provides a highly condensed history of the bill that argues for the validity of that thesis. The second part then critically examines the language of the bill and the strategy used to achieve its enactment. This part of the discussion initially draws heavily upon the critique of rights associated with the critical legal studies (CLS) movement.[2] In its latter stages, however, the second part of the discussion takes up an issue that has received less attention in the CLS critique of rights: the question of empowerment and the way in which the language and theory of rights affect the dynamics of building and sustaining movements for social change by oppressed people.

Finally, the third part of the discussion undertakes what might be termed a countercritique: a defense of the Massachusetts Gay Civil Rights Bill and the strategies used to enact it. The argument is made that securing basic immunities from discrimination and persecution in the present may be the necessary condition for achieving genuine equality in the future.

Origins and Strategies

On November 7, 1989, the Massachusetts legislature approved a civil rights bill for gay and lesbian people. The passage of the Massachusetts Gay Civil Rights Bill was the culmination of a 17-year struggle in which the gay and lesbian community and its allies ultimately overcame both the rhetoric and parliamentary obstructionism of their opponents in the state legislature. Despite significant concessions made to achieve its passage, the Gay Civil Rights Bill stands as one of the most important civil rights victories of the 1980s. At the time, the Massachusetts bill was only the second of its kind to be passed in the United States. Moreover, the bill represents a statewide victory for one of the most despised and persecuted minorities in the United States, at a time when federal courts were singularly unsympathetic to civil rights plaintiffs in general and gay plaintiffs in particular.

The precise origin of the gay rights legislation introduced in 1973 is not entirely clear. Memories have faded over the intervening 17 years, leaving certain only the identity of the official House sponsors. One account, popular in the gay community, holds that Elaine Noble, the first openly lesbian representative to be elected to the Massachusetts legislature, drafted the prototype of the bill one evening while sitting at her kitchen table. This draft was forwarded to Barney Frank—at that time a Democratic state representative from Boston—who introduced the legislation.

From 1973 through 1989 at least 50 different bills aimed at proscribing discrimination against gay and lesbian people were introduced in the legislature. In addition, there was legislation on issues not covered under these bills, including AIDS, foster parenting by gay people, and consensual same-sex activities. Legislation that amended the existing civil rights statutes of Massachusetts by inserting the words "sexual orientation" in the list of categories protected against discrimination in employment, credit, housing, and public accommodations became known as the Massachusetts Gay Civil Rights Bill.

In the early years, 1973–82, the Gay Civil Rights Bill made very little progress on the floor of the legislature. In 1983, however, to the surprise of both opponents and supporters, the bill was approved by the Massachusetts House of Representatives. This was also the first year in which lobbying for the bill became both focused and professionalized. From 1983 onward, the bill progressed in an almost linear fashion, with mounting support culminating in its passage in 1989. The bill's progress, however, took place in two-year increments (1983, 1985, 1987, 1989). The reason for that pattern of development was a conscious decision of the bill's proponents to confine their advocacy to "off years" (i.e., years in which no general elections were held).

In speaking of the bill's proponents, it can fairly be said that no gay community organization was more closely associated with the struggle to pass the Gay Civil Rights Bill than the Massachusetts Gay and Lesbian Political Caucus (the Caucus). The Caucus had its origins in 1973, the first year the bill was introduced, in an informal group of lesbian women and gay men who lobbied for the bill's passage. The impact of the Caucus upon the substance and style of advocacy for the Gay Civil Rights Bill is owed, in great part, to the decision by the Caucus in 1983 to hire a full-time professional lobbyist. This lobbyist, Arline Isaacson, would remain among the bill's chief advocates in the State House until the bill's passage in 1989.

The style of lobbying employed by the Caucus, and encouraged by the bill's advocates within the legislature, can best be described as culturally conservative and strategically nonconfrontational: what might be termed a quintessential "insider" strategy. This style of advocacy had four defining traits.

First, its rhetoric emphasized similarities over differences. Rather than depicting the gay and lesbian community as a distinctive subgroup within society, advocates for the bill, both on and off the floor of the legislature, tended to emphasize that gay and lesbian people were, apart from their sexual orientation, not much different from the general population. Second, the tone of the advocacy was distinctly nonthreatening. Advocates of the bill generally made *requests* for protection from certain harms, rather than *demands* for equal treatment under the law.

Third, the strategy of the proponents was characterized by extreme caution. This caution manifested itself both in the proponents' preoccupation with minimizing press attention (and the consequent public exposure) and in the time and energy expended by the bill's chief lobbyists in assessing and maintaining support on the floor of the legislature. Fourth, the process of lobbying the bill relied heavily on cultivating personal contacts with legislators. This "customized" approach to lobbying paid special attention to the private and political concerns of individual legislators. Besides the daily attention paid to shepherding the bill through the legislature, Isaacson particularly focused her energies on developing personal relationships with members of the House and Senate.

The Caucus also attempted to garner support among other traditional civil rights constituencies. Within the State House, African-American legislators played an important role as advocates for the bill and were among its strongest supporters. In the 1970s, Representative Mel King (D-Boston)[3] had linked the Gay Civil Rights Bill to the civil rights struggles of African Americans and urged its passage. Representative Byron Rushing (D-Suffolk), throughout the 1980s, drew similar analogies between the civil rights struggles of African-Americans and the gay and lesbian communities. Playing perhaps the most central role was Senator Royall Bolling (D-Suffolk), one of the state legislature's most senior African-American members.

The practical significance of marshaling support among other traditional civil rights constituencies—such as women's groups, groups advocating for the elderly, general civil liberties advocacy groups, and even religious groups—had three elements. On the first, most immediate level, this support was part of the effort to gain votes for the bill on the floor of the legislature. On a second level, this broad coalition-building helped develop, or at least gave the appearance of developing, public support for the bill. Lastly, and perhaps most importantly, the support of community organizations and individual legislators from traditional civil rights constituencies gave political credibility and moral force to the arguments on behalf of the Massachusetts Gay Civil Rights Bill.

Though important to the successful passage of the bill, soliciting and maintaining the support of other civil rights constituencies must be seen as auxiliary to the primary efforts of the gay and lesbian community in seeking passage of the bill. Without diminishing the importance of the endorsements of various civil rights groups, it should be recognized that the sustained campaign of lobbying for the bill was almost entirely the work of the gay and lesbian community in Massachusetts.

Moreover, the solicitation of support from individual legislators and community organizations representing traditional civil rights constituencies should not suggest that the arguments of the bill's advocates were framed exclusively in terms of analogies to African-Americans, women, or other groups who have had to struggle for the recognition of their civil rights. In fact, arguments that relied on the analogy between gay and lesbian people and, for example, African-Americans, were in the minority tradition within the 17-year history of debate over the bill. Occasionally, in fact, these arguments were deployed *against* the advocates of the bill.

The majority tradition of rhetoric on behalf of the bill—the sorts of arguments used most frequently by the bill's legislative supporters on the floor of the Massachusetts House and Senate and by the Caucus lobbyists who fought for the bill—relied almost exclusively upon the language of harm avoidance, what might be termed the language of *immunity*.

The central premise of the argument was, regardless of whether being gay or lesbian is natural or unnatural, moral or immoral, it is not so great a harm as to justify discrimination in housing, employment, or the other areas protected by the Massachusetts Gay Civil Rights Bill. Advocates of the bill, in keeping with this line of argument, focused on protecting people from harm or leaving people alone. This sort of argument relies on an appeal to toleration—the idea being that a despised group should be tolerated and protected from certain forms of oppression.

The provisions of the bill itself are almost entirely prophylactic: the bill protects gay and lesbian people *from* being discharged or denied employment, *from* being evicted or denied an apartment, *from* being denied credit or public accommodation on the basis of their sexual orientation. To this extent, the Massachusetts Gay Civil Rights Bill was largely depicted by its supporters as providing limited immunities and not full equality for lesbian and gay people. This position is completely consistent with the actual practice of the bill's advocates in entertaining arguments and accepting amendments that implicitly, and sometimes quite explicitly, denied the fundamental equality of same-sex and heterosexual orientations. From a theoretical standpoint, such a position avoids a defense of the despised group as deserving dignity and respect, which would be tantamount to arguing that the despised group is *wrongly* despised.

The reliance by the bill's proponents on the language of immunity and of harm avoidance was coupled with a strategy of minimizing the alleged effects of the bill. Having committed themselves to a narrowly utilitarian form of advocacy, proponents of the bill were constrained to argue that its residual effects, particularly its potential for approving, legitimizing, or increasing the statistical occurrence of same-sex relations, were absolutely minimal. Perhaps the most oft-repeated contention of the proponents was that the bill would do no more than what the literal text claimed to do: namely, provide narrowly circumscribed forms of legal protection for gay and lesbian people.

By contrast, opponents of the bill repeatedly emphasized the sweeping effects that the legislation would be bound to have upon civil society in the state of Massachusetts. Adopting a basically utilitarian approach, opponents argued that the harm inflicted by the bill would be greater than the good achieved. The argument was made in two manners.

First, opponents often attempted to minimize the goods that the bill sought to realize. This minimization took two forms: (1) denying that acts of discrimination against gay and lesbian people occurred; and (2) contending that, even if such discrimination did occur, existing laws provided adequate remedies and deterrence.

Second, opponents maintained that the bill's detrimental effects on society would far outweigh the goods, if any, it sought to achieve. This second argument is really a set of arguments that can be divided into two subgroups. The first subgroup is grounded in a certain view of property rights. In its simplest expression, the arguments in this sub-group maintain that the limitations on various property rights (by employers, homeowners, insurers, and lending institutions) effected by the bill outweigh in their negative effects the good of nondiscrimination that the bill purported to achieve.

The second subgroup, invoking a more moralistic tone, was grounded in the notion that same-sex relations were fundamentally evil, i.e., that being gay or lesbian was unnatural, harmful, and bad both for the gay or lesbian person and for society. This group of arguments was preoccupied with arguing that the bill would increase the occurrence and practice of gay and lesbian sexual orientation by legitimizing or endorsing it. Advocates of this line of argument devoted considerable attention to the fear that gay and lesbian people would recruit or molest children, that an increase in the statistical occurrence of same-sex relations between men would significantly enhance the rate of infection of AIDS, and that the traditional nuclear family would be destroyed by the increase in same-sex relations allegedly to be brought about by the bill.

Throughout the struggle to enact the bill, but particularly in the years 1983–87, some or all of those themes were prominent. By 1987, however, proponents of the bill had secured a majority in both houses. Proponents, however, were faced with a hostile Senate president and could not translate this majority into passage. Time and again, powerful committee chairmen, who owed their positions to the Senate president, allowed the bill to languish in committee until the legislative session had expired.

The success of those dilatory tactics in killing the bill in 1987 generated enormous resentment within the gay and lesbian community. Ironically, the primary impact of this resentment was not felt by the bill's opponents but by its supporters within the Massachusetts Gay and Lesbian Political Caucus.

From 1985, by which time AIDS had come to public attention, there developed within the gay and lesbian community a resurgence of political activism and the formation of new grassroots organizations. By 1987, some of these groups had taken a strong interest in the Massachusetts Gay Civil Rights Bill and had begun to challenge the dominant rhetoric and lobbying strategy of the Caucus. The most prominent of these groups were Mass ACT-OUT and the Massachusetts Gay and Lesbian Political Alliance (the Alliance).

The differences between the substance and style of these groups and those of the Caucus and its allies in the legislature involved both their professed understandings of the bill and the way in which they advocated the bill's passage. ACT-OUT, the Alliance, and in later years the Coalition for Lesbian and Gay Civil Rights (the Coalition), led by David LaFontaine, understood the bill as possessing tremendous symbolic significance for the gay and lesbian community. Like the bill's opponents, these organizations emphasized that the impact of the bill went well beyond its literal text. For these organizations, then, the bill was primarily about positive recognition and affirmation—what might be termed legitimation—of the gay and lesbian community. In addition, these groups emphasized victory not merely in the passage of the bill but in the establishment of an active community that felt responsible for and enabled by the legislation.

Given this understanding, with its emphasis on the dignity, equality, and substantive moral value of same-sex relations, the Coalition, and groups like it, favored a more aggressive, confrontational approach to lobbying the bill. Unlike the Caucus, these groups encouraged maximum press coverage of the bill and strove to keep it in the public eye. In addition, they did not shy from threatening legislators with defeat if they obstructed progress of the bill.

Perhaps the most graphic contrast between the methods of the Caucus and the methods of the new organizations that made their presence felt in 1987 was the civil disobedience in the Senate gallery on January 4, 1988. Shortly before 5:30 p.m. on that day, one thousand demonstrators from the gay community attempted to enter the Senate gallery. The demonstrators shouted, "Gay rights now," and "Shame, shame, shame," to protest the Senate's inaction. In the action, sponsored by Mass ACT-OUT, 12 people from the gay and lesbian community were arrested for disrupting proceedings from the Senate gallery. In the aftermath of the protest, controversy arose over the rough treatment that the protestors had received at the hands of the State House police. In addition, the action split proponents of the bill over the propriety of such tactics.

The Senate sponsor of the bill, Michael Barrett (D-Cambridge), publicly criticized the demonstration and warned that such actions would only erode legislative and public support for the bill. Barrett went on to remind the gay community that a unified strategy was essential to winning passage of the bill. The protest in the Senate gallery also crystallized gay community dissatisfaction with the Caucus and its insider strategy. Arline Isaacson, probably because of her longstanding identification with both the Caucus and the bill, became a central focus of that dissatisfaction. The tension between new organizations like the Coalition and older organizations like the Caucus would exist until the bill's passage. The dominant style of advocacy for the bill, however, remained that of the Caucus and its legislative allies.

The goal of that strategy would finally be achieved in 1989, a legislative year that began with proponents of the Massachusetts Gay Civil Rights Bill having secured a majority of votes in both the House and Senate. The challenge that lay ahead, as in 1987, was translating those majorities into passage of the bill before the year was over.

In the House, the bill made extraordinarily swift progress. Introduced on January 9 by its sponsor Representative Mark Roosevelt, the bill was immediately referred to the Committee on Commerce and Labor. The committee was chaired by Representative Marilyn Travinski (D-Southbridge) and Senator Lois Pines. Although Travinski had consistently opposed the bill, she had been persuaded by the Caucus to let the bill pass out of the committee. The passivity of Travinski's opposition, coupled with the active support of her co-chair Pines, allowed the bill to start its progress through the legislature six weeks earlier than in 1987.

By March 29, less than one week after it had reached the House from the Committee on Commerce and Labor, the bill was passed 76–72. The remarkably expeditious progress of the bill in the House was due largely to the fact that debate on the bill was confined almost exclusively to two days. This, in turn, was only possible because of the support of the House leadership—Speaker of the House George Keverian (D-Everett) and Majority Leader Charles Flaherty (D-Cambridge).

The speed with which the bill passed the House would not be duplicated in the Senate, but the opposition it encountered foreshadowed many of the issues that would be raised by the bill's adversaries in the upper chamber of the Massachusetts legislature. In the Senate, opponents of the bill would have much more success with using amendments to alter the actual text of the bill and delay its progress toward enactment.

The earliest stages of the bill's passage through the Massachusetts Senate began in April of 1989. The Ways and Means Committee reported favorably on the bill, and then, about one month later, the Steering and Policy Committee placed it on the agenda for debate. Throughout the month of June, opponents and proponents of the bill sparred over an amendment that would have placed the Massachusetts Gay Civil Rights Bill on the ballot as a referendum issue. At 1:00 a.m. on July 11, after extensive debate, the bill was sent to the Committee on the Third Reading, now chaired by bill opponent Senator David McLean.

The bill was largely dormant during the summer of 1989, but on September 27, it was discharged from the Committee on Bills in Third Reading. In an extremely important move, five days after the bill was reported, Senate President William Bulger surprised both opponents and supporters by announcing that all amendments to the bill would have to be registered with the clerk by 5:00 p.m. on October 2. Any amendments offered after 5:00 p.m. would be ruled dilatory.

The debate that took place during the remainder of the month of October reads like a great reprise of all the debates that had, for 17 years, preceded it. Virtually every argument raised by opponents in the time the bill had circulated within the legislature was resurrected in the final weeks of debate. The tone of these arguments, however, took on a somewhat desperate quality as it became clear, to opponents and supporters alike, that passage of the bill was inevitable. But this sense of desperation was also tinged with exhaustion and a begrudging respect for the stamina and endurance of the bill's supporters. One opponent of the bill commented, "I commend the people on the other side for their tenacity. . . . They played the game well. They strategized like the Russians strategized when the Germans entered Russia—they waited for the cold winter to come."

On October 30, 1989, the bill was approved for enactment, 22–13. One week later, as part of a parliamentary formality, the motion of Senator Kirby to reconsider the enactment vote was defeated, 21–9. Seventeen years after it was first introduced, the Massachusetts Gay Civil Rights Bill became law, on November 15, 1989, when it was signed by Governor Michael Dukakis. Proponents of the bill, however, would soon realize that they had one remaining legal battle to win.

Soon after it became apparent that the Gay Civil Rights Bill would pass in 1989, opponents struck upon the idea of waging a public referendum campaign to repeal the bill after it had been enacted into law. This was not the first time opponents had thought to put this issue to the Massachusetts electorate. Throughout the bill's history, amendments were offered, and sometimes accepted, that attached both binding and nonbinding public ballot questions to it. This time, however, opponents began to make concrete preparations for a referendum campaign. Most importantly, Citizens for Family First (CFF), the organization that would manage the campaign to repeal the law, was formed and began operation. On November 16, 1989, the day after Governor Dukakis signed the bill into law, CFF presented a petition to the Secretary of the Commonwealth (the Secretary), to initiate a referendum campaign to repeal it.

In their effort to obtain a popular repeal of the Gay Civil Rights Bill, opponents relied upon Article 48 of the Massachusetts State Constitution, which establishes the process by which laws enacted by the legislature can be repealed through referendum. The power of popular repeal, however, is not unlimited. Certain laws are excluded from the referendum process, the most important of which, in this case, are those relating to "religion, religious practices, or religious institutions." Ironically, it was this provision in the Massachusetts State Constitution that kept the newly enacted Gay Civil Rights Bill from being put to a referendum. The reason is that in the process of securing its passage, proponents of the bill had agreed to an amendment that created a sweeping exemption for religious institutions from the provisions of the Massachusetts antidiscrimination statute.

On July 10, 1990, the highest court of Massachusetts, the Supreme Judicial Court, found that two sections of the Gay Civil Rights Bill dealt expressly with religion, religious practices, and religious institutions. Those provisions granted religious institutions a greater degree of freedom in determining how to operate their organizations. Before the bill was passed, only decisions made by religious institutions regarding employment selection were exempt from coverage; after the bill was passed, decisions affecting virtually any aspect of religious organizations were exempt. Moreover, these new exemptions were not limited to discrimination based on sexual orientation, but also included action based on race, color, religious creed, national origin, sex, ancestry, age, or disability. Concluding that the gay rights law did indeed expand the religious exemption, the court found that it could not constitutionally be the subject of a repeal referendum. With that decision, the Gay Civil Rights Bill was saved from popular repeal.

A Critique of the Bill

The bill is essentially a liberal rights document,[4] and a useful critique of liberal rights has been articulated by the Critical Legal Studies movement. As explained by Mark Tushnet, the critique involves four related claims:

> (1) Once one identifies what counts as a right in a specific setting, it invariably turns out that the right is unstable; significant but relatively small changes in the social setting can make it difficult to sustain the claim that a right remains implicated; (2) The claim that a right is implicated in some setting produces no determinant consequences; (3) The concept of rights falsely converts into an empty abstraction (reifies) real experiences that we ought to value for their own sake; (4) The use of rights in contemporary discourse impedes advances by progressive social forces.[5]

What unifies each of these critiques of rights—instability, indeterminacy, reification, and disutility—is the insight that there is something fundamentally contradictory or untrustworthy about rights. Precisely because of its abstraction, rights language can be consistent with any number of concrete applications. Moreover, there is nothing intrinsic to the language of rights that allows adjudication between conflicting rights. Although rights may be perceived to be and have been used as tools of empowerment by oppressed people, rights and rights language contain the seeds of a radical reversal—the potential for unexpected deployment against the progressive forces that first sought to use them. The exemption for owner-occupied two-family dwellings in the text of the Massachusetts Gay Civil Rights Bill is a perfect example of the way in which the CLS critique predicts that rights language has been and can be deployed against progressive movements.

Late in 1989, Representative Royall Switzler remarked that "our system of rights is a closed system; if you give rights to one group, you take them away from another." Switzler's comment typified a strategy employed by bill opponents throughout the debate over gay rights: making the extension of certain rights to gay and lesbian people appear to entail necessarily the curtailment of rights of other groups in society.

Although one may take issue with the intent of Switzler's comment, his logic is hard to dispute. Even granting that the "right" to exclude persons from one's property, on the basis of their perceived sexual orientation, pales in comparison to the importance of equal access to private accommodations, the import of Switzler's idea—that property owners would lose a certain power over their property—is inescapable.

This logic made its power felt in the Senate debate in 1989, when Senator Arthur Lewis proposed the owner-occupied dwelling exclusion.[6] The premise of the exclusion was obvious: even if gay and lesbian people should be given certain civil rights, it is too much to ask an owner of a two-family dwelling to live under the same roof with such people. Without straying from a utilitarian understanding of rights as immunities—protections from harm—the proponents of the Massachusetts Gay Civil Rights Bill could have argued that the good achieved by the exclusion was outweighed by the harm it imposed in denying housing access to gay and lesbian people. This would have involved either arguing that the harm of restricting access to housing, represented by the exclusion, outweighed any good it achieved; or rebutting the presumption that gay and lesbian people are so intrinsically repulsive that to share the same building with them involves some real harm to their cotenants.

The proponents of the bill, perhaps because of their unwillingness to assert publicly the fundamental goodness of same-sex orientation, were unwilling to challenge the valuation of rights implicit in the exclusion. Because of this, the opponents of the bill were able to deploy property rights not only in opposition to the rights of gay and lesbian people, but to assert those rights as superior to the expanded access to housing that the bill sought to provide.

We now critically consider three aspects of the bill and the process used to enact it. First and most briefly, some attention is given to the text of the bill that was enacted into law. Second, the effects of the strategy used to enact the bill, both the type of lobbying and the rhetoric of advocacy for the bill, are examined in the light of their impact on the attitudes of the public as a whole and on the gay and lesbian community in Massachusetts. Third, some attempt is made to assess the limitations of the language in which the struggle largely took place.

The bill, as enacted into law, provides important protections for gay and lesbian people in the areas of housing, public accommodation, employment, and credit. It is not, however, an equal rights bill for gay and lesbian people. Significantly, one of the most important issues in the gay community in 1985—foster care eligibility—is explicitly excluded from the purview of the law. The legislature made clear that nothing in the law would be interpreted to establish even the presumptive fitness of gay and lesbian people to be foster parents. Moreover, the law explicitly rejects any endorsement of same-sex marriages, or of gay and lesbian people as persons. In short, a law for which the gay and lesbian community struggled for 17 years, a law heralded as a landmark victory in gay and lesbian rights, explicitly renounces any reformative impact on two of the most important aspects of the lives of lesbian and gay people or of human beings in general: romantic intimacy and family. There is even a question whether the law would preempt the sodomy statutes that are still in existence in Massachusetts.

As for the strategy used to obtain the bill's enactment, two distinct criticisms can be made. First, by employing an insider strategy, by carefully keeping the campaign for the bill within the State House walls, and by restricting press attention and minimizing public scrutiny, advocates of the bill managed to achieve an almost exclusively *legal* victory. The impact of the struggle to enact the bill on a *cultural* level was virtually nonexistent. The cautious style of the professional and highly effective advocacy utilized by the Caucus focused almost entirely on the legislators themselves. Relatively little attention was given to altering public perceptions, educating society about gay and lesbian issues, or organizing popular support for the goals of the gay and lesbian civil rights movement. The adamant resistance of the bill's advocates to placing it on the ballot had the unintended consequence of precluding the possibility of a genuine statewide discussion of the merits of the legislation—or the hard realities of the lives of gay and lesbian people in Massachusetts.

This, in turn, left the bill open to popular reversal through the referendum process. Though some polls indicated as much as 66 percent support for the bill within the state, its advocates dreaded the idea of a referendum and fought hard to prevent it. Moreover, the speed with which Citizens for Family First was able to accumulate an unprecedented number of signatures for the referendal repeal of the newly enacted bill can be seen as probative evidence of the strength of homophobia among the electorate.[7]

The second criticism is similar to the first, but focuses on the gay and lesbian community in Massachusetts itself. In an interview on the subject of the referendum, one of the first questions put to one of the leaders of the Coalition, David LaFontaine, was whether the various gay and lesbian groups that had been involved in the struggle for the bill had formed an organization that coordinated preparations for fighting the referendum. LaFontaine explained that the groups had, in fact, met to form such an organization but had never managed to agree on a name. In fact, so contentious were the organizing meetings that no coordinated effort to resist the referendum was ever mounted by a coalition of the major gay and lesbian groups within Massachusetts. The Supreme Judicial Court, when it found the referendum prohibited under the state constitution, saved the bill, *deus ex machina*, from the possibility of repeal. The decision of the court also spared the gay and lesbian community, at least temporarily, from confronting its own divisions. Many of those divisions had been exacerbated by the process of lobbying the bill.

Although it is hard to question the efficacy of the narrowly focused, professionalized lobbying strategy of the Caucus, its impact on the gay and lesbian community, in terms of exclusion and disempowerment, remains to be adequately assessed. Even admitting the ineffectiveness of the strategy put forward by the Caucus's rivals, particularly Mass ACT-OUT, the Alliance, and the Coalition, the process utilized by the Caucus was singularly ineffective in educating, involving, and empowering gay and lesbian people and organizations on a grassroots level. The fact that the gay press was silent for so long on the bill is, in itself, partly a tribute to the Caucus's success in pursuing its State House strategy for enactment.

Beyond these considerations, however, there is the question of the nearly exclusive embrace of the theory and language of immunity in advocating the bill's enactment—the idea that lesbians and gay men were to be protected, not affirmed. The costs of that embrace have yet to be enumerated. Perhaps most obvious, the proponents of the bill were willing to accept a series of homophobic amendments. These include not only the "no endorsement" clauses on marriage, same-sex orientation, and foster care, but also the profoundly insulting caveat (which appears every time the term "sexual orientation" is used in the law) of "except those persons whose sexual orientation involves minor children as a sex object." Such explicit legislative pandering to one of the most pernicious aspects of homophobic ideology, the completely unfounded contention that gay people are likely to be pederasts, is particularly insulting given that it appears in the context of what purports to be a gay and lesbian civil rights law.

Part of the problem of the language of immunity is that it does not capture one of the most important political aspirations of human beings: the desire for equality. Describing the importance of the egalitarian ideal in American history, Kenneth Karst has written:

> It is the presumptive right "to be treated by the organized society as a respected, responsible, and participating member." Every individual is thus presumptively entitled to treatment in our public life as a person, one who deserves respect, one who belongs to our national community. The principle is presumptively violated when the organized society treats someone as inferior, as part of a dependent caste, or as a nonparticipant. The chief citizenship value is respect; the chief harm against which the principle guards is degradation or the imposition of stigma.[8]

Few groups in our society suffer more from "degradation" and "stigma" than gay and lesbian people. Most fundamentally, the inferior status of gay and lesbian people is not so much a function of lacking immunities as a denial of a fundamental dignity or equality. This denial of equality results in a variety of exclusions, including the exclusion from legal recognition for intimate spousal relationships.

When one senator stood and affirmed publicly the goodness of same-sex relations, he was met with silence, and more than clever political maneuvering on the part of the bill's proponents had taken place. The Sir Thomas More of the playwright Robert Bolt tells his jurors that "the maxim of the law is *qui tacet consentire*—silence gives consent."[9] This maxim has been taken up, at least implicitly, by gay and lesbian groups like ACT-UP. The now-famous principle of this AIDS direct action group, "Silence = Death," is but a variation on More's principle: nonresistance in the face of injustice is a kind of complicity with evil. The silence that met Senator Locke's challenge was a kind of consent, an acquiesence in the widespread prejudice that gay people are inferior to heterosexual people.

To some degree, by framing their arguments in the language of immunity and by accepting that language into the text, advocates for the law ran the risk of institutionalizing the homophobic prejudice they left unchallenged. Although it is true that the objectionable amendments discussed above may have no *legal* force, they establish a precedent for further entrenching and providing institutional recognition for the status inequality of gay and lesbian people.

Peter Gabel, in his critical examination of the effects of rights language on progressive social movements among oppressed people, comments that the first intention of such movements is always practical: "When workers demand the right to engage in collective action on the shop floor, or women demand the right to safe abortions, or gay people demand the right to dental care for 'domestic partners' under employee-benefit plans, they want to do things that are good in themselves and will advance practical aims (including the aim of building the movement)."[10] The more fundamental motivation, however, is a yearning for the healing of human community, the striving to gain recognition in public consciousness, to achieve respect, and to realize "the universal and authentic meaning of freedom and equality as that meaning would be realized for everyone through the realization of each movement's particular demands."[11]

This second motivation, however, is often lost after the first, practical set of rights is gained. Rights victories, of their nature, tend to have an ambivalent effect on the social movements that achieve them. While such victories can enfuse a movement with vitality and confidence, they can also increase conservative tendencies, since each victory invariably means that there is now more for the oppressed group to lose. More significantly, however, each subsequent conflict over rights brings society closer to the realization of the inadequacy of a regime of immunities.

Overcoming this inadequacy, Gabel has written, would mean "that we would actually have to change, and in a way that would require us both to open ourselves to each other in a new way and to abandon the forms of substitute connection through which we have defended ourselves against such openness for a long time."[12] Among other things, this would translate into a genuine social struggle to articulate a shared vision of not merely what can be tolerated, but what ought to be affirmed as constitutive of a good life. For all its political acumen and strategic success, the strategy and language of the advocates of the Massachusetts Gay Civil Rights Bill scrupulously avoided precisely this sort of confrontation.

Final Reflections

A critique of the Massachusetts Gay Civil Rights Bill has as its empirical precondition the existence of such a law. Though the principle seems self-evident, its practical importance should not be overlooked. The advocates of the bill achieved something that, at the time, 48 other states had not. The significance of this political achievement necessarily tempers any criticisms that are made of the bill or the process used to secure its enactment. Apart, however, from the cliché that "half a loaf is better than none," several distinct arguments can be made on behalf of the bill and the strategy used to enact it.

First, with regard to changing public consciousness, law itself has an educative function. Whatever the failures of advocates of the bill in educating the public during the 17-year struggle for enactment, the very presence of such a statute, and the public awareness that gay and lesbian people can now invoke the power of the state for protection, can have a powerful impact on cultural perceptions of gay and lesbian people.

Second, with regard to the gay and lesbian community itself, the passage of the bill has represented a kind of public affirmation.[13] The coverage of the bill's passage in the community's press, as well as the outpourings of support for events surrounding the bill's signing into law, is indicative of the significance of its passage to the collective self-esteem of the gay and lesbian community in Massachusetts.

Patricia Williams, reflecting from the perspective of the African-American community, has expressed the importance of the dignity-affirming value of rights. Williams begins by recounting the story of a funeral she attended at a small church in Georgia, where "fans with pictures of Martin Luther King, Jr., on them were passed out."[14] Williams goes on to reflect:

> The icon of King is a testament to the almost sacred attachment to the transformative promise of a black-conceived notion of rights, which exists, perhaps, somewhat apart from the day-to-day reality of their legal enforcement, but which gives rise to their power as a politically animating, socially cohesive force. . . . If one views "rights" as emanating from either that body of "legal" history or from that of modern bourgeois legal structures, then of course rights would mean nothing because blacks have had virtually nothing under either.[15]

Third, it may well be the case that the strategy used by the advocates of the bill is the only one now feasible, given the state of the American electorate. Recent studies have shown that almost 77 percent of Americans believe that same-sex relations between consenting adults are *always wrong*.[16] This represents a slight increase in negative attitudes toward gay people over a ten-year period. Moreover, the Center for Political Studies at the University of Michigan has found, in its "Feeling Thermometer," that fully 61.5 percent of those surveyed in 1984 placed their feelings toward gay and lesbian people at the "coldest" end of the spectrum.[17]

Simultaneously, an increasing number of Americans believe that government should have no part in punishing private, consensual sexual activity between adults.[18] Williams's remark that "in discarding rights altogether, one discards a symbol too deeply enmeshed in the psyche of the oppressed to lose without trauma and much resistance,"[19] may be equally true of the *oppressors*—or at least of those who represent the "dominant" lifestyle within American culture. Precisely because the language of rights is so ingrained in American political consciousness, it may be the most effective rhetoric for protecting the dignity of minorities from the oppression of the majority.

Persuading Americans to recognize the dignity of minorities, particularly gay and lesbian people, may require something like a noble lie. That is to say, the public presentation of the gay and lesbian community may have to be tailored to a nonthreatening, culturally conservative image—much like that projected by the Caucus to the members of the Massachusetts State Legislature.

Such a strategy, as the foregoing analysis has sought to make clear, carries with it high costs. Among those costs is the risk of institutionalizing the indignities inflicted upon gay and lesbian people and excluding those gay and lesbian people who do not conform to the carefully cultivated image that the strategy projects in attempts to secure basic civil liberties. The benefits of such a strategy, however, may be to establish legal precedents from which a broader campaign of cultural reeducation can take place. No less a hater of lies than Immanuel Kant believed that there was no universal obligation to reveal all the information at one's disposal:

> I can make believe, make a demonstration from which others will draw the conclusion I want, though they have no right to expect that my action will express my real mind. In that case, I have not lied to them, because I have not undertaken to express my mind. I may for instance, wish people to think that I am off on a journey, and so I pack my luggage; people draw the conclusion I want them to draw; but others have no right to demand a declaration of my will from me.[20]

For the gay and lesbian community, a selective withholding of information, the presentation of a limited, culturally nonthreatening public persona, may be the precondition for securing basic civil rights in the present political climate.

In concluding this discussion of the history of the Massachusetts Gay Civil Rights Bill, one final question must be posed: Did the bill's advocates indeliberately contribute to the idea that civil rights are a function of majoritarian determination? That is, should civil rights depend upon public acceptance or the quality of organization among the population that seeks those rights?

An earlier legal positivism might suggest as much, at least to the extent that it saw rights as flowing only from real political processes.[21] This positivism, however, has been increasingly rejected by contemporary legal thinkers. In its place has come a notion of rights and of law that makes an appeal to some higher moral principles—to a sense of right and wrong.[22]

Proponents of the Gay Civil Rights Bill, in their preoccupation with what works in obtaining majority support, may have indirectly reinforced the notion that the civil rights of minorities are a function of what the majority is willing to extend. Though this may be true in the context of real politics, devising strategies that take this situation as a given may unwittingly contribute to reinforcing it. The normative power of the argument for gay civil rights, the strength of the arguments that equality for gay and lesbian people is something society *ought* to recognize and extend, may be lost in the preoccupation with what works, with rhetorical and political strategies designed to obtain majoritarian support for gay civil rights.

The point of this concluding observation on the history of the Massachusetts Gay Civil Rights Bill has been to suggest that a distinction ought to be preserved between what is politically efficacious and what is morally right. At a time when civil rights plaintiffs are being advised, often by sympathizers, to abandon the federal courts for other fora, it may be important to recognize that the most dangerous subversive effect of a judiciary that has abdicated its responsibility to protect minorities from oppression would be the acceptance of the idea that civil rights are a function for majoritarian determination.

NOTES

1. New Jewish Agenda, *The Shalom Seders: Three Haggadahs* (New York: Adama Books, 1984), p. 76.

2. See generally Alan Freeman, "Racism, Rights, and the Quest for Equality of Opportunity: A Critical Legal Essay," *Harvard Civil Rights–Civil Liberties Law Review* 23 (1988): 325–35. In these ten pages Freeman touches upon the central themes in the CLS critique of rights: their historical use to protect entrenched property interests, their fundamental abstractness and the consequent indeterminacy and manipulability that are a function of that abstraction, their ineffectiveness in achieving cultural change, and their essentially paternalistic character when "granted" to oppressed people. See also Mark Tushnet, "An Essay on Rights," *Texas Law Review* 62 (1984):1363.

3. The designation following the name of a legislator indicates his or her political party and district. Hence, for Mel King, (D-Boston) indicates Democratic party membership from the city of Boston. Or, as another example, Senator David Locke (R-Wellesley) was a member of the Republican party representing Wellesley.

4. In the original version of this essay we describe in detail several key principles of liberal rights theory.

5. Tushnet, "An Essay on Rights," pp. 1363–64.

6. State House News Service, Senate, November 11, 1989, p. 2.

7. Citizens for Family First, to the great surprise of people familiar with the referendum process, was able to obtain nearly 65,000 signatures in less than two weeks.

8. Kenneth Karst, "Why Equality Matters," *Georgia Law Review* 17 (1983): 247–48. Karst's article is, to a significant degree, a defense of the ideal of equality from attacks analogous to the CLS critique of rights.

9. Robert Bolt, *A Man for All Seasons* (New York: Random House, 1969), p. 152.

10. Peter Gabel, "The Phenomenology of Rights-Consciousness and the Pact of the Withdrawn Selves," *Texas Law Review* 62 (1984): 1588.

11. Ibid.

12. Ibid.

13. Writing in a South African context, prior to the abolition of apartheid and election of Nelson Mandela, Albie Sachs, chief constitutional theorist for the African National Congress, reflected on the symbolic power of law for the self-esteem and sense of empowerment of oppressed people:

> constitutions can have many meanings. In the first place, they establish structures of government, and lay down how political power is to be exercised. Yet a constitution does much more than indicate the political and legal organisation of the state. It serves as a symbol for the whole of society, as a point of reference for the nation. People like to feel that they have constitutional rights even if they do not exercise them. . . . Above all, the constitution is a vehicle for expressing fundamental notions of freedom, at the conceptual, symbolical and practical levels.

Albie Sachs, "The Last Word—Freedom," in *Protecting Human Rights in a New South Africa* (Cape Town: Oxford University Press, 1990), pp. 184–189.

14. Patricia Williams, "Alchemical Notes: Reconstructing Ideals from Deconstructed Rights," *Harvard Civil Rights–Civil Liberties Law Review* 22 (1987): 416.

15. Ibid., pp. 416–17.

16. Kenneth S. Sherrill, Remarks at the Annual Meeting of the American Political Science Association, August 30–September 3, 1989, p. 1.

17. Ibid., p. 2. The "Feeling Thermometer" measures positive and negative *affect* toward certain groups in society. The "colder" the response, the more negative the social affect. The survey cited here indicates that gay and lesbian people rank very low in the public's esteem.

18. See Herbert McClosky and Alida Brill, *Dimensions of Tolerance: What Americans Believe about Civil Liberties* (New York: Russell Sage Foundation, 1983). McClosky and Brill discovered that despite widespread disapproval of same-sex relations between adults:

> when the public is asked whether "homosexual relations in private be-

tween consenting adults" should be left to the individual or forbidden by law, they strongly express the view that they should be left to the individual and are beyond the majority's control. Thus they are saying, in effect, that sexual preference is a private matter and ought not to be forbidden or regulated by the state, however "immoral" it may seem.

Ibid., p. 203. More importantly for this discussion, "a majority of respondents also regard it as consistent with 'the American ideal of human rights for all' to adopt local ordinances that assure gays equality in jobs and housing." Ibid. Admittedly, the McClosky and Brill study was authored before AIDS loomed large in the public consciousness. Nevertheless, it offers probative evidence of the degree to which rights language—and the theory of legally enshrined immunities—have penetrated the public consciousness.

19. Williams, "Alchemical Notes," p. 433.

20. Immanuel Kant, *Lectures on Ethics,* trans. Louis Infield (New York: Harper & Row, 1963), p. 226.

21. The classic example of such positivism is H. L. A. Hart, *The Concept of Law* (Oxford: Oxford University Press, 1961).

22. See, e.g., Ronald Dworkin, *Taking Rights Seriously* (Cambridge: Harvard University Press, 1977). There, Dworkin contrasts legal positivism with the dominant theory of law today, which argues that law is grounded in some moral scheme that is not reducible to the result of a discrete set of empirical political processes.

EIGHT

The year 1995 marks the fifteenth year of uninterrupted Conservative party rule in Britain. While Thatcherism is most often associated with a particular economic agenda, in this essay Davina Cooper and Didi Herman argue that the 1980s also saw significant state intervention in the promotion of the traditional family form. Focusing on initiatives in reproductive technology and education policy, the authors show how law was used to contain lesbian and gay challenges. More specifically, they unpack the political discourse of the period and argue that neither the state nor the law has one identifiable interest. Official responses to lesbian and gay sexuality are contradictory and often the result of compromise and appeasement.

Getting "the Family Right": Legislating Heterosexuality in Britain, 1986–91

Davina Cooper / Didi Herman

IF WE get the family right, all those other things will come right as a spin-off effect. Our prisons will not be bursting; our rate of abortions will not be higher than anywhere else; marriages will not break down; and divorce will not be higher than anywhere else.[1]

Introduction: "Storm over Virgin Births"[2]

In March 1991 the British press exploded with a story that was to occupy the mass media for days. It concerned the provision by clinics of anonymous donor insemination services to women described as virgins. At the controversy's outset, it was unclear whether these so-called virgins were heterosexual or lesbian. Nevertheless, it did not take long for the specter of lesbian mothers to be invoked.

The virgin births outrage is one of several recent British legislative attempts to statutorily fortify a sexual hierarchy of families. These provisions are located at the interface of the public and private, ideo-

This essay is slightly revised and greatly shortened from its original, published in *Canadian Journal of Family Law* 10 (1991): 41. See that version for a more detailed discussion and fuller referencing.

logical and cultural divisions entrenched by the Wolfenden Report and subsequent 1967 Sexual Offences Act. Arguably, it was the disintegration of this dichotomy, highlighted by the current and continuing demands by lesbians and gay men (in most Western countries) for state-derived benefits and the equal facilitation of diverse family forms, that provoked the legislative responses discussed here. The Wolfenden settlement, rooted in the assumptions of containment and inevitable diffusion of a dominant sexual politics, could no longer be relied upon. Legal regulation therefore became necessary to maintain the status quo.

We first briefly set out the legislation and government directives under consideration. We then focus on the authoritative contributions of politicians and professionals to the debates, and, in the final section, we reflect upon the wider political context within which these measures emerged. A comprehensive analysis of recent sexual regulation must situate these initiatives in such a context, and not simply explore the texts themselves, as if they existed independently of social and political action.

The Legislation

Anonymous Donor Insemination: The Human Fertilization and Embryology Act, 1990 (HUFEA)

The HUFEA was the culmination of years of debate and research, including the report of the renowned Warnock Commission in 1984.[3] The act, following on the heels of a 1987 White Paper,[4] adopted many of the commission's recommendations, assumptions, and frames of reference. The HUFEA was directed toward two primary areas of regulation: embryo research and infertility treatment services. It created a statutory licensing body, the Human Fertilization and Embryology Authority, with wide powers to issue and revoke licenses and "police" facilities engaged in research and treatment (Sections 39, 40).

The provisions concerning treatment are most relevant to this discussion.[5] The HUFEA provides for the mandatory licensing of all conception services provided by clinics, with the exception of services that assist conception using sperm from a woman's husband or partner and her own eggs (Section 3). In other words, the licensing only relates to *donated* eggs or sperm, whether anonymous or not. Previously, the services had been voluntarily self-regulated.

The section central to our study is Section 13(5): "a woman shall not be provided with treatment services unless account has been taken of the welfare of any child who may be born as a result of the treatment (*including the need of that child for a father*), and of any other child who may be affected by the birth" [emphasis added]. The incorporation of this section into the act had a somewhat complicated legislative history. During the House of Lords debate on the bill, two amendments were introduced. The first aimed to prohibit all anonymous donor insemination by restricting services to those cases involving only "the eggs of that woman and the sperm of her husband." This was eventually withdrawn in favor of a somewhat less severe amendment intended, instead, "to prohibit the provision of AID [artificial insemination by donor] to unmarried women, lesbian couples or unmarried couples."[6] Although this amendment fell (by one vote), its sentiments were taken into account when the bill returned to the Commons. As a result, Section 13(5) was added.

The interpretation of Section 13(5) has been mediated by the Human Fertilization and Embryology Authority, the statutory licensing body created by the HUFEA. In March 1991, the members issued their draft Code of Practice for consultation. The Authority proposed that where the child will have no *legal* father,[7] "Centres are required to have regard to the child's need for a father and should pay particular attention to the prospective mother's ability to meet the child's needs throughout his or her childhood."[8] The postconsultative and final draft of the code added the following: "and where appropriate, whether there is anyone else within the prospective mother's family and social circle who is willing and able to share the responsibility for meeting those needs and for bringing up, maintaining and caring for the child."[9] In this way, the professional Authority succeeded in moderating the intentions of conservative politicians whose views were that there was no substitute for "father."

Education Policy: Section 46, Education (No. 2) Act, 1986, and Section 28, Local Government Act, 1988

Two additional pieces of legislation, also with implications for lesbian and gay families and the enforcement of heterosexuality, occurred in the field of education. Both were responses to initiatives being developed by a handful of Labour local authorities in the mid-1980s to eradicate discrimination faced by lesbian and gay employees and residents and to make council provision more responsive to their needs.[10] Despite limited implementation, the publicization of these and other "loony left" policies by the mass media and the right led to an explosive backlash. One particular policy occasioning much wrath was that of "positive images"—an attempt to eradicate anti-lesbian and gay discrimination and to provide positive educational materials within the school system.

Government hostility to local council lesbian and gay initiatives was evident from early on. Section 46 of the 1986 Education (No 2) Act, enacted two years prior to the notorious Section 28, mandated, among other things, that local authorities take reasonable steps to ensure sex education be provided within a framework that had "due regard to moral considerations and the value of family life." This was supplemented by a government circular (11/87). It stated that schools were to ensure children learned about "self-restraint" and the "physical, emotional, and moral risks of casual and promiscuous sexual behaviour."[11] Furthermore, "pupils should be helped to appreciate the benefits of stable married and family life and the responsibilities of parenthood." Homosexuality had its own section: "There is no place in any school in any circumstances for teaching which advocates homosexual behaviour, which presents it as the 'norm,' or which encourages homosexual experimentation by pupils" (Section 22).

Shortly after the passage of the Education Act, 1986, the Earl of Halsbury unsuccessfully proposed a Private Member's Bill in the Lords to prohibit local governments from "promoting homosexuality" in schools. Later, a similar bill was resubmitted, becoming Section 28 of the Local Government Act 1988. The section declared that local government could neither intentionally "promote homosexuality" generally in their work nor, more specifically, "promote the teaching in any maintained school of the acceptability of homosexuality as a *pretended family relationship*" [emphasis added].

Parliamentary and Expert Arguments

Conservative Discourse

In advocating the regulation of sexuality and families, conservative approaches were constructed around four key themes. First, the family is the foundation upon which civilization is built, "family" meaning the marriage of a man and a woman, and their children. Second, the welfare of children is best furthered by this unit; any other arrangement causes harm to children and to society. Third, lesbians and gay men are incapable of providing proper role modeling for children; this, in conjunction with their dubious motivations for wanting children, renders them unsuitable as parents. Whilst these last two themes are interdependent, it is helpful to examine their subjects—the child and the parent—separately. Finally, law should be employed as a means of compelling compliance with sexual norms:

> The family is the basis of all civilization. It is also the basis of life itself. All life—people and animals as well—was created by God. It is also the result of a union between a mother and a father. So the child comes into the world as part of a trinity. It emerges as part of a family. If the child is

lucky, there are also brothers and sisters, grandparents, uncles and aunts and all the glorious host of kinsmen, noble and otherwise. It is the love and happiness engendered in our own families which protect and nurture us all and enable us to go out into the world and try to share that love and happiness with others.[12]

These comments, by Baroness Strange, took place during a House of Lords debate on "the family" in 1989. Similar contributions were made in a House of Commons "family policy debate" the subsequent year. On both occasions, members from all sides of the political spectrum echoed the Baroness's sentiments, positions given specificity in the legislative debates around the HUFEA, the Education Act, 1986, and the Local Government Act of 1988 (Section 28).

During the HUFEA debates, various members argued that alternative insemination services violated the sanctity of family and marriage, their views expressing a deep-rooted, conservative Christianity.[13] Right-wing Christians in Britain and North America maintain that the heterosexual nuclear unit is God-ordained; any other arrangement is both evil and dangerous. Explicit in this familial ideology is the articulation of "family" with "nation." Conservative Christians often support restrictive immigration and nationality laws, and part of their opposition to lesbian and gay families is rooted in this traditional need to fortify the Christian home and nation against perceived enemies— within and without. This foundation, however, is usually *publicly* tempered by a more professionally oriented discourse.

In the Lords debate on the Halsbury Bill (precursor of Section 28), Baroness Faithfull claimed to speak for the "sake of the children" who, she argued, need the experience of living alongside a stable father and mother.[14] Like Baroness Faithfull, Lady Saltoun of Abernethy, speaking to her HUFEA amendment four years later, also deployed a child welfare discourse: "I am not really interested in morality, in the rights of women to have children, or in prevalent sexual mores. I am concerned with the best interests of children."[15] While she acknowledged that single women could make good parents, on the whole, she argued, such families inadequately served the child's best interests. For this, the presence of a father was necessary:

> The interests of those who cannot have children in the normal way and want them, and the interests of the children they may have are not necessarily compatible. Under these circumstances, surely the best interests of the children must be the paramount consideration. . . . Children learn primarily from example, by copying what they see. It is by example that a boy learns how to be a responsible husband and father and how to treat his own children in turn. It is by example that a girl learns how to be a wife, from seeing how her mother cares for her father. . . . It is for simi-

lar reasons that the Committee may consider that lesbian couples should not be eligible to receive AID or in vitro fertilization services.[16]

This view of the harm caused to children of nontraditional families was reiterated by conservative "experts." Less explicitly political, an array of medical, psychiatric, educational, and welfare professionals were mobilized to underpin the legislation of heterosexuality. According to one doctor, children of "virgins," for example, might grow up "with a jaundiced view" of sexual relationships.[17] Richard Whitfield, an education professor, wrote that

> for children to stand the best chance of thriving in our culture they need, ideally, to experience the unconditional love of a mother and a father figure who are committed both to the child and to each other. In this way, the youngster daily experiences role models from each gender, helping over a long period, often at margins of awareness, to promote the emergence of a secure sexual identity.[18]

During the "virgin births" scandal, Whitfield's views were disseminated by the press.[19]

Thus far, we have referred to the construction of the child's best interests in conservative parliamentary and "expert" debate and how this construction is rooted in conservative familial ideology. Related to although somewhat separate from this is the depiction of the nontraditional parent. During episodes such as the "virgin births" scandal, heterosexually defined women who declined intercourse were constructed as ill and in need of treatment. According to one psychologist interviewed at the time, "Women who seek to have children without ever having experienced a sexual relationship may be suffering from psychological problems which need treatment."[20]

The refusal of "virgins" (it is unclear whether this meant women wanting children without intercourse or women who had never had intercourse) to be heterosexually penetrated was presented as symptomatic of an underlying disorder or selfishness.[21] This attribution of selfishness to "virgin mothers" (and, in other debates, lesbians) proved a familiar refrain.[22] According to one clinic director, "we have decided not to treat single women outside stable relationships. On the issue of virgin mothers, I would question the motives of a woman who wanted a child but would not enter into a relationship with a man."[23]

This construction of virgins and lesbians is inextricably linked to the articulation of childlessness with infertility. In popular and medical texts, infertility is represented as a condition in need of treatment. This approach is encoded in the HUFEA, which explicitly defines clinic facilities as services for treatment. The assumption is that women are only childless through infertility. Thus, women who do not have children are pathologized. Yet this equation of childlessness with infertility cannot stand in the case of lesbians and virgins who are both fertile and wanting children. Deemed childless by choice, their decision to use medical facilities is seen as taking resources away from women who truly need them.

Underlying the idea that virgins and lesbians selfishly reproduce is the counterclaim that "normal" reproduction is socially beneficial, even altruistic. The "virgin mothers" panic brought out a seldom expressed corollary: that heterosexual intercourse is an obligation, a duty to god and nation, and that only those who perform their duty should reap the rewards (children). The *Daily Mail* headline, for example, decried this "scheme which strikes at the very heart of family life" by giving "women who have never had sex . . . the chance to have a baby."[24] Heterosexual sex has, in this view, nothing to do with women's pleasure. The lesbian or virgin is selfish because she represents the woman for whom pleasure supersedes duty. She will not voluntarily offer herself to satisfy heterosexual men's desires; nor will she assist in reproducing the status quo.

In addition to arguments reliant on constructions of family, child, and parent, others emphasized the immorality of homosexuality and the threat posed by the "permissive society"[25]:

> we have for several decades past been emancipating minorities who claimed that they were disadvantaged. Are they grateful? Not a bit. We emancipated races and got inverted racism. We emancipated homosexuals and they condemn heterosexism as chauvinist sexism, male oppression and so on. They will push us off the pavement if we give them a chance. I am, in their jargon, a homophone [*sic*], a heterosexist exploitationist. The whole vocabulary of the loony Left is let loose in a wild confusion of Marxism, Trotskyism, anarchism and homosexual terminology.[26]

Halsbury's comments explicitly construct an "us" and a "them." The "us" is the white (implicitly not a race), heterosexual population, while races and homosexuals constitute a homogeneous, threatening them (albeit as mutually exclusive categories).

While some on the right might have wished for the recriminalization of "private sphere" homosexual activity, others, such as Halsbury, simply argued that current policies were going too far. Not only were lesbians and gay men "increasingly aggressive," but their agenda was part of a larger one posing a challenge to the status quo, requiring far more from society than simply to be left alone in their bedrooms.

A key discursive strategy was to construct an imaginary past, free of degenerative practices and ideas. Today's Sodom and Gomorrah must be cleansed, the dangers posed by homosexuality eliminated. The

Earl of Halsbury, in moving his amendment prohibiting local authorities from "promoting homosexuality," described the threat at hand:

> Those [homosexuals] who make the worst of their situation are the sick ones who suffer from a psychological syndrome whose symptoms are as follows: first of all, exhibitionism; they want the world to know all about them; secondly, promiscuity; thirdly, proselytizing; they want to persuade other people that their way of life is the good one; fourthly, boasting of homosexual achievements as if they were due to and not in spite of sexual inversion; lastly, they act as reservoirs of venereal diseases of all kinds.[27]

Implicit in Halsbury's speech is (among other things) the equation of morality with societal stability. Patrick Devlin's argument of another era—that without a common morality society will disintegrate—is given new voice by those opposed to the public acceptance and acknowledgment of lesbian and gay sexuality.[28] Sex education was one area in which a "clearly moral framework" was crucial and, the need to present children with a heterosexual imperative key: "Discussing the ifs and buts of homosexuality and promiscuity is obviously dangerous . . . mentioning these subjects at such an early age will tempt a child to find out more and to put into practice at an early age what is best left to a much later age if one has to go down that devious path."[29] Law is not viewed here as a neutral, value-free mode of regulation. On the contrary, the role that the law plays in shaping social relations is recognized; as dominant ideology fragments and "new" practices and ideas come to the fore, the law must be seized and used as a weapon of restraint.

Liberal Discourse[30]

Conservative and liberal paradigms occupied, with few exceptions, the polarities of parliamentary debate. However, a liberal perspective leaves, for many feminists particularly, much to be desired. What is interesting about the political process is the extent to which liberalism becomes the only ideology publicly available to counter conservative attacks. Liberals addressed themselves directly to the two conservative themes discussed above: the family, including child welfare and parental suitability, and the relationship between law and morality. They also added a third element—equal rights.

Although the concept of family may have possessed a less exclusive meaning, liberals nonetheless attempted to outdo their conservative counterparts when it came to extolling familial virtues. A frequent tactic of progressive politicians was to demonstrate how Conservative economic policy had itself posed the greatest threat to the family. For example, in a 1989 House of Lords debate on the family, Lord Carter condemned those aspects of government policy that increased family, and particularly child, poverty.[31] Another peer noted how the Conservative government had presided over a massive increase in homelessness: "this debate has taken as its central theme the importance of the family . . . the family cannot thrive if it has no home . . . the Government have in my view been derelict in their duty toward the family by failing miserably to provide housing for the homeless and better conditions for the badly housed."[32] In this sense, then, liberals fundamentally diverged from conservatives by locating the primary responsibility for child welfare in the public sphere. The majority of the problems faced by children were due to inadequate public provision, not parental immorality or the lack of suitable role modeling.

Liberals therefore started from the premise that social reality did not reflect the rosy picture painted by conservatives. On the contrary, traditional families were as likely to be characterized by crisis as by stability, with children often not receiving the protection and support they were due: "Anyone objecting to homosexuals adopting or fostering children on the grounds that they might interfere with the children is mad. In most cases where children have been molested or sexually abused, the perpetrator has been a heterosexual male."[33]

Other MPs, often deploying the work of sympathetic experts,[34] acknowledged the proliferation of "new" family forms. Guy Barnett MP, for example, found the phrase "nuclear family not merely inaccurate but deeply offensive."[35] Another suggested the term family had "many definitions": "in my view, we should be considering not only the nuclear family but the single parent family, and the extended family, particularly among ethnic groups."[36] Yet, despite their location of social ills in the inadequacy of public provision, liberals nevertheless emphasized the importance of privacy when it came to addressing the relationship between law and morality.

In the Lords HUFEA debates, several speakers explicitly challenged conservative perspectives on the relationship between law and morality. Lord Ennals, for example, arguing against Lady Saltoun of Abernethy's HUFEA amendment, stated there must be preserved "for the individual an area of private morality in which the state may not intervene."[37] Or, as Lord McGregor of Durris put it, "However we define morality in these areas, we shall never be able to enforce it by law."[38] According to Simon Hughes MP in the 1987 Section 28 debates, adults were entitled to make choices so long as others were not harmed.[39]

Liberals' insistence upon a law-and-morality separation, while possibly helpful to lesbians and gay men in past debates concerning the criminal law regulation of sexual behavior, helps less with many contemporary demands. First, this separation is predicated upon homo-sexuality remaining private—*public* lesbian and gay sexual behavior ("flaunting it") has always been considered the law's business within liberal discourse.[40] Second, the issue, for lesbian and gay movements and their liberal supporters, is both one of *resisting* state intervention *and*, just as importantly, achieving an impact upon the character such intervention takes. Reproductive technologies, for example, will be, and arguably should be, regulated. What kinds of families, though, will such legislation condone? It is in response to such concerns that the third theme of the liberal approach emerges.

In the 1987–88 Section 28 debates, John Cunningham MP stated that the Labour party believed in equal rights and equal treatment for all people, including homosexuals, while Simon Hughes, a Liberal Democratic party MP, similarly argued that while there should not be discrimination in favor of lesbians and gay men, neither should they be denied equal treatment.[41] Within a liberal equal rights approach, re-liance is placed on notions of immutability. Sexual orientation is per-ceived as fixed, either prebirth or at an early age, contrasting sharply with a conservative position that emphasizes the fluidity of sexuality and the power of social factors to shape sexual behavior.

Conservative MP David Wilshire, in moving Section 28, argued that there was no "objective evidence" proving sexuality was im-mutable.[42] But Mark Fisher, a Labour party member, replied that les-bians and gay men no more chose their sexuality than heterosexuals chose theirs.[43] For left-winger Tony Banks, homosexuality was a "way of life;" it could not be promoted.[44] A just society does not discriminate against people for something they cannot help, especially where there is no evidence that others (in this case children) are harmed. However, within this pluralistic world view, life styles are *not* equal. Homosexu-ality is still second-rate. In both houses of Parliament, liberals were careful to note that, while opposing Section 28, they nevertheless dis-approved of the "promotion" of homosexuality.[45] On not one occasion, so far as we could discover, did a parliamentarian call into question the promotion of *heterosexuality.*

While liberalism has proved to be the most pragmatically suc-cessful approach for lesbians and gay men in the public sphere, its em-phasis on immutability makes it problematic for those (such as femi-nists) who argue that sexuality is above all a social relation, historically and culturally specific. Feminist theorists have argued that heterosex-uality is not a cross-cultural, biological norm but an institutional prac-tice that perpetuates unequal gender relations. Such an analysis can-not exist within a liberal framework that depoliticizes the construction of sexual attraction. Nor can there exist within this approach a recognition that for many lesbians, and some gay men, their sexuality is a conscious political and social decision and not a manifestation of some innate sexual essence that simply needs to be revealed.

The equal rights theme reveals a tension underlying liberal contributions. On the one hand, it is argued that lesbians and gay men deserve equality. However, liberals leave unaddressed the legislative promotion of heterosexuality. Were they to consider this, they might then be compelled to argue that homosexuality has a right to be *equally promoted*. The failure of the liberal approach to suggest this and its reliance instead on immutability (no one can be persuaded to be homosexual) leave to conservatives the view that sexuality is fluid, that human sexual expression may not be fixed, and that gender identity is precarious. The result is that these ideas only find public expression in a reactionary, unprogressive mode.

Legislative Origins

So far, our discussion has focused on parliamentary and "expert" texts. Yet these, while important, are not sufficient to understand either the form or reasons for the Conservative legislative agenda on sexuality and parenting. Various questions remain unanswered. To what extent were Section 28 and the HUFEA part of Thatcher's moral agenda? What role did right-wing pressure play in the process? What were the practical concerns involved? These are the questions to which we now turn.

Pragmatism

The need to address practical considerations was most evident in the enactment of the HUFEA. The legislation was the outcome of a long process of policy deliberation concerning reproductive technologies—a "growth industry" in need of regulation. Yet to what extent did this apply to anonymous donor insemination? Arguably, its inclusion in the scheme was more an attempt to bring all the infertility services provided by clinics together under one regulatory framework than a fear of technology out of control. There was also a perceived need to sort out questions of paternity: When do sperm donors become legal fathers? How should social fatherhood be legislated? The role and status of men were matters of primary concern. Indeed, Carol Smart has argued that debates over regulating new technologies must be seen within a context of a growing emphasis on fatherhood and paternal rights.[46]

It is also possible that the government's approach to donor insemination—"balancing interests" rather than explicitly prohibitive—reflected lessons learned from the mass mobilizations against Section 28. Senior Conservatives were apparently embarrassed over the furor occasioned by the section's passage.[47] In subsequent legislative developments, such as the HUFEA, the government aimed for an approach that could be validated through professional rather than explicitly political discourse.

Moral Panics

Various writers have noted the frequent call for legislation in response to media-accentuated moral panics.[48] One motivation for Section 28 was clearly the hysteria surrounding the perceived activities of "loony left" councils. The escalation of this fear, completely out of proportion to any actual antidiscriminatory activity, has been well documented.[49] No doubt, the HIV/AIDS panic also played a significant role during this period. Section 28 was, arguably, an ill-conceived attempt by the government to look like it was "doing something." At the same time, the panic itself was partly organized *by* central government to discredit local Labour authorities shortly before the 1987 national election and to woo a section of Labour's traditional constituency.[50]

In the case of the "virgin births" controversy, one can speculate whether, had it exploded one or two months earlier, the HUFE Authority's draft Code of Practice would have looked any different. As it was, the draft was fully prepared (though not yet released) prior to the story hitting the media. Certainly, the Authority did not respond to the panic by delaying and rewriting the guidelines. Furthermore, the final copy of the code might arguably be said to be less severe than its earlier draft. In this case, there is no evidence that panic affected regulatory developments.

The "Moral Right"

Although the tabloid press and media generally were important in drawing attention to "virgin births" and "homosexual lessons," their production of such texts needs to be seen within the context of right-wing pressure within and without the Conservative party. Right-wing demands for legislation that would proscribe homosexual culture, behavior, and parenting and prescribe married, heterosexual, monogamous, Christian life were highly influential. However, the agendas of the government and the moral right do not always coincide. Section 28 was not supported by the government when the right first introduced it as a Private Member's Bill in the House of Lords prior to the 1987 general election. The government argued then that the clause was unnecessary and refused to promote its passage through the House,[51] despite later supporting its reintroduction in the Commons shortly after reelection. Government ambivalence was similarly apparant in the case of the earlier Education (No. 2) Act, 1986 and the 1987 Department of Education interpretive circular, which spelled out the moral right's ideological position more explicitly than the government was prepared to codify in statute.

Section 35 of the HUFEA represents a similar compromise with the moral right. The wording of Section 35(5), including the phrase "a child's need for a father," was only introduced as a government amendment subsequent to the failed Ashbourne and Abernethy amendments in the House of Lords. The addition of "a child's need for a father" symbolizes, again, the appeasement of "pro-family" neo-conservatives. However, the exclusion of self-insemination from the regulatory framework, as well as representing a realistic assessment of the difficulties of enforcement, similarly constituted a refusal by the government to go to the lengths demanded by some right-wing sectors.

Nevertheless, Section 28 of the Local Government Act, 1988, Section 46 of the Education (No. 2) Act, 1986, and, less dramatically, Section 35 of the HUFEA, all represent, to varying degrees, ideological victories of the moral right. In the case of Section 28, writers have argued that it was intended as an appeasement by a government principally concerned with economic, as opposed to moral, restructuring.[52] A senior Tory is quoted as saying that it was "a piece of red meat which we have to throw to our wolves every now and then to keep them quiet."[53] Furthermore, an interpretive circular published shortly after the section's passage stated that "local authorities will not be prevented by this section from offering the full range of their services to homosexuals, on the same basis as to all their inhabitants, so long as they are not setting out to promote homosexuality."[54] It has been argued that this represented a significant undermining of the section.[55]

Yet, was it simply a matter of appeasement and compromise, or was Thatcherism a movement of the moral as well as the economic right? Margaret Thatcher was known to oppose same-sex criminal law reform.[56] In a speech to the 1987 Conservative Party Conference, she expressed dismay that "children who need to be taught traditional moral values are being taught they have an inalienable right to be gay."[57] Although many senior Conservatives prioritized economic as opposed to sexual and familial regulation, their views on such matters were nonetheless traditional. Thus, when the threat of an emergent homosexual counterhegemony was raised, they were prepared to support the ideologues and positions of the vocal "moral majority."

Thatcherite Social Policy

The Education Act, 1986 and Section 28 also need to be seen within the context of the right-wing education agenda in which they were embedded. Conservative education policy was one of the cornerstones of Thatcherism. Developed in the 1970s, it led in the mid-1980s to reforms that included the opportunity for schools to opt out of local authority control, the prohibition of education deemed "political," the entrenchment and formalizing of Christian education; and the imposition of a national testing program and curriculum. Many of these measures, including Section 28, were intended to restrict and curtail local authority power by shifting decision-making responsibility to the central government and other bodies. These reforms took advantage of popular fears about children's education, portraying "loony" local government as responsible for the introduction of absurd and dangerous educational policies.

Thatcher's agenda entailed an attack on the "new professionals"—teachers, social workers, municipal policy makers, and others were viewed as responsible for dangerous new ideas. Section 28 formed part of the right's program to undermine what they perceived to be professional "claptrap" and "half-baked theories." In their place "parental common sense" and "traditional ideas" were extolled by populists, politicians, and "experts" deploying traditional educational epistemologies. Thus, the interests of parents were articulated with those of conservative ideologues.

In contrast to this attack on education and welfare professionals, reproductive technology legislation, while subjecting medical professionals to legal regulation, did so within a context of deferring to their judgment. The HUFE Authority, the overseeing body, is composed of professionals and laypersons, not politicians.[58] The government approach in this area has been to respect the integrity, knowledge, and expertise of, primarily, the legal and medical professions—an approach reflecting the power inequalities and ideological nature of different professionals and their discursive fields.

However, one similarity between Section 28 and Section 35(5) of the HUFEA is that both fit squarely within Thatcherism's social policy agenda for the family. The Conservatives' extensive assault on the welfare state, including a massive privatization program, has resulted in an increasing burden of social provision falling to families. The removal of many long-standing state supports for the young, elderly, ill, and disabled has forced people to look to their families for sustenance. This has necessitated a concomitant resuscitation of familial ideology—the idealization of the heterosexual nuclear unit.[59] The primacy, significance, and naturalness of the family had to be reasserted to render familial responsibility inevitable, and, importantly, necessary to a morally healthy nation. Any failure of families to provide adequately is then posited as the result of individual family dysfunction or abnormality, and any grouping of individuals not fitting the nuclear model, such as lesbian and gay households, are similarly identified.

Conclusion

In this essay, we have highlighted the political context within which recent legislative initiatives in sexuality, parenting, and reproduction have taken place. All of these statutory provisions are both responses to and determinants of the struggles of diverse groupings within various social and political arenas. While Section 28 was an explicit example of a right-wing victory, its very emergence was a response to the increasing visibility and strength of lesbian and gay communities. Our study also suggests that law does not reflect one homogeneous, identifiable interest. Rather, legal regulation embodies contradiction and compromise, and is often directed toward achieving conflicting goals.

One of the key themes of this essay has been the emergence of legal regulation in different spheres. Sandra Bartky, discussing Michel Foucault's work, argues that such developments are characteristic of modernity, an era in which the exercise of power has become increasingly anonymous.[60] Yet is this the case here? Our essay has revealed the ways in which legal measures and regulation have intervened as dominant ideology loses force. Arguably, ideology is one of the most anonymous technologies of power, less easy to contest than legal regulation. However, as alternative practices and ideas gain currency, dominant ideology needs to be supplemented by other techniques. Section 28, for example, was only considered essential once schools and local government education departments began developing a progressive sexual politics. The HUFEA's "need for a father" criterion would be gratuitous and unnecessary if women only reproduced within the nuclear unit.

In discussing the state's response to lesbian and gay demands for publicly provided benefits and status, the emphasis on public support for individual attainment of the good life undermines the traditional liberal separation of public and private. Sex education and reproductive provision fuse two spheres central to the state's regulation of homosexuality. Conservatives, of course, recognize this; hence their call for the legal enforcement of traditional morality in all spheres of life, to stop, as the Earl of Halsbury put it, being "pushed off the pavement."

Liberals deny such a threat exists. Instead, there is room enough in their society to accommodate difference, particularly when such difference is immutable. Yet, difference is only accommodated to the extent that "the other" becomes "the same." Even when restrictive laws are given liberal interpretations, the acceptability of lesbians and gay men may be predicated upon their reproduction of dominant behaviors, values, and culture. The white, middle-class, "coupled" lesbian, with a well-paid, secure job and a spacious home, is more likely to receive treatment services than the ex-prostitute, refused them in one case.[61] As some lesbians and gay men gain admittance into the status quo, familial ideology may be strengthened and others may be further marginalized. These remain important issues in any discussion of state intervention in family life.

NOTES

1. Lord Ashbourne, Lords, *Hansard*, February 6, 1990, col. 767.

2. *The Daily Mail* (London), March 11, 1991.

3. *Report of Inquiry into Human Fertilization and Embryology* (London: H.M.S.O., 1984).

4. Department of Health and Social Security, *Human Fertilization and Embryology: A Framework for Legislation*, Cm. 251 (London: H.M.S.O., 1987).

5. In terms of research, Section 3 permits licensed embryo research up to 14 days gestation.

6. Lords, *Hansard*, February 6, 1990, col. 788.

7. Section 28 of the HUFEA establishes legal paternity. Briefly, there are two presumptions when sperm has been anonymously donated and a woman has given birth as a result: (1) The husband or male common law partner is presumed to have consented to the "procedure" and, in the absence of contrary evidence, acquires paternity; and (2) an anonymous sperm donor is not the legal father.

8. Human Fertilization and Embryology Authority, *Code of Practice: Consultation Document*, March 1991, clause 3.13. Clause 3.10, however, stated that prospective clients must be given a "fair and unprejudiced assessment."

9. Ibid., Section 3.16(b) (Section 3.13 in draft).

10. See Davina Cooper, *Sexing the City: Lesbian and Gay Politics Within the Activist State* (London: Rivers Oram, 1994).

11. Department of Education, London: Circular No. 11, 1987.

12. Baroness Strange, Lords, *Hansard*, November 29, 1989, col. 478–80.

13. "The heart of the problem is that Britain has ceased to be a Christian country." Julian Brazier, Commons, *Hansard*, March 16, 1990, col. 826. Such sentiments, for various reasons, are rarely expressed in public forums. See Didi Herman, *Rights of Passage: Struggles for Lesbian and Gay Legal Equality* (Toronto: University of Toronto Press, 1994), chap. 6.

14. Lords, *Hansard*, December 18, 1986, col. 329.

15. Ibid., February 6, 1990, col. 801.

16. Ibid., col. 788–89.

17. Quoted in J. Mullin, "Wish to Avoid Sex May Hide Neurosis," *The Guardian*, London, March 12, 1991.

18. Richard Whitfield, "Don't Give In to Pressure," *Community Care*, January 24, 1991, p. 16.

19. See A. Sage, "Can Gay Couples Be Good Parents?" *Independent on Sunday*, London, March 10, 1991. See also psychologist Joan Freeman quoted in "Is This Right for Children?" *Sunday Express*, September 30, 1990.

20. Quoted in Mullin, "Wish to Avoid Sex."

21. Conversely, by implication, that having *once* been penetrated, having the status of nonvirgin equipped women for motherhood. One of the few feminist contributions reported by the media was that of psychologist Sheila Kitzinger: "The unpenetrated woman has not been possessed. A woman has proved that all she needs is access to semen, and it's hitting men where it hurts." *The Guardian*, March 13, 1991, quoted in Jill Radford, "Immaculate Conceptions," *Trouble and Strife* 21 (1991): 8.

22. Rebecca Klatch's study of right-wing women in the United States shows the frequent articulation of feminism with selfishness in their world view. See her *Women of the New Right* (Philadelphia: Temple University Press, 1987). See also J. Isaac, "The New Right and Moral Society," *Parliamentary Affairs* 43 (1990): 209; and Sarah Franklin, "Deconstructing Desparateness: The Social Construction of Infertility in Popular Representations of New Reproductive Technologies," in Maureen McNeil, ed., *The New Reproductive Technologies* (London: Macmillan, 1990), p. 200.

23. Peter Brinsden, medical director of Bourn Hall clinic, quoted in *The Guardian*, March 12, 1991.

24. Cited in Radford, "Immaculate Conceptions," p. 8

25. Earl of Halsbury, Lords, *Hansard*, February 6, 1990, col. 795. See also Earl of Lauderdale, ibid., p. 794.

26. Earl of Halsbury, Lords, *Hansard*, December 18, 1986, col. 310.

27. Ibid. Halsbury notes his comments only apply to male homosexuals.

28. Patrick Devlin, *The Enforcement of Morals* (Oxford: Oxford University Press, 1965).

29. Peter Bruinvels, Commons, *Hansard*, October 21, 1986, col. 1066.

30. By "liberal," we do not mean members of the Liberal Democratic party but, rather, those holding pluralist, welfare-oriented perspectives—including members of the Labour party.

31. Lords, *Hansard*, November 29, 1989, col. 439–42.

32. Ibid., col. 457.

33. Labour MP Joan Lestor, quoted in "Is This Right for Children?"

34. See, e.g., Susan Golumbuk et al., "Children in Lesbian and Single Parent Households: Psychosexual and Psychiatric Appraisal," *Journal of Child Psychology* (1983): 551.

35. Commons, *Hansard*, October 21, 1986, col. 1973.

36. Ibid., March 16, 1990, col. 808. See also Chris Smith MP's defense of pluralism and democracy in ibid., December 15, 1987, col. 1008.

37. Lords, *Hansard*, February 6, 1990, col. 791.

38. Ibid., col. 793.

39. Commons, *Hansard*, December 15, 1987, col. 994.

40. The oft-cited liberal H. L. A. Hart argued in favor of legal intervention to protect "ordinary citizens" from the "public affront" of homosexuality in *Law, Liberty, and Morality* (Oxford: Oxford University Press, 1963).

41. Commons, *Hansard*, December 15, 1987, col. 995–6, 992.

42. Quoted in Stephen Jeffrey–Poulter, *Peers, Queers, and Commons: The Struggle for Gay Law Reform from 1980 to the Present* (London: Routledge, 1991), p. 239.

43. Ibid. Labour MP Joan Ruddock commented that in "an all pervasive culture of heterosexuality," homosexuals struggle to become heterosexuals, but *"they do not succeed, of course."* Commons, *Hansard*, December 15, 1987, col. 1003. See also Frank Dubbs MP, ibid., May 8, 1987, p. 1014, col. 995–6.

44. Ibid., p. 1022.

45. See Labour Peer, Lord Graham of Edmonton, Lords, *Hansard*, December 18, 1986, col. 327; and Baroness David in the same debate, ibid.,

col. 331. See also Labour MPs Cunningham, Commons, *Hansard,* December 15, 1987, col. 1021; and Radice, ibid., October 21, 1986, col. 1061.

46. Carol Smart, " 'There Is of Course the Distinction Dictated by Nature': Law and the Problem of Paternity," in Michelle Stanworth, ed., *Reproductive Technologies: Gender, Motherhood, and Medicine* (Cambridge: Polity, 1987), p. 98.

47. See Jeffrey-Poulter, *Peers, Queers,* p. 227.

48. The pioneering work is Stanley Cohen's *Folk Devils and Moral Panics: The Creation of the Mods and Rockers* (London: MacGibbon & Kee, 1972).

49. See, e.g., Sue Sanders and Sue Spraggs, Section 28 and Education," in Carol Jones and Pat Mahoney, eds., *Learning Our Lines: Sexuality and Social Control in Education* (London: Women's Press, 1989). See also David Evans, "Section 28: Law, Myth, Paradox," *Critical Social Policy* 27 (1989–90): 85. A poll taken in 1988 at the time Section 28 was introduced showed that the percentage of people agreeing with the legalization of homosexual relations between consenting adults had dropped from 61% in 1985 to 48%. See Jeffrey–Poulter, *Peers, Queers,* p. 226. The effects of the HIV/AIDS panic must also be considered.

50. See Ken Jones, *Right-Turn: The Conservative Revolution in Education* (London: Hutchinson, 1989), chap. 1.

51. Government spokespeople contended that Halsbury's clause was too widely drawn. See Sanders and Spraggs, "Section 28."

52. See, e.g., Martin Durham, "The Thatcher Government and the Moral Right," *Parliamentary Affairs* 42 (1989): 59. See also N. Flynn, "The 'New Right' and Social Policy," *Policy and Politics* 17 (1989): 97.

53. Quoted in *Capital Gay,* London, March 18, 1988.

54. Cited in Jeffrey–Poulter, *Peers, Queers,* p. 227.

55. Ibid.

56. Ibid., p. 138.

57. Quoted in Evans, "Section 28," p. 74.

58. At the time of writing, the Authority had 19 members, 11 of whom were women. The dominant professions were law and the medical field of obstetrics and gynecology.

59. For analyses of welfare state issues under Thatcher, see generally John Clarke et al., eds., *Ideologies of Welfare: From Dreams to Disillusion* (London: Hutchinson Education, 1987). For discussions of familial ideology in the British context, see Robert Lee and Derrick Morgan, *Birthrights: Law and Ethics at the Beginning of Life* (London: Routledge, 1989), p. 150; Miriam David, "Moral and Maternal: The Family in the Right," in Ruth Levitas, ed., *The Ideology of the New Right* (Cambridge: Polity Press, 1986), p. 136.

60. Sandra Bartky, "Foucault, Femininity, and the Modernization of Patriarchal Power," in Irene Diamond and Lee Quinby, eds., *Feminism and Foucault* (Chicago: Northeastern University Press, 1988). For further discussion, see Davina Cooper, *Power in Struggle: Feminism, Sexuality and the State* (New York: New York University Press, 1995).

61. See *R. v. Ethical Committee of St. Mary's Hospital* [1988] 1 F.L.R. 512. Note that this case was not decided under the HUFEA.

NINE

The focus of much lesbian legal theorizing has been lesbian discrimination. Thus, theory and strategy about lesbians and the law have tended to be developed with a particular sort of lesbian in mind. In this essay, Ruthann Robson argues that, as a result of this focus, the specific context of lesbian criminal defendants and prisoners has been left unaddressed. With her article she seeks to begin a dialogue to remedy this situation. Robson, first considering lesbian criminality in the context of equality theory, then explores the construction of lesbian identity in criminal trials. In a final section she begins to envision a lesbian legal theory of criminal justice.

Convictions: Theorizing Lesbians and Criminal Justice

Ruthann Robson

THOSE of us engaged in the practice of lesbian legal theorizing have been disinclined to address the multitude of issues provoked by the lesbian as criminal defendant. In the explicitly sexual context, the dominant assumption has been that lesbians were rarely, if ever, prosecuted for sexual crimes; I have elsewhere argued that this assumption is mistaken.[1] In the nonexplicitly sexual context, two contradictory assumptions coexist. First, the pairing of the words "lesbians" and "criminal" is metaphorical at best,[2] with lesbians inhabiting a gendered realm of privatized tranquillity. Second, the pairing of these terms is stereotypical at worst, with lesbians being stock characters in films and fiction about vampires, prisons, and ax murders. Yet these assumptions are not the only deterrents to theorizing lesbians as criminal defendants. More importantly, conceptualizations of equality and identity often operate as obstacles to theorizing lesbians accused or convicted of nonsexual crimes. This piece is an attempt to articulate and confront these obstacles, as well as to begin a specifically lesbian legal theorizing of the relationships between lesbianism and criminal justice.

I am grateful to Victoria Brownworth for sharing her work, information, and insights on lesbians and murder. I am also grateful to participants who commented upon earlier portions of this work during presentations at CUSH (Columbia University Seminar on Homosexualities) and Colloquium CLAGS (Center for Lesbian and Gay Studies, City University of New York), as well as at the conference on Homosexualities and Social Sciences, New York. I am also grateful for the editorial comments of Didi Herman and Carl Stychin.

180

The Politics of Equality

Politically, it has seemed most urgent for lesbian, gay, and bisexual legal theorists to theorize equality, with the result that many other projects are relegated to a subordinate status. The political importance of theorizing equality, however, is not only an obstacle in terms of allocating energies and resources, for the theorizing of lesbians as criminal defendants may be incompatible with a political agenda of achieving equality.

To theorize legal equality is to theorize the necessity of a departure from legal censure, especially the criminal penalties that have attached to lesbianism. The criminalization of lesbians through statutes that outlaw our sexual expressions is often considered the foundation upon which our discrimination rests. In cases involving the custody of children, for example, the existence of a sodomy statute supports the cross-examination of the lesbian parent regarding her sexual conduct and a judicial finding that she is an admitted felon as well as a sexual deviant. Repeal of the so-called sodomy statutes has thus been an explicit goal of the lesbian and gay legal reform movement: Distance from criminality is a necessary condition of equality.

The pursuit of equality has a rhetorical inconsistency with criminality. By focusing on equality, the lesbian and gay civil rights movement has sought to present images of what I call "but for" lesbians, who, "but for" their lesbianism, are "perfect." These "but for" images of lesbians are intended to contradict the pathological depictions of lesbians advanced by conservatives. However, conservatives have evinced the ability to pathologize even these "but for" images, often relying upon lesbian- and gay-produced theorizing, cultural production, and research. For example, lesbian and gay work on the economic status and political power of our communities is routinely harnessed against antidiscrimination laws in a strategy with disturbing similarities to stereotypical anti-Semitism.[3] Such a climate understandably produces a reluctance to theorize on issues so easily manipulated by conservatives. While our own theorizing might attribute the disproportionate number of lesbians on death row in the United States[4] to social biases and discrimination, conservative explanations would certainly link lesbianism and murder as social—and moral—pathologies, both deserving state condemnation through legal mechanisms.

The "but for" lesbian is not merely a rhetorical strategy; she is necessary doctrinally, especially as discrimination theory has developed in the United States. In the relatively rare event that there exists a legal bar to discrimination on the basis of sexual orientation, a discrimination plaintiff must demonstrate that "but for" her lesbianism, she would have been granted the benefit, such as housing or employment. The lesbian with a criminal conviction is not a preferred plaintiff under these circumstances. As employers and others become more sophisticated, the articulation of an acceptable reason to discriminate becomes more important. A criminal conviction is not only socially unacceptable, it is enshrined in the positive law of many jurisdictions: Conviction of a felony can foreclose the right to vote and own a firearm, and is admissible as evidence of veracity. Thus, the lesbian "criminal" is inconsistent with particular litigation to achieve equality, just as a more general focus on lesbian criminality is inconsistent with the overall rhetorical strategy of normalization to achieve equality.

The overarching nature of equality discourse is also implicated in a propensity to conceptualize lesbians as victims (persons being subjected to homophobic violence) rather than as possible perpetrators of violence: rights for innocent victims are much more palatable than special rights for morally culpable actors. Even violence between lesbians is often articulated in terms of equality: The battered lesbian is entitled to the same social services, legal remedies, and criminal defenses as her heterosexual counterpart. The lesbian perpetrator remains relatively untheorized, except to the extent that she is implicitly subjected to an equality claim that she should be treated as her heterosexual counterpart—the male batterer—and prosecuted to the full extent of the law. She must thus be delesbianized: She is a "common criminal," a "stranger," a "man." In the context of criminal justice, our theoretical and political energy is directed almost exclusively to the lesbian we can valorize as the victim.

Even when a lesbian perpetrator is theorized, she tends to be recast as a victim. The case of Annette Green is illustrative. Green is reportedly the first American lesbian allowed to raise a battering defense in the prosecution for the murder of her lover. The judge accepted the defense argument that battered "woman" meant battered "person," thus allowing evidence of battering. The prosecutor argued that the battering defense was inappropriate, despite his admission that Green had been "battered. She was shot at before by the victim. She had a broken nose, broken ribs." The jury rejected the battering defense summarily, taking only two-and-a-half hours to deliberate, which included the time necessary to agree upon a jury foreperson. One interpretation of the failure of the battering defense in the case of a lesbian is due to a reluctance to believe that lesbians can be victims.[5]

The lack of success of victimization as a trial strategy for individual lesbians is certainly worth exploring. However, I am interested in the import of the strategy's insistence on a formal and neutral version of equality—as well as further reifying the already rigid American model of equality—that rejects (or hopelessly distorts) previous theoretical formulations of domestic violence that rely upon a gendered dynamic of power. In the convoluted scenario exemplified by Annette Green, the perpetrator—this time the lesbian who has been murdered—is again relegated to the realm of the untheorizable.

The situation of Green as well as many other lesbian criminal defendants demonstrates the disjuncture at the metatheoretical level between equality paradigms and criminal justice concerns. Theorizing lesbians involved in the criminal justice system does not fit neatly into equality structures, because there is no congenial category of similarly situated persons who are consistently being afforded more favorable treatment. Feminists have confronted a similar problem in attempting to theorize female criminals; the male criminal is not an appealing normative category and may even be afforded less favorable treatment in some circumstances.[6] Further, many feminists have correctly identified equality itself as a problem, rather than a solution, for women. For example, women accused of murdering their male partners could rarely meet the classic male-defined criteria for self-defense. In response, feminists developed the battered-woman-syndrome defense, the same defense Green sought unsuccessfully to translate into the lesbian context.

Despite its problems, equality retains a fundamental appeal. Some feminist legal theorists have, for example, criticized the battered-woman-syndrome defense on the basis that it is predicated upon (and therefore perpetuates) female inequality.[7] Some feminist criminologists have posited an equality, or liberation, theory of female criminality linking women's claims for equality with hypothesized increases in women's criminal activity. Empirical findings that women are prone to be convicted more frequently, receive harsher sentences, and remain incarcerated for longer periods validate the theoretical subject; just as similar empirical findings regarding lesbians in comparison to nonlesbian women validate the theoretical subject. Such invocations of equality suggest their own problems: The battered women's syndrome defense has assisted some women; the liberation theory is consistent with an anti-equality backlash; and contrary or inconclusive empirical data trivialize any theoretical inquiry.

The problems and appeals of theorizing equality have been articulated by feminists as the sameness/difference conundrum. This conundrum also structures lesbian/gay legal theorizing and strategizing.[8] As many have argued, this conundrum, with its concomitant requirement of rights, often rigidifies our theorizing and stalls our activism. Such arguments have a magnified resonance in the criminal justice context. In criminal law, the other side of the equality equation is always the state—not other criminal defendants.[9] Thus, we must be especially skeptical of the capacity of civil rights equality discourse to dominate our theorizing and our ultimate goals in the criminal context.

In one circumstance, however, the politics of equality should be given more attention rather than less in the criminal justice context. The theorizer and the theorized subject occupy a vexing relation of inequality. By theorizing, we risk exploiting and sensationalizing real lesbians involved in ugly and tragic events who often face prolonged incarceration. Such theorizing inures to the benefit of the relatively insulated and privileged academic or other writer and ultimately entertains (often through educative pleasure) the audience.

The most flagrant example is Aileen Wuornos, known (incorrectly) as the first female serial killer.[10] Even to attempt to theorize about her is to risk further exploiting and sensationalizing a person who has been so repetitiously exploited and sensationalized that her very exploitation is sufficiently notorious to warrant a documentary film: *Aileen Wuornos: The Selling of a Serial Killer.* Most media accounts are not so self-conscious, of course. The media frenzy over Wuornos produced a superficially fictionalized American made-for-TV movie, *Overkill: The Aileen Wuornos Story,* as well as segments on U.S. TV tabloid shows such as "Hard Copy," "Dateline," and "Inside Edition," a segment on Court TV, talk show interviews, and pieces in popular magazines such as *People, Glamour,* and *Vanity Fair.*

Such media exploitation and sensationalization are not independent of the legal process. In Wournos's case, for example, how is the legal process affected when sheriffs and an (ex)lover/co-defendant are marketing the story; a public defender is negotiating a deal with a producer; a producer is paying childhood acquaintances for exclusive rights to their memories; and an "adopted mother" and new attorney are negotiating interviews from death row? Given such events, the court proceedings not only become secondary but may also become more subject to the forces of market than the interests of justice.[11] Unfortunately, Wuornos's situation is not unique.[12]

I am not suggesting that lesbian theorists occupy exactly the same position as those betraying confidences for movie deals. Neither am I suggesting that defendants or prisoners possess no agency, personality, or power, nor that lesbian theorists should refrain from theorizing about lesbian criminal defendants. What does worry me, however, is that our treatments of lesbians accused or convicted of murder will be distinct but not sufficiently different from more obvious types of exploitation. The power differentials between theorist and inmate are vast.

Our possible exploitation of theorized subjects is related to the political dangers of promoting an aestheticization of violence through
sensationalization. This aestheticization has attached to our cultural
notions of serial killers in particular and of murderers in general.[13] The
social problems derived from being a woman, from being a lesbian, and
from being economically disadvantaged are sublimated into a romanticized version of the outlaw. The outlaw is supremely individual, effectively erasing the social aspects of her condition. She can then be
romanticized through "true crime" books, media reports, and even theories. She becomes an excitingly individual problem solved through
resort to the rationalized procedures of criminal investigation and prosecution. Even as we criticize and theorize these criminal justice processes, her peril may still become our profit. Notions of equality, then,
in terms of this relation, continue to be useful and relevant.

Conceptualizing Identities

In addition to the political and ethical problems with theorizing lesbians and criminal justice, there are methodological problems that are
concretized versions of the postmodernist problematics of identity that
have so preoccupied lesbian and "queer" theorizing. The first layer is
the problem of identifying a lesbian presence in newspaper reports,
trial transcripts, and appellate opinions; what criteria do we use? For
example, the identification of lesbians on death row in the United
States depends upon an (implicit) articulation and application of operative criteria. Of the 17 women who are "implicated as lesbians" by
Victoria Brownworth, only a few have consistently maintained a lesbian self-identity before the circumstances leading to their conviction,
during the trial and related proceedings, and as prisoners on death row.
While sexual identity is arguably always socially constructed, it is difficult to fathom more "constructing" circumstances than the threat of
being executed. In other words, if one's very life is at stake, it seems
one might reconceptualize one's identity to comport with identities
that maximize the chance of survival. At the very least, living on death
row, isolated from previous communities and intimacies, might cause
one to change one's sexual identity.

Any self-identity must always be evaluated in the context of the
relevance of lesbian identity at trial. Lesbian identity can be important
as part of the prosecution's theory of the case. In the example of murder, the importance of the defendant's lesbian identity can vary with
the gender of the victim. If the victim is a woman, then the (lesbian)
defendant committed the crime out of sexual passion: The victim was
the defendant's lover, former lover, or sexual threat to the defendant's

relationship. If the victim is male, then the (lesbian) defendant committed the crime out of her antipathy for men.

A few recent murder prosecutions in the United States demonstrate this. In Annette Green's case, the prosecutor secured her conviction for the murder of her lover by stressing the defendant's intimate relationship to the victim, alluding to sexual jealousy rather than self-defense as the motive for Green's violence. In the cases of Aileen Wuornos and Ana Cardona, both presently on Florida's death row for murdering males, the lesbian-as-man-hater approach is never explicitly articulated but virtually floats from the transcript pages. Thus, sexualized banalities of lesbians—and women in general—as jealously possessive ("hell hath no fury") or as man-haters may fluctuate with the gender identity of the victim, but can be marshaled toward a finding of guilt.

Another problematic aspect of lesbian identity as deployed in prosecutions is its proof. In the cases of Green, Wuornos, and Cardona, the defendant's lesbianism was not contested by the defense. In cases in which the defendant does contest her lesbian identity, the prosecutor must prove it in order to sustain that portion of the theory of its case. In the absence of a living lesbian lover who can testify to the existence of her relationship with the defendant—an issue discussed below—the evidence used to prove lesbianism is extremely troublesome and clichéd. One type of evidence is that of gender conformity. The defendant "dressed like a man, kept her hair cut like a man, wore men's clothing, including men's shoes."[14] While this strategy may become less effective in contemporary urban courtrooms, many women remain imprisoned for crimes proved in part by such references. Another type of evidence is that of nonheterosexuality. The defendant has no apparent heterosexual activity—no "boyfriend"—so must therefore be a lesbian. This strategy may be gaining ascendancy, if its popularity outside of the criminal context is any indication.[15]

Defining and applying criteria for lesbian identity do not entirely resolve the methodological issues posed by identity problems. An additional difficulty arises from determining the relevance of lesbian identity. This question is usually posed to me as, "Are you saying that these women are convicted *because* they are lesbians?" While I cannot sustain any claim of legal causation, it would also belie credulity to maintain that lesbianism plays no role in convictions. One of the few empirical studies that has been done concludes that lesbians are more likely to be convicted and serve longer sentences than heterosexual women.[16] The statistical abnormality of the number of women "implicated as lesbians" on death row in the United States is also probative.[17] As one death row expert has cautiously opined, "all other things being equal, a female offender's lesbianism would be a disadvantage rather than an advantage in the capital punishment process."[18]

Nevertheless, numerical correlations are ultimately unsatisfactory for theorizing lesbians in the criminal justice system. Problems of methodology include not only defining lesbian identity but isolating lesbianism as a factor. Similar to other lesbians, a lesbian criminal defendant is not exclusively a lesbian. Statistically, a lesbian who is a criminal defendant is probably also a woman of color and disadvantaged economically.[19] Positing ethnic, racial, or class status as the cause of prosecution and conviction is facile; however, empirical data that point to the statistical overrepresentation of disempowered groups within the criminal justice system confirm a social observation. There is little reason to suspect that lesbianism operates radically differently from other minority identities as a derationalizing, dehumanizing wedge between the criminal defendant and the criminal justice system as embodied by prosecutor, judge, and jury.

In addition to its connection with other identities, lesbianism is difficult to isolate as a consistent factor within the criminal justice system, because crimes and their trials are exceedingly particularized. Variables include the circumstances of the crime, the situations of the defendant and victim, and the location of the trial. The manner in which lesbianism is deployed may be inconsistent with its deployment in a different trial or even within the same trial. The criminal defendant may not be the only incarnation of lesbian identity, and the prosecution may also have to grapple with lesbianism. In some instances, the victim may be implicated as a lesbian; the prosecutor must thus maintain that a crime against such a person is worth punishing. In other instances, the prosecution's star witness may be a lesbian, in which case the prosecution must maintain that she is credible. In such situations, neither the prosecution nor defense strategy can consist of a simple condemnation (or valorization) of lesbian existence. Thus, it becomes necessary to differentiate between good lesbians (worthy of protection and believable) and bad lesbians (worthy of punishment and disbelief).

As used by the prosecution, the tropes manipulated to differentiate between good lesbians and bad lesbians demonstrate an amazing versatility.[20] One of the most interesting manipulations occurred in the prosecution of Ana Cardona for the murder of her child. Cardona was portrayed as a feminized, attractive, and popular lesbian as contrasted with her (former) lover, Olivia Gonzalez-Mendoza, who was portrayed as mesmerized by Cardona. Such a construction reverses the stereotypical one of identifying the bad lesbian as the more "male"-identified partner, lack of gender conformity being a sign of deviance, and maleness being an indicator of a propensity toward violence.[21] Interestingly, however, the construction of Ana Cardona was consistent with the *femme fatale* trope so prominent in murder prosecutions of heterosexual women.

Further, the *femme fatale* construction was conjoined in the Cardona case with another trope prominent in murder prosecutions of heterosexual women: the bad mother.[22] For although the defense argued that the actual murderer of the child was Gonzalez-Mendoza and although there was testimony to support such an argument (especially at the separate penalty phase of the trial, in which the jury considered the imposition of the death penalty), Cardona, as the biological mother of the victim, was the person prosecuted, convicted, and sentenced to death for a capital crime. The state attorney offered Gonzalez-Mendoza a relatively generous plea bargain in exchange for her agreement to testify against Cardona. As an editorial from the *Miami Herald,* entitled "Deserved the Death Penalty," opined: "Cardona may have been the weaker partner in this union, but she was something that Gonzalez was not. She was Baby Lazaro's mother. She had the moral, legal, and every other responsibility for his welfare. She was not too weak to call the police, or HRS [the state agency responsible for child welfare], or somebody to come and get the baby."[23] In a similar case in California, the court held that the biological mother's "legal duty" to protect the child from the behavior of her lesbian lover satisfied the requirements for first-degree murder, although there was no evidence the biological mother ever physically harmed the child.[24]

Yet lesbianism itself may be understood as a trope in the murder prosecution of Cardona. From a different perspective, centering the trope of bad mother, lesbianism becomes an enhancement of that category. Especially in the press accounts of Cardona's trial, "lesbian" functioned as a suppressed intensifier, not unlike "cocaine-user" or "selfish." Similarly, in the prosecution and press coverage of Aileen Wuornos, "lesbian" functioned as an adjective for "prostitute," negating the possibility that Wuornos was any storybook "heart of gold" streetwalker. In both the Cardona and Wuornos cases, the lesbian identity amplified another identity—(bad) mother or prostitute—and became submerged into it.

This submersion of lesbian identity into another disparaged identity renders methodological purity impossible. Perhaps this submersion is a testament to the progress—or at least superficial shift—in contemporary life that renders it publicly treacherous to link lesbianism and murder as correlated pathologies. From a prosecutor's perspective, such an explicit linkage could risk losing the conviction (depending on the attitudes of the jurors, judge, or appellate judges) or some political prestige (depending on the attitudes of one's superiors, the local press, and voter population). Thus, as in discrimination discourse, legal actions that are detrimental to lesbians can appear to be only coincidentally related to their lesbian identities. The assertion of the irrelevance of lesbianism can serve the state's interest.[25]

The danger for lesbian legal theorists, reformers, and activists is that we will be daunted by methodological complications. Theorizing lesbians within the criminal justice system is a rather messy project given the blurring of lesbian identities and the relevance of such identities. Despite these methodological obstacles and the political and ethical problems previously discussed, I believe we must move toward theorizing the connections between lesbianism and criminal justice systems.

Toward a Lesbian Legal Theory of Criminal Justice

Identifying the obstacles to theorizing lesbians and criminal justice marks a preliminary path. Some of the equality-related problems of theorizing lesbians as criminals can be surmounted by a more expansive and radical interpretation of equality. The adages about a society being appropriately judged by its treatment of its criminals and freedom being realized only when the least fortunate are free are applicable to lesbian legal theorizing. Theorizing for the exclusive benefit of "but for" lesbians is partial at best. Thus, I maintain that we must attempt to theorize—and incorporate in our legal reform agendas—lesbians accused or convicted of crimes, including violent crimes. While the project of theorizing lesbians and criminal justice with "lesbian" as its centrifugal force arguably reinstates the previously discussed obstacles to theorizing, lesbian legal theory must take up the case of criminal justice in general and criminal defendants in particular. If it does not, then it risks being a "but for" theoretical position, which "but for" its lesbian emphasis, could be a normalized theory. Lesbian legal theory in this regard should take heed of feminist legal theory's history, a history considered by many to be marred by its accentuation of legal issues important to professionalized women. Nevertheless, in making criminal justice an important subject of inquiry and advocacy, we should not make equality a shibboleth that obscures the differences between civil rights and criminal justice.

Our ambitions of equality should also appropriately extend to our own work. Our theorizing must not only address but must reflect an attention to the possibilities of exploitation of criminal subjects. Further, we must be wary of the sensationalization and aestheticization of violence. Lesbians convicted of murder should not be glamorized as outlaws just as they should not be dismissed as irrelevant. Both options tempt the theorist, who can make particular crimes into a "sexy" presentation at a prestigious conference, or who can decide that the issue of crime is not one that deserves attention in the present scholarly climate. The issue of advocacy in cases in which lesbianism is implicated also merits examination. While I believe our practical intercession in the area is important, I remain uncertain about the terms and conditions of that intercession. As always, it seems to me that subjecting our own involvements to rigorous reflection is extremely vital. I am not suggesting a spectacle of mutual trashing, or even self-flagellation. Instead, I believe we can aspire to (if not always achieve) an ethical consciousness about the impact and consequences of our own stake as theorizers in the realm of criminal justice.

Methodological obstacles resulting from the imposition of identity criteria can be surmounted by adopting expansive definitions. I suggest that we should be less interested in the consistent or even articulated self-identified lesbian identities of various actors than in the specter of lesbianism whenever it is introduced into criminal justice proceedings, however obliquely. Ultimately, I am less concerned with whether an individual defendant is "really" a lesbian than with the manner in which her lesbianism becomes pertinent. The question I am thus interested in posing is: To what effect is lesbianism—as trope, stereotype, theory of the case, prejudice—articulated during the criminal process?

This expansive definition of identity also means that combinations of identities, be they ethnic, racial, economic, or constructed as similar to "prostitute" or "bad mother," also merit attention. Nevertheless, I believe we must be wary of the way in which other identities are utilized to trump lesbian identity. Lesbianism becomes irrelevant for those who argue that a particular case is really about prostitution or mothering or economic status. My wariness extends to the manner in which theories of the female offender can suppress considerations of lesbianism. My argument is certainly not that prostitution or mothering or economic status or gender is irrelevant. My argument is simply that we must consistently entertain the relevance of lesbianism.

Further, we must expand our methodologies. We must address complicated and particularized situations as such. While statistics can be useful, we must be wary of reasoning from statistics. We should also be wary of adopting criminal justice definitions as our own. The very definition of "crime" must be vigorously questioned. Given the erratic and bizarre ways in which our sexual acts have been and continue to be defined as crimes, we have more than sufficient cause to be similarly distrustful of other constructions of crime. In terms of our inquiries, we must also expand our concerns from the more easily researched and potentially glamorous crimes such as murder to the more mundane crimes of shoplifting, fraud, and drug offenses. We must also expand the subject positions to be theorized. While the purpose of this essay has been to focus upon lesbians as criminal defendants, the positions of all lesbians within the criminal justice system merit interrogation. The position of the lesbian as victim of a crime has received the most previous attention, and we should not abandon that project. However, I believe further expansion is necessary. For example, what does it mean for a lesbian to prosecute other lesbians within the criminal justice system?

Theorizing lesbians and criminal justice as a matter of lesbian legal theory must put lesbians at the center of its theoretical perspective. In this regard, such theorizing is no different from theorizing child custody or immigration as a matter of lesbian legal theory. At least as I conceptualize it, lesbian legal theory allows lesbians to become the centrifugal force around which all else is problematized.[26] Thus, in the criminal justice system context, it requires an examination of the entire system in light of its impact upon lesbians and its use of "lesbianism" in the achievement of its own goals. Such a project can benefit from the extensive work done by criminal justice critics, including feminist criminologists who continue to examine the complicated impact on women of the criminal justice system and its use of gendered stereotypes. If we consider the criminal justice system from the perspective of lesbianism—and more particularly of the survival of lesbians and lesbianism—what theoretical conceptualizations of criminal justice do we develop? If we apply our politics of equality and our interrogations of identity to the categories "criminal" and "justice" as rigorously as we have applied them to the category "lesbian," how do our theories of crime and punishment alter? Once we begin the serious task of taking criminal justice as a subject for lesbian legal theory, perhaps we will be able to intervene in actual criminal trials in ways that promote lesbian survival.

NOTES

1. Ruthann Robson, *Lesbian (Out)Law: Survival Under the Rule of Law* (Ithaca, NY: Firebrand Books, 1992), pp. 29–45.

2. The power of this perception was demonstrated to me by another gay/lesbian legal scholar who assumed that my presentation entitled "Lesbians as Criminals" concerned lesbians and child custody.

3. In the legal literature, this argument was recently made in Robert Duncan, "Who Wants to Stop the Church: Homosexual Rights Legislation,

Public Policy, and Religious Freedom," *Notre Dame Law Review* 69 (1994): 393, 407–11.

4. There are approximately 2,887 persons on death row—convicted of a capital crime and sentenced to death—in the United States. Of this number, 41 are women (approximately 1.4%); however, of the 41 women approximately 17 are 'implicated' as lesbians (approximately 41%). See Victoria Brownworth, "Dykes on Death Row," *The Advocate*, June 15, 1992, pp. 62–64.

5. Green's defense attorney, William Lasley, believes that the verdict is explainable by homophobia. Lasley also reports that prospective jurors were heard expressing the desire to be selected as jurors in order to "hang that lesbian bitch" and that Green was subjected to homophobic treatment by state personnel.

The statements of the prosecutor, Assistant State Attorney Bob Johnson, are quoted in *Gay Community News*, September 17–23, 1989, p. 1. The prosecutor also charged Green with the highest degree of murder allowable under the applicable law, despite circumstances that comprise classic examples of lower degrees of murder, such as battering, mutual fighting, intimate relation, and diminished capacity (because of alcohol). I further discuss this case in Robson, *Lesbian (Out)Law*, pp. 158–60.

6. The feminist literature on female offenders is vast. Important works include: Freda Alder, *Sisters in Crime: The Rise of the New Female Criminal* (New York: McGraw Hill, 1975); Susan S. M. Edwards, *Women on Trial* (Manchester: Manchester University Press, 1984); Coramae Richey Mann, *Female Crime and Delinquency* (Birmingham: University of Alabama Press, 1984); and Anne Worrall, *Offending Women: Female Lawbreakers and the Criminal Justice System* (London and New York: Routledge, 1990). A comprehensive anthology including women as offenders, victims, and workers is Barbara Raffel Price and Natalie J. Sokoloff, *The Criminal Justice System and Women*, 2nd ed. (New York: McGraw Hill, 1995). A useful overview of two decades of the literature occurs in Sally S. Simpson, "Feminist Theory, Crime, and Justice," *Criminology* 27(4) (1989): 605–31.

7. See, e.g., Phyllis Crocker, "The Meaning of Equality for Battered Women Who Kill Men in Self-Defense," *Harvard Women's Law Journal* 8 (1985): 121; and Elizabeth M. Schneider, "Describing and Changing: Women's Self-Defense Work and the Problem of Expert Testimony on Battering," *Women's Rights Law Reporter* 9 (1986): 195.

8. For a discussion of this conundrum in the context of family, see Brenda Cossman, "Family Inside/Out," *University of Toronto Law Journal* 44 (1994): 1.

9. There is an argument that the other side of the equality equation is always the state, even in civil litigation. However, even to the extent that we recognize the state's implicit position with regard to civil litigation, such a recognition undergirds rather than diminishes any recognition of the power of the state's explicit position in criminal law.

10. For a discussion of whether Aileen Wuornos fits any criteria of a serial killer, such as killing for pleasure, see Phyllis Chesler, "A Woman's Right to Self Defense: The Case of Aileen Carol Wuornos," *St. John's Law Review*

66 (1993): 933, 946–48. Even if Wuornos does fit the criteria, she is certainly not the first woman to do so; see ibid., p. 946, citing Eric Hickey (between 1800 and 1988 a total of 34 female serial killers have existed). See also Ann Jones, *Women Who Kill* (New York: Holt, Rhinehart & Winston, 1980), esp. pp.129–39 (discussing many cases, including Belle Paulson, a woman who lured a succession of men to her farm and murdered them for pecuniary gain).

11. Chesler outlines some of these events in "A Woman's Right," pp. 961–62. Her most damaging observation is that because childhood acquaintances were offered payments for exclusive interviews with a producer, they may have interpreted the terms of these deals to include not cooperating with Wuornos's defense attorneys.

12. In a case involving the death sentence for a woman accused of the kidnapping murder of a young girl with whom she had sex, the defendant argued at trial that she suffered from battered-woman-syndrome and had procured and killed the girl at the insistence of her husband. In a recent appeal, she contended that her attorney's negotiation of publicity contracts directly influenced his trial strategy. At trial, the attorney conducted a four-day direct examination of the defendant, eliciting "lurid facts" previously ruled inadmissible. Such facts were central to his "copyrighted, 400-plus page 'appellate brief' that he has attempted to market as the basis of a book or movie." *Neelley v. State,* 1994 W.L. 248245 (Ala. June 10, 1994).

13. The work of Jane Caputi, *The Age of the Sex Crime* (Bowling Green, OH: Bowling Green University Press, 1987), articulates this point with relation to male serial murderers whose victims are predominantly women.

14. *Perez v. State,* 491 S.W. 2d 672, 673,675 (Tex. Crim. App. 1973).

15. As I discuss elsewhere, this strategy was employed in recent U.S. politics to raise the specter of lesbianism on unmarried women nominated for political office. See Ruthann Robson, "The Specter of a Lesbian Supreme Court Justice: Problems of Identity in Lesbian Legal Theorizing," *St. Thomas Law Review* 5 (1993): 433.

16. Robert Leger, "Lesbianism Among Women Prisoners: Participants and Nonparticipants," *Criminal Justice and Behavior* 14(4) (1987): 448.

17. See n. 4.

18. Victor Streib, "Death Penalty for Lesbians," *National Journal of Sexual Orientation Law* 1 (1994): (an electronic journal).

19. See generally Pat Carlen, *Women, Crime, and Poverty* (Milton Keynes: Open University Press, 1988); and Coramae Mann Richey, "Minority and Female: A Criminal Justice Double Bind," *Social Justice* 16(3) (1989): 160–72.

20. Defense strategies have been less explicit because of the burden of the prosecution to prove its case and the complimentary lack of burden on the part of the defense.

21. This stereotyped construction is most operative in cases in which the "bad" lesbian is accused of murdering her lesbian partner.

22. Marie Ashe examines the legal construction of the bad mother in "The 'Bad Mother' in Law and Literature: A Problem of Representation," *Hastings Law Journal* 43 (1992): 1017. For a discussion of how the criminal law "enforces the subordinating aspects of motherhood and punishes women's resis-

tance," see Dorothy E. Roberts, "Motherhood and Crime," *Iowa Law Review* 79 (1993): 95.

23. Editorial, *The Miami Herald,* April 3, 1992, p. 26A.

24. *People v. Martin,* 4 Cal. Rptr. 2d 660 (5th Dist. 1992).

25. For example, the state objected to the National Center for Lesbian Rights' motion for leave to file an amicus brief on behalf of Aileen Wuornos relating to the homophobia that may have denied her a fair trial. The state argued that lesbianism was irrelevant.

26. My notions of lesbian legal theory here depend on my earlier work, notably Robson, *Lesbian (Out)Law.*

TEN

William F. Flanagan examines the challenges posed by the emergence of a distinct identity politics around HIV and AIDS and the conflicts that have developed between this disability politic and the more traditional politics of the lesbian and gay communities. He traces the history of AIDS service organizations and radical activist groups, and he raises the question of who is entitled to assert "ownership" of AIDS in setting public policy and the direction of activism. Furthermore, Flanagan demonstrates that, as the demographics of the epidemic shift, the strains in the direction of activism between treatment research and prevention/health care are exacerbated. He argues that the diverse needs of those who are at risk of HIV and who are living with HIV and AIDS may not be met within a single activist agenda. Finally, Flanagan concludes that AIDS discourse should not be limited to a politic of either disability or sexual orientation.

People with HIV/AIDS, Gay Men, and Lesbians: Shifting Identities, Shifting Priorities

William F. Flanagan

Introduction

It is difficult to describe the endless, relentless impact AIDS has had on the lives of gay men. It is now hard to recall how we lived before AIDS; many gay men today have never known a time free of a constant threat of illness and death. Although AIDS continues to profoundly affect gay men, along with the many lesbians and others who joined in the struggle against this disease, in the Western world the impact and meaning of AIDS now extend beyond the gay and lesbian communities. In short, the conflation of gay and lesbian activism with AIDS activism is no longer sustainable.

This essay describes the origin and evolution of AIDS activism, its roots in the gay and lesbian communities, its current stresses and tensions, and its possible directions in the future. What emerges is a story of a developing identity of people living with HIV and AIDS, and an evolving and distinct disability politic around that identity. As this identity has taken shape and found a collective voice, it has increasingly asserted a politic independent of, and occasionally in conflict with, the more traditional politics of the lesbian and gay communities. Although welcomed by many people with HIV and AIDS, for some in the gay and lesbian communities this development has been resisted, as the "ownership" of AIDS has been increasingly challenged. This development has also posed particular issues for gay men with HIV, who are caught between an identity centered on sexual orientation and an emerging identity centered on disability. There is increasingly an effort to articulate the intersection of these occasionally conflicting identities and to explore the meaning of this multiplicity of identities. Finally, this essay explores the difficult question of whether AIDS activism will be ultimately strengthened or weakened by this evolution.

A Coming of Age

Like many gay men, I can now trace the history of AIDS to the summer of 1981, when the first media reports about a strange new illness affecting gay men surfaced. I was 20 years old and had, only months before, begun to explore what I found to be the extraordinarily exotic and liberating world of gay life. At the time, the reports of this puzzling disease were very few, and no one, including government institutions of public health, paid any particular attention. For someone just coming out, such as myself, there was no information at all.

Before entering the University of Toronto Law School in the fall of 1982, I made my first visit to New York City at the age of 21. I recall meeting a medical student, a tall, handsome, intriguing man, who at one point in an intimate encounter suddenly began to examine my lymph nodes. I found this most curious. Apparently satisfied with the results of his examination, he mentioned something about an illness affecting the lymphatic system of some gay men. I scoffed. I had never heard of any such thing and assumed that medical school was responsible for his neurotic concern about disease. I entirely forgot about this incident, my first brush with the coming of AIDS, until several years later.

Continuing my study of gay life, I traveled to San Francisco in the summer of 1983. I met a charming Australian who took me for romantic drives around the city in his convertible. When I returned home to Canada, I discovered that he had slipped some condoms in my backpack. I was entirely puzzled by this. I had never even known anyone who used condoms and could not imagine why he had given them to me. It made me uneasy, but I eventually passed it off as a San Francisco quirk.

That same year, in New York, Michael Callen and Richard

Berkowitz wrote their ground-breaking pamphlet "How to Have Sex in an Epidemic," with a preface by Dr. Joseph Sonnabend, advocating for the first time the use of condoms on the assumption that this new disease was sexually transmitted. One year later, in 1984, the human immunodeficiency virus (HIV) was isolated, and the means of transmission of the new disease started to become alarmingly clear. In 1985, what came to be known as the "safer sex" campaign began in earnest.

AIDS came into our lives deceptively slowly, until it suddenly seemed to be everywhere all at once. Seemingly overnight, ever-larger numbers of completely healthy young men would suddenly develop pneumonia and die within a matter of days. With the introduction of the HIV test in 1985, epidemiological studies soon made clear how widespread was this lethal disease. We now know that it was during the early years of this epidemic, 1980–85, when little was known and precautions were few, that as many as 50 percent of all gay men in most urban centers in North America became HIV-infected. With an incubation period of ten or more years, most of these men have yet to develop AIDS. Our unimaginable losses of the past may be dwarfed by even greater losses in the next five years.

AIDS Service Organizations: The Gay and Lesbian Communities Respond

Ever suspicious that this reported new disease was simply another plot to restrict a sexual freedom that had been so recently won after tremendous effort, the gay community was at first quick to minimize the significance of AIDS and to reassert the right to sexual freedom and autonomy. Nevertheless, early in the epidemic, gay community–based AIDS service organizations (ASOs) were established. For me, as a past resident of New York City currently in Toronto, the most familiar examples include the Gay Men's Health Crisis (GMHC), formed in New York City in the fall of 1981,[1] and the AIDS Committee of Toronto (ACT), established in 1983.

The goal of these early groups was to provide care for people with AIDS, many of whom were very ill, to educate the public in order to reduce irrational fears of transmission, and to educate those at risk. At this time, when more than a few public figures were advocating drastic measures such as quarantine, ASOs played a critical advocacy and activist role. Conscious of the dangers of being forced into a dependent "patient" role by the emerging ASOs, people living with AIDS were also quick to identify a shared interest and a need to develop autonomous self-help organizations. This model appealed particularly to gay men with AIDS who were familiar with the coming out and community self-empowerment politics of the gay and lesbian movement. In 1983, at a lesbian and gay health conference held in Denver, a group of people with AIDS issued the Denver Principles condemning the label of "victim" and coining the term "people with AIDS" (PWAs) to describe themselves. The group recommended that people with AIDS "form caucuses to choose their own representatives, to deal with the media, to choose their own agenda, and plan their own strategies."[2]

In addition to the gay community–based AIDS service organizations and the PWA movement, communities of color and native communities began to address AIDS. Rather than adopting an AIDS-specific project model, many of these communities first developed AIDS services within existing multiservice agencies.[3] The gay community tended to view AIDS as an entirely new issue demanding unprecedented resources and attention. In communities of color, AIDS was viewed in the context of a community already struggling with poverty and a lack of access to health care and education.[4]

The early ASOs, grassroots in origin and activist in direction, remained closely linked to the larger gay and lesbian political movement. Education efforts were largely gay-focused, including some material targeted at the lesbian community, and consciously affirmed a "pro-sex" ideology. The staff and volunteers were almost entirely gay and lesbian. Consequently, ASOs devoted few, if any, resources to education about the risks of heterosexual transmission.

The AIDS Committee of Toronto was largely established by former gay and lesbian members of *The Body Politic*, the internationally recognized gay and lesbian liberationist journal that played an integral role in the gay and lesbian movement from the journal's foundation in 1973 until its eventual demise in 1987. GMHC, as its name indicates, was from its origin unequivocally identified as a gay organization. ACT, on the other hand, was somewhat slow to acknowledge publicly its obvious and vital connection to the gay community, likely due to a lingering concern that this would only further link AIDS and homosexuality in the public mind. It was only in 1990, with a speech by Stephen Manning, ACT's then executive director, that ACT proclaimed that the gay and lesbian community, as the group most affected by AIDS, was entitled to assert "ownership" of AIDS. According to Manning, this ownership gave the gay and lesbian community a unique "moral right" to participate in shaping society's response to AIDS. ACT acknowledged what it had always believed: AIDS-phobia and homophobia were virtually indistinguishable. ACT had finally come out of the closet.

Between 1983 and 1987, ASOs were on the forefront of early AIDS activism, working to reduce public fear and encourage a compassionate, reasoned response. However, this objective came to be seen as too timid and restricted. As AIDS grew more threatening, many gay men started to focus on the need for radical measures to bring government attention and resources to bear on the growing epidemic. The ASOs were becoming viewed as part of the growing AIDS establishment, indistinguishable from other mainstream nonprofit health organizations. AIDS activism and AIDS service organizations began to diverge.

In New York, AIDS activists began to accuse GMHC of being too conservative and unwilling to aggressively challenge the scientific and state organizations responding to AIDS. New York AIDS activism began to develop an independent identity.[5] The founding of the AIDS Coalition to Unleash Power (ACT UP) in 1987 marked the beginning of what was to become over the next three years an enormously successful and influential AIDS activist movement in the United States and abroad.[6]

Radical Action

In the fall of 1987, I moved to New York and started graduate work in law at Columbia University. I was assisting a fellow student who was involved in an important *pro bono* AIDS discrimination case representing a pharmacist with HIV who had been dismissed from his hospital job at the Westchester County Medical Center.[7] As part of our lobbying strategy to influence the hospital, we decided to approach ACT UP, this new, radical activist group apparently composed of people with AIDS who had nothing to lose and who were becoming famous for daring street protests.

I had no idea what to expect. The image of crazed radicals, kamikaze AIDS pilots, came to mind. Instead we found a remarkably dynamic, sophisticated, and immensely dedicated group of about 300 people for whom the AIDS crisis was a matter of life and death. With the assistance of ACT UP, we organized a successful demonstration at the Westchester County Medical Center, protesting its AIDS employment policies. Thus began my three-year involvement as a member of ACT UP.

At ACT UP, disdain ran high for GMHC, harshly perceived as a timid organization dedicated merely to helping people die. "Silence = Death" was ACT UP's famous rallying cry, a powerful equation requiring no explanation for gay men in New York. We seized America's center of finance, throwing our bodies on the road and staging a "die in" on Wall Street to underscore the lack of leadership on AIDS from corporate America. We surrounded the Federal Drug Administration in

Washington, DC, demanding action on research and access to experimental treatment. We grabbed the podium at the 1989 International AIDS Conference in Montreal and read to the worldwide AIDS establishment our Montreal Manifesto, a bill of rights for people living with HIV and AIDS.

AIDS Action Now!, a somewhat less colorful although no less sophisticated Toronto AIDS activist group, was a little astonished by these brash Americans taking over the Montreal AIDS conference. Although few of the Americans had any idea who Canada's then Prime Minister Brian Mulroney even was, once informed of his dismal record on AIDS, ACT UP members vigorously protested his speech at the conference, as if Mulroney were one of ACT UP's own AIDS villains. I had the impression AIDS Action Now! was slightly embarrassed and annoyed at this typical display of American imperialism. As a temporary resident of New York, I decided to drop my natural Canadian reserve and join in the fray.

Like the ASOs that preceded it, ACT UP remained closely linked to the gay and lesbian communities. Although, whenever the question arose, ACT UP was insistent that it was first and foremost an AIDS activist organization and not a gay organization, "Silence = Death" posters always included a pink triangle, the mark by which the Nazis identified gay men in the concentration camps. Composed primarily of gay men, ACT UP also included a fairly large number of committed lesbians. Noting the emerging radical sexual identity that was later to give rise to "queer" politics, some lesbian AIDS activists were delighted by "that delicious outrageous queer decadence indulged by gay men as a survival strategy."[8] Other lesbian activists saw ACT UP as an opportunity for a strategic alliance between lesbians' skills in community organizing and gay men's access to money and media visibility.[9]

Although the self-help PWA movement had begun as early as 1983, ACT UP was not an organization composed exclusively, or even primarily, of people with AIDS. The PWA movement, which involved seriously ill people diagnosed with AIDS, was largely focused on immediate treatment issues and peer support. This was perceived as distinct from ACT UP's broader activist agenda to attract and sustain state involvement in the fight against AIDS.

Nonetheless, it was understood that most of ACT UP's members were gay men at risk of developing AIDS, often described as the "worried well." At this time, of course, the HIV antibody test, only first made available in 1985, was not widely used. From the time of ACT UP's start in 1987 until at least 1990, a politic around HIV status had yet to develop. In retrospect, it appears that during this time most members were either unaware of their HIV status or kept this knowledge to themselves. Perhaps this information was not perceived as relevant, as it was felt that all members were equally at risk. On the other hand, those aware of their HIV infection might have felt it unsafe to reveal that information, even within ACT UP. At any rate, at the time there was no particular sense that activists with HIV might share interests or a political agenda that would in any way differ from those of other members. If there was, it was unarticulated.

When introduced in 1985, the HIV test immediately became hugely controversial. Although associated with AIDS, it was not known how many people with HIV would ever develop AIDS. Hopes, later disappointed, were that the number would be very few. At the time, there were also no available treatments for HIV infection, and the test carried the enormous risk that it could be used to identify and discriminate against HIV-positive people. For these reasons, there was little incentive to take this test, and widespread resistance in the gay community.

In 1988, once effective treatments for some opportunistic infections had been identified, along with the more controversial antiviral treatment AZT, AIDS service organizations began to encourage people at risk to seek an HIV test. Fears remained that the results might be used to discriminate against people with HIV, especially in those jurisdictions that required that the results be reported to public health officials. Unlike New York State, which in 1988 enacted laws protecting the confidentiality of this information, Ontario and other jurisdictions continued to require the mandatory nominal reporting of all cases of HIV infection to public health authorities.[10]

Although a politic around people with AIDS emerged as early as 1983, a politic for people living with HIV was slower to develop, and indeed only became possible once the HIV test became more widely used in the years following 1988.

Shifting Demographics and Priorities

In 1990, I graduated from Columbia and left New York to take up a teaching position in Toronto. At this time, ACT UP was showing signs of the strain that would eventually lead if not to its demise, at least its radical reformulation. When ACT UP was founded in 1987, gay and bisexual men (most of whom were white) constituted 70 percent of Americans with AIDS. Five years later, in 1992, such men made up only 55 percent of people with AIDS, and the number continues to decline. In the United States, ever increasing numbers of new and frequently overlapping populations were being affected, including IV drug users, people of color, and women, presenting a wide variety of new and difficult challenges for prevention education and HIV treatment.

The shifting demographics of AIDS are much less dramatic in Canada and in other Western nations. In Toronto, for example, over 90 percent of people with HIV are still gay and bisexual men, most of whom are white.[11] However, the fact remains that the epidemic is moving beyond the gay community, a factor that poses enormous challenges for preventive education, health care, and HIV/AIDS activism.

Although ACT UP had involved itself quite deeply in a number of prevention issues, most notably a highly controversial needle exchange program, the core of its work remained advocacy around research issues and the development of new treatments. This was a natural focus for a group of gay men, some of whom were discovering they were HIV-positive and most others fearing they might be. Better treatment, and fast, was the only real hope. The focus of ACT UP's most famous demonstrations—at Wall Street, the Federal Drug Administration, and the International AIDS Conference—reflected this overriding concern with research and development.

In the United States, research was not the sole or even primary issue for communities of color and women, where prevention and health care remained urgent concerns. This tension was even apparent within the gay male community, as gay men of color increasingly articulated a need to address prevention issues specific to them, including language, literacy, and cultural barriers, a matter that had been largely overlooked in the earlier prevention efforts of the gay community. On an international level, in Africa and Asia the importance of prevention was becoming even more apparent.[12] In many of these countries, where the annual per capita health care budget is often less than $10, expensive AIDS treatments, even if they are eventually developed, will never be widely available. For some activists the focus on research was beginning to appear short-sighted, if not elitist.

Despite a lack of state support, and notwithstanding a fairly specific initial focus on literate, white gay men, prevention efforts targeted at the gay community enjoyed considerable success following 1985. With the introduction of safer-sex guidelines, the rate of new infections drastically declined. Recent evidence indicates that this rate is once again climbing, particularly among young men under 25, illustrating the real difficulty in sustaining safer-sex behavior and the need to develop new prevention programs targeted at gay men.[13] Nonetheless, from the start of ACT UP in 1987, prevention was not its most pressing priority. For similar reasons, Toronto's AIDS Action Now! set as its sole mandate political action directly relevant to people living with HIV and AIDS, expressly excluding activism around prevention issues.

With tension developing between activism around prevention

and activism around treatment research, activists with HIV were discovering that their priorities were no longer universally shared by all AIDS activists at ACT UP. The demographics of AIDS had shifted, and the challenges were growing increasingly diverse. Seriously addressing prevention and health care issues relevant to communities of color (including gay men of color) and women (including women of color) required nothing less than a radical reexamination of poverty, racism, and sexism, the real barriers to preventing the spread of AIDS in these communities and providing treatment for those infected. For many activists living with HIV, this shifting focus suggested that AIDS was simply becoming yet another intractable social problem not easily amenable to change and likely to inspire fatigue and indifference on the part of society as a whole. For people living with the imminent threat of serious illness and death, this shifting focus appeared nothing less than life threatening.

Lesbian AIDS Activists

The strains in AIDS activism were also reflected in the relationship between AIDS activism, the lesbian community, and the gay community. It was in the lesbian and gay communities that AIDS activism first began, most notably in the establishment of the gay and lesbian community–based ASOs. Lesbian feminists and gay men had long experienced an uneasy alliance during the era of liberationist politics of the 1970s. Strategies for change, priorities, and modes of operating were frequently at odds. Many lesbian feminists felt silenced and marginalized by the largely gay male leadership, and some opted for working within the women's political movement rather than developing alliances with gay men.

Nonetheless, lesbians played an important role in the early years of the development of the ASOs, whether out of a sense of solidarity with gay men, or, as one woman said, out of the traditional role of women as nurturers, raised to "despise ourselves and belittle our own needs, while holding those of men to be important."[14] This prominent role was evident even though the incidence of AIDS within the lesbian community was and remains extremely small, largely linked to IV drug use and not sexual behavior. The AIDS Committee of Toronto consciously reflected its roots in *The Body Politic*, a journal that made great efforts, with varying degrees of success, to foster a political alliance between lesbians and gay men. From its inception, lesbians played a central role in ACT's development. Likewise, lesbians had played an important role in the success of ACT UP.

Nonetheless, some lesbians began to question their involvement in what seemed to be largely a gay male health crisis, suspecting that once again the lesbian and gay political agenda was really being directed predominantly by the concerns of gay men. Other lesbians increasingly identified with the emerging prevention and treatment issues for women with AIDS, including strategies to enable heterosexual women to negotiate safer sex with their male partners. For these lesbian AIDS activists, the AIDS agenda needed to broaden to address systemic issues of sexism and poverty.

An Emerging Disability Politic

In the United States, AIDS activism eventually splintered between research issues and prevention/health care issues, with the establishment of an independent AIDS treatment and research activist group in New York, the Treatment Action Group (TAG) in 1992, and a similar group in San Francisco. In part, this development can be traced to the need of people with HIV to articulate a set of interests and objectives that might be distinct from a larger AIDS politic.

The last four years have also witnessed significant shifts in the direction of HIV/AIDS activism in Canada, although these changes have surfaced in different ways. Unlike the substantial investment in AIDS research and treatment development in the United States, Canada's AIDS research program has always been marginal. Although Canadian AIDS activists have developed a sophisticated system to monitor international treatment and research advances, most notably the widely circulated *Treatment Update* newsletter of the Community AIDS Treatment Information Exchange, research and development issues have never been the center of AIDS activism in Canada. Instead, the AIDS activism of AIDS Action Now!, for example, has long focused on access to health care and experimental treatment for people with HIV and AIDS,[15] insurance issues, discrimination, and social assistance. For this reason, AIDS activism in Canada has not experienced ACT UP's wrenching division nor the establishment of independent AIDS treatment and research activist groups. Nevertheless, for a variety of reasons, in Canada activists with HIV have also begun to assert a shared identity and a shared politic, one distinct from the AIDS activism of the past.

Over ten years into the epidemic, in May of 1992, the Canadian AIDS Society, an umbrella group representing ASOs across Canada, organized the first annual national conference held in Canada that was exclusively composed of persons with HIV and AIDS. This conference recognized the growing influence of people with HIV and AIDS, the development of a new disability politics around HIV (and not just AIDS), and the importance of providing people with HIV and AIDS with an opportunity to organize, share experience, and set priorities.

An activist movement of people with HIV and AIDS has emerged only recently for a number of reasons. As in the United States, the controversy around the introduction of the HIV test in 1985 and the uncertain meaning of an HIV-positive result effectively prevented the development of any common identity between people with HIV and people with AIDS until the early 1990s. Likewise, the legal conception of HIV infection as a disability was slow in developing. For two or three years after the introduction of the HIV test, it was an open question whether asymptomatic HIV infection could even be regarded as a disability under the law, because, unlike most cases of AIDS, it did not result in any manifest symptoms or impairment.[16] It was not until 1988 that Canadian law first recognized that asymptomatic HIV infection, as well as AIDS, were both physical disabilities, with the result that all people with HIV were entitled to protection under the antidiscrimination provisions in Canadian disability rights law.[17]

This emerging identity met with considerable resistance. For many, AIDS was so closely identified with the gay community that it seemed unnecessary and counterproductive to make distinctions between an identity politic around HIV and AIDS, and a liberationist politic around sexual orientation. AIDS was an issue for the entire gay community; the two were inextricably linked. As expressed in 1990 by the Executive Director of the AIDS Committee of Toronto, homophobia and AIDS-phobia were virtually indistinguishable. Any gay man or lesbian committed to the fight against homophobia was necessarily a part of the fight against AIDS. The idea of an emerging and distinct disability politics around HIV and AIDS seemed absurd.

For many HIV-negative gay and lesbian leaders in the "AIDS establishment," the implications of this emerging identity were threatening, occasionally sparking a harsh reaction. It appeared to place their leadership position, and their "ownership" of AIDS, in question. People with HIV, particularly gay men, who began to articulate an HIV disability politics were accused of internalized homophobia, trying to distance AIDS from the historic leadership provided by the gay and lesbian communities, and to whitewash its association with sexual difference. As members of a community devastated by AIDS, HIV-negative gay men questioned how their involvement could be any less invested or profound than that of gay men with HIV. Lesbian AIDS activists, virtually none of whom were HIV positive, feared this was an attempt to marginalize and devalue their participation.

For others, this development seemed utterly self-destructive. It was inexplicable that gay men with HIV would apparently seek to abandon an identity around sexual orientation to embrace an identity even more loathed and feared: HIV and AIDS. For many gay men with HIV, a disability politic also posed the risk of becoming isolated from the gay and lesbian communities and possibly even shunned by AIDS-phobic members within these communities. These larger communities might eventually abandon AIDS as an issue.[18] Why place at risk this close association with the most important allies of people with HIV and AIDS?

Why a Disability Politic?

Given the risks and tensions inherent in the articulation of a distinct identity politic around HIV and AIDS, it might seem extraordinary that such a politic has even begun to develop. Nevertheless, a number of reasons can be suggested for this development. At the beginning of the AIDS epidemic, most of the gay community, in partnership with many in the lesbian community, recognized the enormity of the threat posed by AIDS. This threat was, on the whole, felt equally by all those involved in the struggle. With so little known about AIDS, it appeared that the entire community was at risk. There was unanimous agreement about the most pressing issues: compassionate, effective, and accessible care for the sick, and prevention education for gay men at risk. There was little reason for any tension between the goals of care and prevention.

As the AIDS epidemic has grown, the needs of those living with HIV, and the needs of the increasingly diverse communities at risk, can no longer easily be met within one AIDS activist agenda. The people most directly affected, those infected with the virus, are no longer simply composed of the very sick and dying, as in the early days of the epidemic. People with HIV, surviving ten or more years without any symptoms of illness, have recognized that they may have to articulate a specific agenda around HIV treatment, research, and care issues that is distinct from a larger AIDS politic where their interests might be marginalized or patronized. This explains in part the independent activism around research and treatment issues in the United States within ACT UP, and in Canada where AIDS Action Now! has long articulated its mission as excluding prevention issues.

At the same time, activists with HIV are also recognizing shared interests distinct from, or even at odds with, the larger gay and lesbian politic. These tensions arise in at least three areas: disclosure to sexual partners, the direction and priorities of ASOs, and the ongoing project to secure the legal recognition of same-sex spouses.

Disclosure

In January 1993, publishing the results of an entirely unreliable survey of callers who had bothered to phone in, Toronto's local gay and lesbian magazine, *Xtra!*, reported that a substantial majority of callers believed that people with HIV should either refrain from all sex or in all cases disclose their HIV status to their partners before engaging in sex.[19] At the time, I wondered how many gay men might be foolish enough to engage in unprotected sex, simply assuming that their partner was HIV-negative because he had not disclosed otherwise. To me, the poll seemed to suggest a disturbing level of ignorance and AIDS phobia in the gay community.

Later that year, reports surfaced in the Toronto media about a young gay man who had been charged with criminal negligence and detained on the grounds that he had allegedly infected another young gay man through unprotected sexual intercourse without ever disclosing that he was HIV positive.[20] This was the first time in Canada that criminal charges had been brought against a gay man for engaging in unprotected sex with another man.[21] It was suggested that the complainant had pressed for criminal charges in the hopes of securing some kind of monetary award from the Ontario Criminal Injuries Compensation Board.[22] The facts of the case were sketchy: It was not known whether the accused had actively misrepresented his HIV status, or whether he had simply chosen not to disclose and, for whatever reason, the parties had engaged in unsafe sex.

Reaction in the gay community was mixed. Consistent with the results of *Xtra!*'s survey earlier in the year, more than a few were of the view that the prosecution was appropriate and should proceed.[23] Michael Leshner, a well-known gay Crown prosecutor, had allegedly volunteered to prosecute the case on behalf of the Crown. In 1992, Leshner had won a high-profile case against the provincial government requiring the extension of the province's employee family benefits package to his same-sex partner.[24] In choosing Leshner, it appeared that the provincial government was carefully positioning itself to secure the support of at least some members of the gay community for this prosecution.

Before any real debate could occur, and for reasons never disclosed, the prosecution did not proceed, and the accused was released. Both AIDS Action Now! and the AIDS Committee of Toronto (of which I was by then the chair of the Board) were preparing for an explosive debate in the gay community. At least two issues arose: obligations, if any, to disclose, and the role, if any, of criminal charges relating to unprotected gay sex.

Consistent with its longstanding education policy, ACT took the position that safer sex practices imposed an equal obligation on all gay men, both HIV positive and negative, to protect themselves. When the parties were aware of the risks inherent in sex between men and of the need to take precautions, disclosure was unwarranted, unnecessary, and unrealistic. In our view, unprotected sex, increasingly common among younger gay men, was a public health issue requiring creative and relevant education efforts, not criminal charges.

We recognized that criminal law might be a measure of last resort when persons who have no particular reason to suspect they might be at risk engage in sex with someone who knowingly and deliberately takes advantage of their ignorance and places them at risk.[25] However, in the case of these two gay men, there was no doubt that they were both fully aware of the risks inherent in unprotected sex between men. Criminalization of the conduct in this case would only turn the accused into a scapegoat. Moreover, the incidence of unprotected sex might actually increase if gay men began to rely on criminal law, rather than condoms, to protect themselves. The criminalization of unprotected sex might provide cold comfort to some HIV-negative gay men, erroneously thinking it offered them protection. We regarded it as a direct assault on people living with HIV.

Before this debate arose in the gay community, Voices of Positive Women, a Toronto-based support group for women living with HIV, had already articulated a policy around disclosure. Recognizing the power imbalance between men and women, and the threat of violence that might follow disclosure, Voices had taken the position that women with HIV were not required to disclose their HIV status to their male sexual partners.

The inevitable debate around disclosure and criminal charges underscores the potential for a painful split between AIDS activism and many members of the gay community. On the whole, activists with HIV, including both women and gay men, strongly oppose any general disclosure obligation and see only a very limited role for criminal prosecution.[26] At the same time, more than a few members of the gay community express shock and outrage that gay men with HIV are even having (safer) sex, let alone doing so without informing their partners of their HIV status. With this level of AIDS phobia within the gay community, the conflation of AIDS phobia and homophobia, as articulated by ACT in 1990, becomes increasingly problematic.

Priorities and Power in AIDS Service Organizations

AIDS service organizations (ASOs), largely founded by nonprofessional volunteers in the gay and lesbian communities in the early 1980s, have undergone wrenching change in the past four years. The inevitable shift away from the original grassroot foundation and toward increased formal accountability and bureaucratization has been much criticized and lamented, with more than a hint of nostalgia for the old days.[27] The original coalition of gay men and lesbians is becoming much less prominent as many lesbians gradually leave the field, either burnt out or no longer attracted to working in an organization appearing to shift away from its activist direction.[28] Ever increasing numbers of straight women, most professionally trained social workers, are replacing those leaving.

Like AIDS activism, ASOs are also facing great pressure to respond to the diverse range of issues faced by women, people of color, and people with HIV, groups that increasingly overlap and intersect. The oldest and largest ASOs, originally developed to serve the needs of a largely white gay male community, had two main objectives: care for the very sick and prevention education for gay men. These same ASOs are now facing the challenges of responding to a more diverse community with a broader and more complex range of needs.

Perhaps more than any other group to date, people with HIV have been the most vigorous in challenging the direction of ASOs. At ACT, members with HIV have led a reexamination of its assertion in 1990 that the gay and lesbian communities were entitled to "ownership" of AIDS and thus to a unique role in setting policy and direction. For many people with HIV, ACT had overlooked their own obvious claim to "ownership" of AIDS, a matter that has only grown more significant as tensions rise between AIDS activism and certain interests in the gay and lesbian communities. The Board of ACT, a majority of whom were gay men with HIV, eventually rejected ACT's earlier position, and in a 1993 newsletter to the membership, the Board stated that "it is time to recognize a stronger claim than that of the gay and lesbian community —the claim of all people actually infected with HIV."

In the view of the Board, of which I was a member, ACT's focus on AIDS had become blurred, and its service and education efforts were suffering. People with HIV, including the gay men for whom the programs were largely designed, were being poorly served. ACT's service programs were historically directed at caring for the ill and tended to develop chronic dependence on specific staff or volunteers in the organization. People with HIV, most of whom were in good health and determined to stay that way, were demanding more diverse services designed to foster long-term well-being, self-determination, and independence. ACT's old model of care was proving inadequate.

ACT had also failed to address the needs of women with HIV and women at risk. Given its lesbian and gay identity, ACT's prevention education programs for women were disproportionately focused on lesbians rather than on straight women who faced much higher HIV-related risks. ACT's Women and AIDS program had also historically failed to attract any substantial participation of women with HIV, almost all of whom were straight.

In an important example of an emerging distinct politic around

HIV, the Board was determined to place all people with HIV at the center of ACT's work. Nevertheless, this goal was met with considerable suspicion by an old guard more comfortable with the historic identification of ACT as a gay and lesbian organization in which people with AIDS were clients, not participants in setting the direction of the agency.

Same-Sex Spousal Recognition

In addition to the debate around disclosure and the direction of ASOs, at least one other area of potential conflict can be identified. In 1994 in Ontario, gay and lesbian activists actively lobbied the provincial government to extend most of the rights and obligations of spousal status to include same-sex couples, culminating in the dramatic defeat in June 1994 of the government's proposed Bill 167.[29] Among other things, the bill would have imposed spousal support obligations on same-sex couples who had cohabitated for three or more years, would have extended intestate succession privileges to same-sex couples, and would have granted to a same-sex partner the right to make medical decisions on behalf of his or her incapacitated partner.[30]

Although recognizing the importance of matters such as the substitute treatment decision provisions and intestate succession provisions, AIDS activists consistently raised the concern that spousal recognition could have the adverse effect of lowering the social assistance paid to people with HIV and AIDS, if their same-sex partner were deemed a spouse under the relevant social assistance legislation.[31] In this case, the income of this deemed spouse would act as a reducing factor for the other spouse's benefits, possibly even eliminating any eligibility.[32] Same-sex couples curiously benefit from the current law, because their relationships are effectively ignored by social assistance agencies when determining eligibility. There is no expectation that the same-sex partner will provide any income security to the applicant.

Of course, the effect of including the income of the deemed spouse has disastrous consequences for many heterosexual couples by eliminating eligibility for social assistance. This raises a larger issue of when, if ever, the income of an applicant's partner should ever be considered in the context of social assistance. Many AIDS activists argued that the spousal recognition project should be stayed until this issue could be adequately resolved for both same-sex and heterosexual couples dependent on social assistance. However, the Coalition for Lesbian and Gay Rights largely ignored the issue in its lobbying efforts.[33] In the end, it appeared that securing spousal recognition for same-sex couples took precedence over income security for people living with HIV and AIDS.

Conclusion

A distinct identity politic around HIV and AIDS is developing and is in turn reshaping AIDS activism. A decade ago, when I first encountered AIDS, it was effectively indistinguishable from gay men, and gay and lesbian activism. Within dominant culture, this conflation likely remains largely unchallenged but is increasingly difficult to sustain. People with HIV and AIDS are recognizing a shared identity that crosses lines of sexuality, gender, race, and class. The old partnerships in AIDS activism—between the lesbian and gay communities, and between prevention and research/health care issues—are being reexamined. A broader range of occasionally conflicting priorities is becoming more evident, and out of this conflict a distinct HIV disability politic is being articulated.[34]

Identity politics, although a powerful tool for disadvantaged groups to gain access to power, is also fraught with danger. It tends to emphasize difference at the expense of shared goals, focusing on factors that separate rather than unite. Categories of identity risk becoming fixed and essential; rigid lines are drawn. Men cannot be feminists; whites cannot be partners in antiracist efforts; HIV-negative lesbians and gay men cannot be AIDS activists. Identity politics also tends to become further complicated when identities overlap and intersect: women of color with HIV, gay men with HIV.[35] Identity politics seems to demand that a choice be made: are you gay? HIV? a person of color? In particular, the unique experience of those with multiple identities, such as gay men with HIV, or black women, is marginalized and unarticulated, one identity always seeming to subsume, or silence, the other.

For gay men with HIV, an AIDS discourse limited to disability threatens to erase sexual orientation and marginalize the real and unique challenges faced by gay men in dealing with a disability or illness, such as the ability to make substitute decisions on behalf of an incapacitated partner, or the barriers thrown up by homophobic health care, scientific, or state institutions. Likewise, an AIDS discourse limited to sexual orientation can marginalize the voice of gay men living with HIV and AIDS around such issues as disclosure, the direction of ASOs, and spousal status recognition. The challenge for gay men with HIV and AIDS is to articulate a multiplicity of identities, one without abandoning the other.

Identity politics have always played a powerful part in political struggles, in the past focusing on ethnicity, religion, and class, and in contemporary times focusing on race, gender, sexual orientation, and disability. Identity politics have proven useful in articulating shared interests and creating the potential for collective action, particularly among those suffering a disadvantage or an injustice. Women and people of color have been notably successful in employing identity politics to articulate a distinct voice and secure a measure of political power. Those with multiple identities, such as lesbians and women of color, have learned to minimize one identity and maximize another, depending on the challenge faced and the desired objective.[36] People with disabilities, in particular gay men with HIV and AIDS, can learn from this example. Yet, in doing so, people with HIV cannot overlook the partnerships essential to collective action around HIV with the gay and lesbian communities, feminists, disability groups, and others. However, when people with HIV and AIDS, including gay men, identify divergent interests that are occasionally in conflict with those of other groups, it is not to be lamented that people with HIV and AIDS, a group uniquely disadvantaged and stigmatized, have increasingly articulated a distinct and assertive politic.

NOTES

1. Philip M. Kayal, *Bearing Witness: Gay Men's Health Crisis and the Politics of AIDS* (Boulder, CO: Westview Press, 1993), p. 1.
2. Michael Callen, ed., *Surviving and Thriving with AIDS: Collected Wisdom*, vol. 2 (New York: People with AIDS Coalition, 1988), pp. 294–95.
3. Cindy Patton, *Inventing AIDS* (New York: Routledge, 1990), pp. 10–11.
4. Harlon L. Dalton, "AIDS in Blackface," *Daedalus* 118 (1989): 205.
5. Larry Kramer split with GMHC in what became a famous open letter published in January 1987, accusing GMHC of inaction and incompetence. See Larry Kramer, *Reports from the Holocaust: The Making of an AIDS Activist* (New York: St. Martin's Press, 1989), pp. 100–116.
6. Larry Kramer played an important role in establishing ACT UP, calling for direct action in the form of protests, pickets, and arrests in an address at the Gay and Lesbian Community Center in New York on March 10, 1987. See ibid., pp. 127–39.
7. *Doe v. Westchester County Med. Center* (N.Y. State Div. Human Rights, December 12, 1990). See *New York Law Journal*, December 26, 1990, p. 30. The tribunal found that there was no evidence of any significant risk to patients. The pharmacist was awarded $30,000 in damages and was reinstated.
8. Maria Maggenti, "Wandering Through Herland," in Arlene Stein, ed., *Sisters, Sexperts, Queers: Beyond the Lesbian Nation* (New York: Penguin, 1993), pp. 245, 248.
9. Ruth L. Schwartz, "New Alliances, Strange Bedfellows: Lesbians, Gay Men, and AIDS," in Stein, ed., *Sisters, Sexperts, Queers*, pp. 230, 239.
10. This was the subject of my graduate thesis at Columbia University School of Law. See W. F. Flanagan, "Equality Rights for People with AIDS: Mandatory Reporting of HIV Infection and Contact Tracing," *McGill Law Journal* 34 (1989): 530. Notwithstanding the Ontario government's repeated

promise to amend the law to permit testing without reporting names (anony-mous testing), the law remains unchanged to date. The government continues negotiations with AIDS activists and public health officials in an effort to set guidelines outlining when the reporting of the names of infected persons should be required. In the meantime, the many Ontario doctors who refuse to comply with the mandatory reporting provisions remain liable for prosecution under the Ontario Health Protection and Promotion Act, R.S.O. 1990, c. H.7.

11. Ted Myers, Donald McLeod, and Liviana Calzavara, "Responses of Gay and Bisexual Men to HIV/AIDS in Toronto, Canada: Community-Based Initiatives, AIDS Education, and Sexual Behaviour," in Mitchell Cohen, ed., *Changing Sexual Behaviours in the Shadow of AIDS: A Survey of Gay and Bisexual Men in Communities Throughout the World* (forthcoming). See also Ted Myers, *Men's Survey: The Canadian Survey of Gay and Bisexual Men with HIV Infection* (Ottawa: Canadian AIDS Society, 1994).

12. The 1994 International AIDS Conference held in Tokyo largely focused on the growing rate of HIV transmission in Asia, a "looming explosion." See "AIDS Virus Infects 3 Million in Year," *The Globe and Mail*, Toronto, August 9, 1994.

13. Myers, *Men's Survey*.

14. Schwartz, "New Alliances, Strange Bedfellows," p. 231.

15. The establishment of the Emergency Drug Release Program by the Canadian Ministry of Health in February 1989, permitting in some cases the early release of experimental treatment, was an important victory. "Drugs for the Treatment of AIDS," Press Release and Circular Letter to Doctors from Health Protection Branch, Health and Welfare Canada, February 8, 1989.

16. Flanagan, "Equality Rights for People with AIDS," pp. 576–80.

17. *Biggs v. Hudson* [1988] 9 C.H.R.R. D/5391, was the first decision of a human rights tribunal in Canada finding that both HIV infection and AIDS were to be considered disabilities for the purposes of the British Columbia Hu-man Rights Act, S.B.C. 1984, c.22. Likewise, the U.S. Supreme Court held in *School Board of Nassau County v. Arline*, 480 U.S. 273 (1987), that a person with a communicable disease (in this case tuberculosis) was entitled to the protec-tion available under the federal Rehabilitation Act of 1973, Pub. L. No. 93-112, 87 Stat. 357 [codified as amended at 29 U.S.C.S. 701–96(1982)]. Three years later, Congress passed comprehensive legislation prohibiting discrimination on the basis of physical disability, including HIV infection: Americans with Dis-abilities Act, Pub. L. No. 101–336, 104 Stat. 327 (1990).

18. Jeffrey Schmalz, "Whatever Happened to AIDS?" *The New York Times Magazine*, November 28, 1993. Schmalz, who died of AIDS three weeks before the article was published, argued that the gay community has largely lost in-terest in advocating around AIDS. HIV-negative gay men "do not want a dis-ease to be what defines their community." According to Schmalz, as hopes for improved treatment become ever more remote, interest is waning, and AIDS activism is being overcome with despair.

19. "Tel-Xtra," *Xtra!*, no. 187, January 15, 1993; 74% of callers believed people with HIV should disclose their status.

20. Widely discussed in the community, this case was first reported in a local television broadcast on "CITY TV News," October 29, 1993.

21. There have been a number of cases of criminal charges in the case of heterosexual transmission. See *R. v. Mercer* [1993] 43 C.C.C.3d 41 (Nfld. C.A.), where the accused engaged in unprotected sex with two women, both of whom became HIV-infected. He pleaded guilty and was sentenced to 11 years in prison. In *R. v. Ssenyonga* [1992] 73 C.C.C.3d 216 (Ont. Prov. Ct.), the accused allegedly infected three women through unprotected intercourse. The accused died before a verdict was rendered, and the case was stayed. See also *R. v. Kreider* [1993] 140 A.R. 81 (Prov. Ct.); and *R. v. Summer* [1989] 99 A.R. 29 (C.A.), aff'g 98 A.R. 191 (Prov. Ct.), both cases involving guilty pleas to charges of common nuisance and sentences of one year in prison.

22. In January 1994, the Ontario Criminal Injuries Compensation Board awarded one of the complainants in the *R. v. Ssenyonga* case $15,000 for damages suffered (Dec. No. 922–034759, January 21, 1994).

23. Another "Tel-Xtra" poll published on September 3, 1993, indicated that 70% of callers believed that people who failed to disclose their status should be charged with a criminal offense.

24. *Leshner v. Ontario* [1992] 16 C.H.R.R. D/184 (Ont. Bd. of Inquiry).

25. This appears to have been the situation in *R. v. Ssenyonga*, where the accused allegedly deliberately and knowingly misrepresented his HIV status, refused to use a condom despite repeated requests by his sexual partners, and engaged in intercourse with women who were presumably unaware of any particular risks.

26. There is also potential for a split between some feminists, who might favor a broad disclosure obligation for straight men with HIV (and the liberal use of criminal law for those who fail to disclose), and women with HIV who oppose general disclosure obligations.

27. See Brent Ledger, "ACT at 10," *Xtra!*, March 19, April 2, 1993; and Coleman Jones, "The Feud Within," *NOW*, June 10, 1993.

28. Schwartz, "New Alliances, Strange Bedfellows," p. 242.

29. *An Act to Amend Ontario Statutes to Provide for the Equal Treatment of Persons in Spousal Relationships*, 3rd Sess., 35th Leg. Ont., 1994.

30. Ontario law expressly recognizes the right of same-sex partners, defined as two persons who "have lived together for at least one year and have a close personal relationship that is of primary importance in both persons' lives," to make health care decisions for an incapacitated partner. See Substitute Decision Act, S.O. 1992, c. 30. "Spouses" enjoy the same privileges under the act. Bill 167 would have simply amended the definition of "spouse" under this act to include a same-sex couple, rather than granting this status to make substitute decisions on the basis of a distinct "partner" relationship, as is currently the case.

31. Family Benefits Act, R.S.O. 1990, c. F.2.

32. In British Columbia, a lesbian was denied access to social assistance on the grounds that her lesbian partner was employed and had a good income. "A Lesbian's Relationship Is Finally Recognized, but Only So the Government Can Deny Her a Welfare Cheque," *Xtra!*, no. 257, September 2, 1994.

33. Patricia Lefebour, "Same Sex Spousal Recognition in Ontario: Declarations and Denials: A Class Perspective," *Journal of Law and Social Policy* 9 (1993): 272.

34. It is interesting to consider the potential for developing alliances with other disability groups. The link between HIV and hemophilia provides one obvious example of a now rather well-developed coalition. The Ontario provincial government is currently funding a feasibility study to establish a nonprofit viatical company that would effectively enable people suffering from a life-threatening condition to cash in their life insurance policies while still alive. Cancer and ALS organizations have expressed some interest in participating in the study, which might lead to the establishment of a nonprofit viatical company managed by the disability groups directly affected.

35. For example, Kimberlé Crenshaw has extensively explored the political and theoretical issues created by the intersection of race and gender, and the "ideological and political currents that combine to first create and then to bury Black women's experience." See Kimberlé Crenshaw, "Demarginalizing the Intersection of Race and Sex: A Black Feminist Critique of Antidiscrimination Doctrine, Feminist Theory, and Antiracist Politics," *University of Chicago Legal Forum* (1989): 139, 160.

36. Vera Whisman, "Identity Crises: Who Is a Lesbian Anyway?" in Stein, ed., *Sisters, Sexperts, Queers: Beyond the Lesbian Nation*, p. 47. In considering the question posed by the title, Whisman notes that consistently maximizing a lesbian identity risks constructing a "rigid, suffocating, and at least implicitly racist understanding of 'the lesbian' and her culture, ethics, and politics." According to Whisman, this identity occasionally must be "minimized" in order to maximize an identity as a woman, or as queer, to push against and challenge a lesbian identity: "We need to minimize *and* maximize, create unities and simultaneously see them as false, build boundaries around ourselves, and, at the same time, smash them" (ibid., p. 59).

About the Editors and Contributors

The Editors

DIDI HERMAN teaches law at Keele University in Britain. She is the author of *Rights of Passage: Struggles for Lesbian and Gay Legal Equality* (Toronto: University of Toronto Press, 1994) and *Normalcy on the Defensive: The Christian Right's Anti-Gay Agenda* (Chicago: University of Chicago Press, forthcoming).

CARL STYCHIN teaches law at Keele University. He is the author of *Law's Desire: Sexuality and the Limits of Justice* (London and New York: Routledge, 1995) and of numerous articles on sexuality and legal discourse.

The Contributors

KATHERINE ARNUP teaches Canadian studies and women's studies in the School of Canadian Studies at Carleton University, Ottawa. She is the author of *Education for Motherhood: Advice for Mothers in Twentieth-Century Canada* (Toronto: University of Toronto Press, 1994) and of articles on lesbian mothers and child custody, donor insemination, and child-rearing advice for mothers. She is the editor of *Lesbian Parenting: Living With Pride and Prejudice* (Charlottetown, P.E.I.: gynergy books, 1995). She is the mother of two girls, Jesse and Katie.

SUSAN BOYD is chair in feminist legal studies at the University of British Columbia, Vancouver, where she teaches feminist legal studies and family law. She is the author of articles on child custody law, women's work, the primary care-giver presumption, feminist legal theory, and privatization themes in family law.

217

PETER M. CICCHINO, BRUCE R. DEMING, AND KATHERINE M. NICHOLSON graduated from Harvard Law School, Cambridge, in 1992. Cicchino is presently the Coordinator of the Lesbian and Gay Youth Project of the Legal Action Center for the Homeless in New York, an outreach project for gay and lesbian street youth.

DAVINA COOPER teaches law at the University of Warwick. Her publications include *Sexing the City: Lesbian and Gay Politics Within the Activist State* (London: Rivers Oram, 1994) and *Power in Struggle: Feminism, Sexuality, and the State* (Ballmoor, Bucks: Open University Press, 1995). She also does sociolegal research on local government and was an elected council member in London in the 1980s.

MARY EATON is a doctoral student at Columbia Law School in New York. She has written extensively on the connections among law, sexual orientation, race, and gender.

WILLIAM F. FLANAGAN is an assistant professor of law at Queen's University in Kingston. He was a member of ACT UP New York from 1987 until 1990, and served on the Board of the AIDS Committee of Toronto from 1991 to 1995. He was Chair of the Board from 1993 to 1995.

LEO FLYNN is a lecturer in the School of Law in King's College of the University of London. He is a graduate of the National University of Ireland and Cambridge University. His research interests include the theory and practice of equality law.

SHELLEY A. M. GAVIGAN is a member of the Faculty of Law at Osgoode Hall Law School of York University in Toronto. She is currently the Academic Director of the Intensive Program in Poverty Law at Parkdale Community Legal Services in Toronto.

LESLIE J. MORAN is a lecturer in law at Lancaster University, where he teaches courses in gender and the law, lesbian and gay legal studies, and law and the body. His primary research interests are legal practices of sexuality, theory, and human rights. His book, *The Homosexuality of Law*, will be published in 1996 by Routledge, and his current field of research is legal responses to homophobic violence.

CYNTHIA PETERSEN is professor of law at the University of Ottawa where she teaches a seminar on lesbian and gay legal issues and a course on lesbian theory and feminism. Her work focuses on issues of law that affect the lives of lesbians and gay men. She will be representing EGALE (Equality for Gays and Lesbians Everywhere), a Canadian national organization, in a forthcoming Supreme Court of Canada case involving same-sex spousal recognition.

RUTHANN ROBSON is professor of law at the City University of New York. Her recent work includes *Lesbian (Out)Law: Survival Under the Rule of Law* (Ithaca, NY: Firebrand Books, 1992), numerous articles addressing the possibilities of lesbian legal theory, and two books of lesbian fiction, as well as a forthcoming novel focusing on a lesbian attorney who represents lesbians accused of murdering their children.

Index